Forensic Epidemiology

INTERNATIONAL FORENSIC SCIENCE AND INVESTIGATION SERIES

Series Editor: Max Houck

Firearms, the Law and Forensic Ballistics
T A Warlow
ISBN 9780748404322
1996

Scientific Examination of Documents: methods and techniques, 2nd edition
D Ellen
ISBN 9780748405800
1997

Forensic Investigation of Explosions
A Beveridge
ISBN 9780748405657
1998

Forensic Examination of Human Hair
J Robertson
ISBN 9780748405671
1999

Forensic Examination of Fibres, 2nd edition
J Robertson and M Grieve
ISBN 9780748408160
1999

Forensic Examination of Glass and Paint: analysis and interpretation
B Caddy
ISBN 9780748405794
2001

Forensic Speaker Identification
P Rose
ISBN 9780415271827
2002

Bitemark Evidence
B J Dorion
ISBN 9780824754143
2004

The Practice of Crime Scene Investigation
J Horswell
ISBN 9780748406098
2004

Fire Investigation
N Nic Daéid
ISBN 9780415248914
2004

Fingerprints and Other Ridge Skin Impressions
C Champod, C J Lennard, P Margot, and M Stoilovic
ISBN 9780415271752
2004

Firearms, the Law, and Forensic Ballistics, Second Edition
Tom Warlow
ISBN 9780415316019
2004

Forensic Computer Crime Investigation
Thomas A Johnson
ISBN 9780824724351
2005

Analytical and Practical Aspects of Drug Testing in Hair
Pascal Kintz
ISBN 9780849364501
2006

Nonhuman DNA Typing: theory and casework applications
Heather M Coyle
ISBN 9780824725938
2007

Chemical Analysis of Firearms, Ammunition, and Gunshot Residue
James Smyth Wallace
ISBN 9781420069662
2008

Forensic Science in Wildlife Investigations
Adrian Linacre
ISBN 9780849304101
2009

Scientific Method: applications in failure investigation and forensic science
Randall K. Noon
ISBN 9781420092806
2009

Forensic Epidemiology
Steven A Koehler and Peggy A Brown
ISBN 9781420063271
2009

INTERNATIONAL FORENSIC SCIENCE
AND INVESTIGATION SERIES

Forensic Epidemiology

Steven A. Koehler
Peggy A. Brown

CRC Press
Taylor & Francis Group
Boca Raton London New York

CRC Press is an imprint of the
Taylor & Francis Group, an **informa** business

CRC Press
Taylor & Francis Group
6000 Broken Sound Parkway NW, Suite 300
Boca Raton, FL 33487-2742

© 2010 by Taylor and Francis Group, LLC
CRC Press is an imprint of Taylor & Francis Group, an Informa business

No claim to original U.S. Government works

Printed in the United States of America on acid-free paper
10 9 8 7 6 5 4 3 2 1

International Standard Book Number: 978-1-4200-6327-1 (Hardback)

This book contains information obtained from authentic and highly regarded sources. Reasonable efforts have been made to publish reliable data and information, but the author and publisher cannot assume responsibility for the validity of all materials or the consequences of their use. The authors and publishers have attempted to trace the copyright holders of all material reproduced in this publication and apologize to copyright holders if permission to publish in this form has not been obtained. If any copyright material has not been acknowledged please write and let us know so we may rectify in any future reprint.

Except as permitted under U.S. Copyright Law, no part of this book may be reprinted, reproduced, transmitted, or utilized in any form by any electronic, mechanical, or other means, now known or hereafter invented, including photocopying, microfilming, and recording, or in any information storage or retrieval system, without written permission from the publishers.

For permission to photocopy or use material electronically from this work, please access www.copyright.com (http://www.copyright.com/) or contact the Copyright Clearance Center, Inc. (CCC), 222 Rosewood Drive, Danvers, MA 01923, 978-750-8400. CCC is a not-for-profit organization that provides licenses and registration for a variety of users. For organizations that have been granted a photocopy license by the CCC, a separate system of payment has been arranged.

Trademark Notice: Product or corporate names may be trademarks or registered trademarks, and are used only for identification and explanation without intent to infringe.

Library of Congress Cataloging-in-Publication Data

Koehler, Steven A.
　　Forensic epidemiology / Steven A. Koehler, Peggy A. Brown.
　　　　p. ; cm. -- (International forensic science and investigation series)
　　Includes bibliographical references and index.
　　ISBN 978-1-4200-6327-1 (hardcover : alk. paper)
　　1. Forensic epidemiology. I. Brown, Peggy A. (Peggy Ann), 1955- II. Title. III. Series: International forensic science and investigation series.
　　　[DNLM: 1. Epidemiology. 2. Forensic Medicine. W 750 K77f 2010 2010]
RA1165.K64 2010
614'.1--dc22
　　　　　　　　　　　　　　　　　　　　　　　　　　　　　　　　　　　　　　2009022574

Visit the Taylor & Francis Web site at
http://www.taylorandfrancis.com

and the CRC Press Web site at
http://www.crcpress.com

Table of Contents

Series Preface	xv
Preface	xvii
Introduction	xxi
The Authors	xxvii

1 The Basics of Epidemiology ... 1

    Introduction ... 1
    History of Epidemiology ... 1
    Definition of Epidemiology ... 2
    Types of Epidemiology ... 7
        Aging Epidemiology ... 7
        Cancer Epidemiology and Cancer Control and Prevention Programs ... 7
        Cardiovascular/Diabetes (Chronic Disease) Epidemiology ... 8
        Environmental Epidemiology ... 8
        Infectious Disease Epidemiology ... 8
        Reproductive, Perinatal, and Pediatric Epidemiology ... 9
        Injury Epidemiology ... 9
        Genetic Epidemiology ... 10
        Psychiatric Epidemiology ... 10
        Physical Activity Epidemiology ... 10
        Forensic Epidemiology ... 11
    Epidemiology: Education and Experience ... 11

2 Forensic Epidemiology ... 13

    Introduction ... 13
    Brief History of Forensic Science ... 13
    Development of Forensic Epidemiology ... 14
    Roles of Forensic Epidemiologists ... 16
        Medical Examiner's or Coroner's Office ... 16
        Health Department ... 17
        Public and Private Organizations ... 17
            SIDS Deaths ... 17

	Drug Prevention Programs for Middle and High School Students	18
	Private Consultant	18
	Expert Witness	18

3 The Role of the Forensic Epidemiologist in the Medical Examiner's or Coroner's Office — 19

	Introduction	19
	Role of a Forensic Epidemiologist in a Medical Examiner's or Coroner's Office	19
	Death Investigation Data	19
	Forensic Medicine Data	20
	Crime Laboratory Data	22
	Outside Agencies	23
	Local and National News Agencies	23
	Drug Enforcement Administration	23
	Drug Abuse Warning Network	23
	Law Enforcement	24
	Death Review Boards	25
	Mentoring	26
	Teaching	27
	Conferences	27
	Research and Publication	27
	Peer-Reviewed Journals	28

4 The Operations of a Medical Examiner's or Coroner's Office — 31

	Introduction	31
	Death Investigation Systems in the United States	31
	The Coroner's Office	31
	The Medical Examiner's Office	32
	The Death Call	32
	What Constitutes a Reportable Death in an ME/C Case?	33
	Number of Cases Investigated by ME/C Offices	34
	ME/C Death Cases	35
	Death at a Residence	35
	Death in a Hospital	36
	Death at a Nonresidence	37
	Office Will Issue (OWI)	38
	Morgue Cases	38
	Direct Release to the Funeral Home	39

Table of Contents   vii

    Forensic Examinations   39
        External Examination   39
            Photographing   40
            Clothing   40
        The External Body Examination   40
            Special Processing of the Body   42
        Types of Complete Forensic Examinations   42
    The Complete Examination (Virchow Technique)   43
        Heart   43
        Lungs   44
        Liver   45
        Pancreas   45
        Kidneys   46
        Spleen   46
        Other Internal Organs   46
        Gastrointestinal Tract   46
            Stomach Contents   46
        Central Nervous System (CNS)   47
            Brain   47
            Spinal Cord   48
        Skeletal System   48
    Final Pathological Diagnosis Report   49

5   The Death Certificate   51

    Introduction   51
    Definition   51
    Functions of the Death Certificate   51
    Completion of the DC   52
        Types of Death Certificates   53
    Anatomy of the Standard Certificate of Death   53
        Part 37: Manner of Death   61
    Anatomy of the Medicolegal Death Certificate   64
        Part 27: Cause of Death   68
    Pathway of the DC   71
    Advantages of Using the DC   73
    Disadvantage of Using the DC   74

6   Natural Deaths   75

    Introduction   75
    Definition   75
    Fatalities   75
    Natural Deaths Not Reported to the ME/C Office   76

Natural Deaths Investigated by ME/C Office	77
Forensic Investigation of Natural Deaths	78
Types of Natural Deaths	80
Cardiovascular System	80
Respiratory System	81
Hepatobiliary System	81
Nervous System	82
Organ Weights	82
Stored Tissue and Microscopic Slides	82
Forensic Epidemiological Investigation of Natural Deaths	82
Strengths and Weaknesses of ME/C Natural Death Data	89
Natural Death and the DC	89
Sudden Infant Death Syndrome (SIDS)	90
Introduction	90
Definition	90
Fatalities	91
Foundations of SIDS	91
Forensic Investigation of a SIDS Death	92
Methods of Investigation	93
Prebirth Factors	93
Birth Factors	93
Postbirth Environment	93
Postbirth Parental Behaviors	94
Infant Characteristics	94
Death Scene Reports	94
Manner: Natural or Undetermined?	94
Research	95
Application of Forensic Epidemiological Investigation of SIDS	95
Sleep Position	97
Soft Bedding	97
Bed Sharing	98
Ethnicity and Socioeconomic Status	98
Forensic Epidemiological Investigation of SIDS	99

7   Accidental Deaths   105

Introduction	105
Accidental Drug Overdose Deaths	105
Definition	105
Fatalities	106
Fundamentals of Drug Overdose Deaths	106
Forensic Investigation of an Accidental Drug Overdose	107
Mechanism of an Overdose	109

Forensic Analysis of Drug Overdose	111
Body Fluids Collected	111
Toxicological Analyses	112
Forensic Epidemiological Investigation of Drug Overdose Deaths	112
Advantages and Limitations of Forensic Epidemiological Investigation of Drug Overdose	118
Motor Vehicle Accident	122
Definition	122
Fatalities	122
Fundamentals of MVA Accidents	123
Causes of MVAs	123
Types of MVA Impacts and Associated Injuries	123
Front Impact	124
Side Impact	124
Rollover	124
Rear Impact	125
Forensic Investigation of MVA Deaths	125
Forensic Epidemiological Investigation of MVAs	127
Fatality Analysis Reporting System (FARS)	135
Advantages and Limitations of Forensic Epidemiological Investigation of MVAs	137
Falls	138
Definition	138
Fatalities	138
Fundamentals of Deaths by a Fall	138
Forensic Investigation of Death from a Fall	139
Forensic Epidemiological Investigation of a Fall	141
Advantages and Limitations of Forensic Epidemiological Investigation of Falls	145
Fire	146
Definition	146
Fatalities	146
Fundamentals of Deaths by Fire	146
Mechanisms	148
Forensic Epidemiological Investigation of Fires	149
Advantages and Limitations of Forensic Epidemiological Investigation of Fires	152
Industrial Deaths	152
Definition	152
Fatalities	152
Fundamentals of Industrial Deaths	153
Forensic Epidemiological Investigation of Industrial Deaths	153

Advantages and Limitations of Forensic Epidemiological Investigation of Industrial Deaths	154
Medical Misadventure Deaths	155
Definition	155
Fatalities	156
Fundamentals of Medical Misadventure Deaths	156
Forensic Epidemiological Investigation of Medical Misadventures	158
Advantages and Limitations of Forensic Epidemiological Investigation of Medical Misadventure	158
Drowning	159
Definition	159
Fatalities	160
Fundamentals of Drowning Deaths	160
Mechanism of Drowning	161
Forensic Epidemiological Investigation of Drowning	161
Advantages and Limitations of Forensic Epidemiological Investigation of Drowning	164

8 Death by Suicide — 165

Introduction	165
Definition	165
Fatalities	165
Fundamentals of Deaths by Suicide	166
Investigation of Suicide Deaths	168
Mechanisms of Suicides	169
Suicide by Firearm	170
Suicide by Asphyxiation	171
Suicide by Carbon Monoxide	172
Suicide by Overdose	173
Suicide by Vehicle	174
Suicide by Train	174
Suicide by Exsanguination	174
Forensic Epidemiological Investigation of Suicides	175
Advantages and Limitations of the Forensic Epidemiological Investigation of Suicides	184

9 Death by Homicide — 187

Introduction	187
Definition	187
Types of Homicide	188
Fatalities	189

Fundamentals of Homicide Death Investigation	189
Mechanism of Homicide	192
Forensic Analysis by Method of Homicide	193
Homicide by Firearm	193
Distance from the Victim	195
Homicide by Suffocation	195
Homicide by Fire	196
Homicide by BFT	197
Homicide by Fear	198
Homicide by OD	198
Homicide by Vehicle	198
Homicide by the State	199
Lethal Injection	199
Electric Chair	199
Gas Chamber	200
Firing Squad	200
Hanging	200
Delayed Homicide	200
Forensic Epidemiological Investigation of Homicide	201
National Violence Data Reporting System	212
National Databases	212
FBI Uniform Crime Report (UCR)	212
Supplementary Homicide Report (SHR)	213
National Incident-Based Reporting System (NIBRS)	217
Advantages and Limitations of Using ME/C Data and the DC	218
ME/C Data	218
Death Certificate Data	220

10 Stages of Decomposition: Methods of Determining Identity, Cause of Death, and Undetermined Manner of Death   221

Introduction	221
The Determination of Identity	222
Early Stages of Decomposition	222
Visual Identification	223
Clothing and Personal Effects	223
Fingerprints	224
Moderate Stages of Decomposition	225
Internal Identification	226
Medical/Surgical Implants and Procedures	226
Disease Conditions	226
Advanced Stages of Decomposition	226

	X-ray Comparison	227
	Dental Comparison	227
Extreme Stages of Decomposition		229
	Skeletal Identification	229
	Superimposition Facial Reconstruction	230
Special Cases of Decomposition		230
	DNA	230
Cause of Death Known but Manner Undetermined		231
Cause of Death Undetermined and Manner Undetermined		233
Forensic Epidemiological Investigation of Undetermined Deaths		234

11 Special Types of Investigations — 237

- Introduction — 237
- Homicide–Suicide — 237
- Russian Roulette—Death by Suicide or by Accident? — 238
- Psychological Autopsy — 239
  - Introduction — 239
  - Definition — 239
  - Brief History of Psychological Autopsies — 240
  - The Use of Psychological Autopsy — 240
  - Conducting a Psychological Autopsy — 241
- Bioterrorism: Real-Time Surveillance — 241
  - Introduction — 241
  - Definition — 242
  - Brief History of Bioterrorism — 242
    - Biological Terrorism Agents — 242
    - Chemical Terrorism Agents — 242
  - The Role of the Forensic Community — 244

12 Structure of a Forensic Paper — 247

- Introduction — 247
- Structure of a Manuscript — 247
  - Abstract — 247
  - Introduction — 248
  - Materials and Methods — 249
  - Results — 251
  - Conclusion — 252
  - References — 252
- Types of Manuscripts — 253
  - Research Articles — 253
  - Case Presentations (Case Reports) — 253

	Review Articles	254
	Letters to the Editor	255
	Peer Review	255
	The Peer Review Process	256

13 The Forensic Epidemiologist: Consultant and Expert Witness — 259

Introduction	259
Forensic Epidemiological Consultant	259
Forensic Epidemiologist as Expert Witness	261
The Court Experience	263
The Federal Rules of Evidence	264
The Admissibility of Expert Evidence and Testimony	264
Becoming a Forensic Epidemiologist	266

Bibliography — 269

Appendix A: Normal Weights of Internal Organs, Standard Deviations, and Ranges for Males — 279

Index — 281

International Forensic Science Series

The modern forensic world is shrinking. Forensic colleagues are no longer just within a laboratory but across the world. E-mails come in from London, Ohio and London, England. Forensic journal articles are read in Peoria, Illinois and Pretoria, South Africa. Mass disasters bring forensic experts together from all over the world.

The modern forensic world is expanding. Forensic scientists travel around the world to attend international meetings. Students graduate from forensic science educational programs in record numbers. Forensic literature—articles, books, and reports—grows in size, complexity, and depth.

Forensic science is a unique mix of science, law, and management. It faces challenges like no other discipline. Legal decisions and new laws force forensic science to adapt methods, change protocols, and develop new sciences. The rigors of research and the vagaries of the nature of evidence create vexing problems with complex answers. Greater demand for forensic services pressures managers to do more with resources that are either inadequate or overwhelming. Forensic science is an exciting, multidisciplinary profession with a nearly unlimited set of challenges to be embraced. The profession is also global in scope—whether a forensic scientist works in Chicago or Shanghai, the same challenges are often encountered.

The International Forensic Science Series is intended to embrace those challenges through innovative books that provide reference, learning, and methods. If forensic science is to stand next to biology, chemistry, physics, geology, and the other natural sciences, its practitioners must be able to articulate the fundamental principles and theories of forensic science and not simply follow procedural steps in manuals. Each book broadens forensic knowledge while deepening our understanding of the application of that knowledge. It is an honor to be the editor of the Taylor & Francis International Forensic Science Series of books. I hope you find the series useful and informative.

Max M. Houck
Series Editor

Preface

Interest in the field of forensic science has exploded, due in part to television programs such as *CSI, Crossing Jordan, Forensic Files,* and *Cold Case.* The interest has also been bolstered by public criminal trials such as that of O. J. Simpson, which showed how forensic evidence is collected, analyzed, interpreted, and presented in a court of law. The field of forensic science has traditionally involved areas such as death investigation, fingerprints, serology, ballistics, forgery, and trace evidence. However, within the past few years a new field called *forensic epidemiology* has emerged.

This book is based on the authors' first-hand experience in developing the importance of the science of forensic epidemiology within the medical examiner's office. In addition, it shows how forensic epidemiologists play a major role as communicators between those within the science field and those within the law enforcement community.

Forensic Epidemiology is ideal for forensic scientists, those in the field of public health, injury prevention specialists, law enforcement personnel, lawyers, and forensic consultants:

- Chapter 1, "The Basics of Epidemiology," provides an overview of the science of epidemiology, highlighting the basic principles and the different fields within this discipline.
- Chapter 2, "Forensic Epidemiology," provides a brief history of forensic science and traces the development of the field of forensic epidemiology.
- Chapter 3, "The Role of the Forensic Epidemiologist in the Medical Examiner's or Coroner's Office," describes the role of the forensic epidemiologist and his or her function within the office of the medical examiner or coroner (ME/C). Data collection, analysis, and interpretation are discussed. In addition, the chapter expands upon the forensic epidemiologist's role as liaison officer between the ME/C office and outside agencies.
- Chapter 4, "The Operations of a Medical Examiner's or Coroner's Office," provides an overview of the development of the coroner system and operations of a modern ME/C office, including data generated from the office.

Chapter 5, "The Death Certificate," provides an in-depth examination of the multiple functions of the death certificate and a detailed examination of its various sections.

Chapter 6, "Natural Deaths," describes the role of forensic epidemiologists in the investigation of deaths from natural causes. This chapter highlights how forensic epidemiological studies of sudden infant death syndrome (SIDS) plays a key role in dramatically reducing such deaths.

Chapter 7, "Accidental Deaths," examines a wide range of deaths from accidental causes and how forensic epidemiologists investigate such deaths.

Chapter 8, "Death by Suicide," provides an examination of various methods of committing suicide and the application of forensic epidemiological investigation to suicides.

Chapter 9, "Death by Homicide," defines various types and methods of homicide, fundamentals of death investigation of a homicide, various mechanisms of homicide, and the methods used by a forensic epidemiologist to investigate and interpret homicide data.

Chapter 10, "Stages of Decomposition: Methods of Determining Identity, Cause of Death, and Undetermined Manner of Death," describes the stages of decomposition and various methods used to establish positive identity. This chapter also discusses cases in which positive identification and the cause and/or manner cannot be determined and the impact of such a situation on forensic epidemiological analysis.

Chapter 11, "Special Types of Investigations," examines a number of unique types of deaths and special methods used to determine the cause and manner of death.

Chapter 12, "Structure of a Forensic Paper," contains a detailed description of the structure of a scientific manuscript and the manuscript review process.

Chapter 13, "The Forensic Epidemiologist: Consultant and Expert Witness," defines the role of a forensic epidemiologist functioning as a consultant or as an expert witness, the Federal Rules of Evidence, and the experiences faced by an expert witness during a trial.

Our motivation for writing this book is twofold: to attempt to remedy the underutilization of ME/C data as well as the lack of understanding of the types of data available for research. The vast amounts of information collected by the ME/C office during the many phases of its investigation typically sit in file cabinets or electronic storage systems. Only a small fraction of these valuable data is used to advance the fields of science, public health, or law enforcement. One possible reason for this underutilization is a general lack of understanding of the types of collected data associated with a death investigation and the depth of the data collected. Finally, there is a failure to understand how these data can be used to improve health, safety, and quality of life.

Steven A. Koehler

Peggy A. Brown

Introduction

In order to understand the field of forensic epidemiology, one must first have an understanding of the history of the death investigation system. The modern death investigation system can trace its origins back to medieval England. The formal establishment of the position of the coroner was set forth in Article 20 of the "Articles of the Eyre" in September 1194 in England. The term *coroner* is derived from the Latin word "corona" for *crowner* (appointed by the king or Crown). The original coroners were knights who owned property and had a sizeable income. They were elected for life and were unpaid.

The duties of coroners included conducting inquests over dead bodies, hearing appeals, inspection of an individual's wounds, recording the accusation against another individual, and, if the wounds appeared likely to be fatal, arresting the accused individual. The coroner was also authorized to arrest witnesses or suspects and to appraise and safeguard any lands or goods that might later be forfeited by reason of guilt of the accused. During medieval times, the inquest was conducted on the spot, with the body nearby. The jury consisted of all males, age 20 and over, from nearby towns. In 1259, the jury size was decreased in number to only 20–25 males. In 1877, the inquest system was enacted, requiring an inquest to be conducted whenever the coroner had reasonable cause to suspect violent or unnatural death or when the cause of death was unknown. However, these first death investigators lacked any type of medical training in anatomy, physiology, the causes of disease, or how to ascertain the cause and manner of death.

When the colonists arrived in the New World from England, they brought the coroner system as it existed in the early 1600s to the new continent. The earliest record of a coroner's inquest was in the colony of New Plymouth, New England, in 1635. During this early period, the coroner's office was one and the same as the sheriff's office. Income was provided by the collection of property taxes, poll taxes, and other levies, and the coroner usually received 10% of the collection. Autopsy examinations of bodies were recorded in Massachusetts as early as 1647. The medicolegal application of an autopsy was recorded in Maryland on March 21, 1665. The earliest teaching of medical jurisprudence in the New World appeared to be by Dr. Benjamin Rush of Philadelphia, who presented lectures with titles such as "On the Study of Medical Jurisprudence." The first formal use of physicians in connection with the workings of the coroner's office occurred in Maryland in 1860.

In 1877, the Commonwealth of Massachusetts adopted a statewide system requiring that the coroner be supplanted by a physician known as a medical examiner. At that time, the jurisdiction of the medical examiner was confined to "dead bodies of such persons only as are supposed to have come to their death by violence."

In 1918, New York City eliminated the coroner's office and created a medical examiner system and authorized investigation of deaths resulting from criminal violence or suicide, sudden death among apparently healthy individuals, death of an individual who had not been attended by a physician, death of a prisoner, or death in any suspicious or unusual manner. The medical examiner had the authority to decide as to the necessity of an autopsy.

Currently, two main death investigation systems operate in the United States: the older coroner system and the newer medical examiner system. Whether an individual is examined at a coroner's office or a medical examiner's office is dictated by the laws of the jurisdiction in which the body was pronounced dead. The type of death investigation system varies from municipality to municipality and from state to state. In the United States, 21 states (plus the District of Columbia) have a statewide medical examiner system, 18 states have a mixture of medical examiner and coroner systems, and 11 states have a coroner system (9 of which have county coroners and 2 have district coroners).

In states and counties utilizing a coroner as the medicolegal investigator, the coroner is elected every 4 years, must be 18 years of age or older, and must be a U.S. citizen. The coroner typically employs the assistance of one or more deputy coroners. These deputies examine the death scene and the body, and they create a detailed report of the circumstances surrounding the death. The coroner is responsible for ruling on the cause and manner of death in cases that come under his or her jurisdiction, including violent, sudden, unexpected, and suspicious deaths; medically unattended deaths; deaths involving drugs and toxic substances; deaths during medical treatment; deaths during employment; deaths during interaction with law enforcement agencies; and deaths in which a physician is not present at the time of death. The medical training that a coroner receives ranges from virtually none to only a few weeks of training. The coroner may also employ a forensic pathologist to conduct postmortem examinations.

The coroner's office, unlike the medical examiner's office, is empowered to hold a coroner's inquest, which is conducted by the coroner's solicitor, who is an attorney. The hearings are fact finding in nature and open to the public. An inquest is generally a formal procedure for inquiring into the cause, manner, and circumstances of any death resulting from violence or occurring under conditions that give reason to suspect that the death may have been due to a criminal act or criminal negligence. The power of the inquest includes the authority to question persons under oath, subpoena witnesses, and require them to present all documents relevant to the investigation.

Inquests are also conducted for death resulting from the actions of law enforcement officers, for fires where there was a loss of life or property, or at the direction of the state's *attorney general*. A coroner's jury is impaneled and, at the end of the hearing, jurors are instructed as to the law by an attorney and directed to deliberate on the evidence presented and return their findings in the matter. These findings consist of a formal determination of the cause and manner of death. When identifiable persons are determined to be criminally responsible for the death, they are held for further court proceedings. A court reporter provides a transcription of the proceedings— one to the coroner and one to the office of the district attorney. If the coroner decides that a *prima facie case* exists against any person for an indictable offense, he or she can recommend that a person be brought to trial in the *district* court. The function of the inquest is also to serve as a forum to bring about changes in laws and regulations and to create public awareness of health and safety issues.

The medical examiner system was first introduced in the United States in 1877 in Massachusetts; the first modern-day medical examiner system came into existence in New York City in 1918. In the 1940s, the medical examiner gained the right to order an autopsy of a decedent. The head of a medical examiner's office is the chief medical examiner, who is appointed by the director of the Department of Health, the governor (statewide systems), or the chief executive (local systems) for a 5-year term. The *chief medical examiner* must be a licensed physician and a member of the American Board of Pathology (ABP) in anatomic and forensic pathology with experience in forensic medicine and pathology. (Note that forensic pathology did not become a board-certified subspecialty until 1959.)

The chief medical examiner appoints a *deputy chief medical examiner,* who must also be a licensed physician and have completed an ABP-approved fellowship in forensic pathology. Today's ME office is responsible for the investigation of all sudden and unnatural deaths. The office is supplemented by crime laboratories, such as toxicology, fingerprints, ballistics, trace evidence, and entomology laboratories. In the last several decades, the medical examiner system has been slowly replacing the coroner system in the United States in several jurisdictions.

Death investigations begin when an individual's life comes to an end and the cause and manner of that death are in question or unknown. Upon discovery of the body, a well structured sequence of events occurs. In most regions, the first to arrive at the scene—the "first responders"—are emergency response teams composed of emergency medical technicians (EMTs), paramedics, and firemen. They are followed by the police.

Once a person has been declared dead, the ME/C office takes jurisdiction of the body and the death scene. The police at the scene are responsible for sealing the residence and/or encircling the death scene with yellow "DO

NOT CROSS" tape and waiting for arrival of the death investigation team. The examination of the death scene will determine how the investigation will proceed and what other forensic specialists may be required at the scene. The framework of the death investigation involves three phases. Phase 1 involves a detailed scene investigation conducted by scene investigators, scene photographers, and specially trained forensic examiners. Phase 2 is a thorough postmortem examination by a forensic pathologist. Phase 3 is detailed examination of the trace evidence collected from the scene and the victim.

Not all deaths are investigated by the ME/C office. Each year, approximately 20% of deaths in the United States undergo some type of postmortem examination. Each office has guidelines as to which types of deaths require a forensic investigation. In general, most jurisdictions are interested in deaths that involve sudden, unexpected, unexplained, and traumatic or medically unattended deaths.

The initial phase of the medicolegal death investigation is to send two death investigators and a scene photographer to the scene. The role of these death investigators is to protect the body and the surrounding environment from being mutilated, altered, or contaminated in any way that could affect the forensic evidence at that scene. They obtain information by interviewing the next of kin, family, friends, and witnesses, as well as by thorough examination of the body and scene.

They will also record the condition of the body, noting the stage of decomposition, the position of the body, and the condition and appearance of the clothing. They then write a report that provides a detailed description of the circumstances leading up to the death and offers possible scenarios or preliminary theories that may be of importance, along with the facts that have been established. The role of the forensic photographer is to document the scene via film, digital photos or recording, or video recording; this includes the position of the body, injuries, location of weapons, and how they related to each other at the time the body was discovered.

Depending on the type of evidence present at the scene and the level of complexity, requests for specialized personnel to respond to the scene may be warranted. If deemed necessary, a forensic pathologist, forensic anthropologist, forensic entomologist, or criminalists such as latent print examiners, serologists, blood spatter experts, ballistics experts, or trace evidence examiners may be called to utilize their expertise in the case.

The processing of a death scene involves the application of scientific methodology to the reconstruction of events, criminal or otherwise, in order to assist in the resolution of legal issues in question. The accurate reconstruction of a crime scene, however, may only be achieved through the correct interpretation of physical facts and accurately placing them in proper sequence. Because some physical evidence is fragile, fleeting, and easily destroyed, it is critically important that those who arrive first at the crime scene are aware of the significance of such physical evidence and are competent to make appropriate decisions about the handling, identification, and preservation of all such items. In many cases, forensic scientists are able to determine the most likely sequence of events from the circumstances at the scene; this in turn enables them to reconstruct the elements of a crime scene.

The purpose of any forensic investigation is to establish whether a crime has occurred and, if it has, to provide this evidence in a court of law for a judge or jury to determine the guilt or innocence of the accused.

Once all the forensic evidence has been photographed and collected from the body and the scene, the forensic investigation moves from the scene of the death to the morgue and crime laboratories. Here, the body undergoes a forensic postmortem examination and the evidence collected undergoes a scientific examination.

The postmortem examination consists of an external examination followed by an examination of the internal organs. This procedure is conducted by forensic pathologists. A forensic pathologist is a physician with specialized medical training focusing on understanding the causation of injuries and mechanisms that cause natural and unnatural deaths. The role of the forensic pathologist is to perform forensic autopsies, review medical records, interpret toxicology and other laboratory studies, certify the cause and manner of death, and provide court testimony in criminal and civil law proceedings.

The role of all ME/C offices is first to make a positive identification of the victim and, second, to determine the cause and manner of death. The method chosen for this determination is dictated by the condition of the body. The methods of identification range from a simple photo identification to sophisticated computer-enhanced, three-dimensional facial reconstruction. The simplest method is to compare the body on the examination table to the image on a driver's license. However, in cases of a plane crash or of having only fragments of human remains (e.g., after the September 11 terrorist attacks), identification can only be made through DNA matching. Readers will be given information as to the different methods that pathologists have available to determine the positive identification of an unknown body.

The second role is the determination of cause and manner of death. The cause of death can be thought of as the event that resulted in death. Examples of the cause of death include gunshot wound to the head, asphyxiation from a ligature, stab wound to the heart, or occlusion of the coronary arteries. This determination is made from the external examination of the body, internal examination of the organs, and analysis of body fluids. The manner of death can be thought of as the intent of the act that resulted in death. For example, if the cause of death was blunt force trauma to the chest from a height, the possible manners of death include accident—the victim lost his balance and fell off the bridge; suicide—the victim was depressed, wanted to end his life, and jumped off the bridge; or homicide—the victim was pushed off the bridge. The forensic pathologist does not work in isolation, but rather is aided by other traditional forensic scientists and by two newly emerging positions in the science: sexual assault nurse examiners and forensic epidemiologists.

Readers are taken through the doors into the autopsy suite to see the roles of the autopsy technician and the photographer and to experience the step-by-step autopsy procedure. They will understand the role of the forensic pathologist and follow the steps the pathologist takes to determine the cause and manner of death. They will understand the information revealed by an external examination and the step-by-step procedure of the internal examination, starting from the first incision to sewing up the body cavities. Readers will vicariously examine each internal organ and seek the clues the forensic pathologist is looking for in his or her quest to ascertain the cause of death. They will follow the thinking processes of a forensic pathologist as he or she weighs the scientific evidence to determine the cause of death and the manner of death. Readers will take a detailed look at the certificate of death and the information it contains and how that information is used.

Traditionally, the primary roles of the medical examiner's or coroner's office were to determine the positive identity of the victim, ascertain the cause and manner of death, and then issue a death certificate. The case was then closed. Normally, the mountains of anatomical, epidemiological, geographical, physical, and psychological data were placed in file cabinets or computer files and never examined again. Recently, a new field of science called *forensic epidemiology* has emerged; it focuses on this vast amount of previously unexamined data.

Forensic epidemiology involves the application of the principles and science of epidemiology to forensic data and issues. The results of careful examination of these data can be used by law enforcement agencies, public health officers, and researchers. Through this precise and painstaking research of the data, future epidemics and diseases may be discerned or a population saved due to the results of research and the actions taken. Forensic epidemiological research also plays a major role in the planning and evaluation of health and crime prevention programs. The at-risk population is determined with a focus on changing outcomes. Overall, forensic epidemiology is an important part of any forensic investigation. It is a career that does not exist in the limelight, but rather is behind the scenes.

The Authors

Steven A. Koehler, MPH, PhD, is a professor of forensic science at Point Park University, Pittsburgh, Pennsylvania, and CEO of a forensic science consulting company. His expertise is in the fields of forensic epidemiology, death investigation research, and forensic investigation. He is the former head of the Forensic Epidemiological Department and was the chief forensic epidemiologist at the Allegheny County Medical Examiner's Office in Pittsburgh, Pennsylvania. He teaches forensic science and research methods and conducts research in many fields of forensic science. Dr. Koehler has a BS in biology and psychology from Washington and Jefferson College, an MPH in public health, and a PhD in forensic epidemiology. He is an adjunct associate professor of epidemiology at the University of Pittsburgh Graduate School of Public Health and at the Duquesne School of Law.

Dr. Koehler has held seats on the Suicide Death Review Committee, Child Death Review Committee, the Firearm Death Review Board, and the Internal Monitoring Committee for the Center for Injury Research and Control. He is currently a founding member of the *Journal of Forensic Nursing,* where he is on the editorial board and managing editor of his column, "Death Investigation." He has been listed in *Who's Who in Medicine and Health.* Dr. Koehler has presented at numerous conferences, including the National Injury Prevention and Injury Conference, International Association of Forensic Nurses, National Medical Examiner Association, U.S. and Canadian Academy of Pathology, Food and Drug Administration, and American Academy of Neurology. He is also a pathology assistant at the Veterans Administration hospital in Oakland, Pennsylvania. Dr. Koehler is the founder and executive director of a forensic consulting company and the former assistant chief deputy coroner for Washington County. He can be reached at Point Park University, 201 Wood Street, Pittsburgh, Pennsylvania, 15222; e-mail at sakoehler100@hotmail.com

 **Peggy A. Brown** is a talented freelance writer and independent training/learning consultant. Her BS degree is in human resources and her MS degree is in organizational leadership. She has been listed in *Who's Who for Women in Business*. Peggy has spent the past 20+ years in the training arena directing training, developing training programs and curriculum, creating training departments, and serving as a project manager. She has expertise in diverse subject areas, including safety, airlines, insurance, telecommunications, sales, management training, time management, organizational skills, design strategy, leadership training, team training, personality training, diversity training, promotional work, and domestic abuse, to name a few. She can be reached at peggybrown13@hotmail.com

The Basics of Epidemiology

1

This chapter will provide a brief overview of the science of epidemiology, highlight basic principles, and provide a summary of different fields within the broad general domain of epidemiology, as well as outline the education and experience required of an epidemiologist.

Introduction

Welcome to forensic epidemiology. This is the behind-the-scenes world where possible cause and effect are studied to change and save lives. Through studies of statistical data of such things as cancer, smallpox, car crashes with and without seatbelts, motorcycle deaths with and without helmets, healthy aging, airborne illnesses, homicides, natural deaths, suicides, and so on, a possible risk population or pattern may be determined. Once the at-risk pattern or population is determined, a safer alternate model may be put in place to prevent injury and save and change lives. Scientific method, compiled data, studies, and research are heavily used to determine specific, documented, and verifiable facts in order to deter or stop future outbreaks or occurrences.

History of Epidemiology

The coroner was the forerunner of the forensic epidemiologist and the position can be traced back to medieval times. The original coroners were medieval knights with no formal training in the forensic science of determining the cause or manner of death. Their function was to keep detailed records of crimes, deaths, and property, in order to assess potential revenue for the Crown (the king). The initial powers of the coroner, such as forfeiture of property, sanctuary, abjuration, and appeals, were removed in 1483. By the sixteenth century, the only function that remained for coroners to perform was the investigation of sudden and unexpected deaths.

When the early colonists came to America, they brought the coroner system from England with them. However, they realized that the investigation of violent and unexplained deaths required that the individual in charge have a specific academic background. In 1877, the then current coroner system was replaced by the medical examiner system in Massachusetts. The current U.S.

coroner system can trace its origin back to England when, in September 1194, the position of the coroner was formally established by Article 20 within the *Articles of Eyre*.

The science of epidemiology was first developed to discover and understand the possible causes of contagious diseases like smallpox, typhoid, and polio among humans. Over time, it expanded to include the study of factors associated with nontransmissible diseases like cancer and of poisonings caused by environmental agents. In order to understand disease, the risk factors associated with the disease became the major focus of epidemiological studies. Once risk factors are identified, epidemiologists conduct studies that modify these risk factors in order to assess whether there is a significant change or reduction in the frequency of a specific disease. Epidemiologists may be compared to detectives due to the role they play in public health, clinical research, and preventive medicine by searching out and identifying risk factors that may have a critical influence on the occurrence of disease within a specific population.

Definition of Epidemiology

Epidemiology has been defined as the study of the distribution of a disease or a physiological condition in the human population and the factors that influence this distribution. Epidemiology uses the scientific method to locate and describe these patterns of disease in a defined population and identify factors that may play a role. Focus on the patterns of disease is in terms of *time, place,* and *person*.

- *Time:* An attempt is made to determine whether there are increases or decreases in incidence of a specific disease over a set period of time.
- *Place:* Efforts are exerted to establish whether a specific geographic region has a higher frequency of a disease than another similar region and, if so, then why.
- *Person:* Work is completed to determine personal characteristics that distinguish those that develop a disease from those that do not.

Person features may be further subdivided into *personal, biological,* or *socioeconomic* characteristics.

- *Personal* features include age, sex, and race. Also included are personal habits such as tobacco, alcohol, and drug use; diet; and physical exercise.
- *Biological* features include blood analysis, enzyme studies, physiological functioning of the internal organs, and genetic profile.
- *Socioeconomic* features include income, education, and occupation.

Therefore, epidemiology can be considered as the science involving the sequence of reasoning concerned with the biological inferences derived from observations of disease occurrence and how it relates to human population. In other words, by observing the *who, what, when,* and *where* of an occurrence of disease and applying simple reasoning, one is most likely to find the *why*.

Epidemiological studies have three main purposes: (1) to determine etiological factors, (2) to evaluate a hypothesis using epidemiological data, and (3) when strong statistical association is found, to determine a preventative path.

- The first step is to elucidate the etiology of a specific disease by using epidemiological data and information from the other sciences such as genetics, biochemistry, and microbiology. For example, if an outbreak of food poisoning occurred in a restaurant, the etiological factors would be used to determine which food was contaminated by microorganism and a chemical analysis would be conducted on the served food.
- Next, it is necessary to evaluate a hypothesis of the etiology of a disease based on epidemiological data by clinical study or by laboratory experiment. For example, a few epidemiological studies have shown an association between the use of oral contraceptives and myocardial infarction. This reported initial relationship leads to the design and implementation of multiple, large-scale studies designed to obtain data to support or not support the cited association. If no association is shown, these studies attempt to explain the association with other noncontraception-related factors.
- Finally, when a strong statistical association is reported, the development and evaluation of preventive procedures to reduce the risk factors or behaviors associated with a disease are conducted. Once a solid association has been shown, clinical trials commence. In brief, a *clinical trial* is one in which individuals are randomly allocated to an experimental or a control group. The experimental group is given the drug to be evaluated; the control group receives a placebo ("sugar pill") of the drug. Then the two groups are compared to ascertain whether the drug had any effect on the disease. Confounding variables, biases, and other factors must always be controlled within these groups to avoid incorrect conclusions.

  If either the frequency of disease or behavior in the experimental group is significantly lower when compared to the control group, the researcher can state that, within a specific population, the modification resulted in a reduction in the risk of disease. The researcher further qualifies this using a stated level or a certain percentage drop in a specific behavior. An example of such a clinical trial could be one examining deaths associated with a high-fat diet. Multiple autopsy studies had reported that victims who died from a cardiac event had a high percentage of occlusions of their coronary arteries. Biochemical analysis of these plaques determined that they were formed by a diet high in fat. A clinical trial would compare a group with a high-fat diet to one with a low-fat diet. The participants would be followed for a number of years and thus the numbers that died from a cardiac event could be ascertained.

Epidemiological studies may further be classified as *observational* or *experimental*. *Observational* studies are descriptive epidemiological studies that can be divided into two basic types depending on (1) whether the events have already happened (retrospective) or (2) whether the events may happen in the future (prospective). In a *retrospective* study, the disease has already occurred and the interest is in determining whether the prior exposure is etiologically important in developing the disease. A retrospective study, or case-control study, is the study of a comparison between two groups where one group has the disease ("cases") and the other does not ("controls").

RETROSPECTIVE STUDY: SILICOSIS

An example of a retrospective study could be a study on the development of silicosis among a population of gold miners. Silicosis is a disease of the lungs caused by prolonged inhalation of silicon particles. The study would be carried out in the following manner:

1. Obtain a list of all those employed in a gold-mining operation and divide that population into those with and without the disease.
2. Collect a detailed work history on each miner in the study, including total years working in the mine, specific job title and duties, location within the mine, level of protection, and age at disease onset.
3. Determine a profile of risk factors that were associated with development of the disease and behaviors that offered protective factors against developing the disease.

In this study, maybe wearing a mask was the only variable that differentiated the two groups.

> **RETROSPECTIVE STUDY: VEHICLES CRASHING INTO TREES**
>
> An example of a retrospective study in the forensic arena is the investigation of drivers involved in a motor vehicle accident in which the vehicle hit a tree. Cases include drivers that were not wearing a seatbelt; controls would be drivers that did wear their seatbelts. The epidemiological investigation compares the injuries (including severity) and the number of deaths between those using and not using a seatbelt.

In a *prospective* study, the disease or behavior under study has not yet occurred. The study population is selected because of a particular characteristic or exposure to possible etiological agents and observations over a period of time until the disease or the behavior under study manifests or death occurs.

> **PROSPECTIVE STUDY: RESIDENTS LIVING DOWNWIND OF A PESTICIDE FACTORY**
>
> An example of a prospective study includes following the population who live downwind of a pesticide factory where an accidental release of a known carcinogen into the atmosphere has occurred.

> **PROSPECTIVE STUDY: ADULT WOMEN FORMERLY ABUSED BY THEIR MOTHERS**
>
> Another instance of a prospective study includes studying the behavior of adult mothers that were abused as children by their mothers who now have a newborn child. The women that meet this requirement are recruited into a study framework and will be followed for about 15 years. Data will be collected regarding the mothers' coping ability, daily self-reporting of inflicting any level of injury to their infants, number of visits to the emergency room, monthly physical examinations by a health care nurse to assess infant health, police reports, and death certificates. The goal of this type of study is to assess the rate of abuse among mothers who themselves were victims of abuse.

The strength of any epidemiological study depends on the number of cases and controls included in the study. The more individual cases included in the study, the more likely it is that a significant association will be found between the disease and a risk factor. Just as important is to identify correctly the variable believed to be associated with the disease or behavior that is attempting to be modified. If inappropriate factors are chosen and the real factors are missed, the study will not provide any useful information. Confounding variables must be identified and control parameters input either in the design of the study or by statistical methods. The interpretation of the results of any study must be made with caution as to whether the results can be generalized and the limitations of the study. Thus, it is very important that epidemiologists choose the proper factors to study at the outset and not study too many factors at once because the possibility of finding confounding factors increases with the addition of more variables.

Epidemiology relies heavily on statistics for establishing and quantifying the relationships between risk factors and disease and for establishing whether or not a particular disease is occurring excessively in a specific geographic area. Medical records can provide invaluable historical data for establishing trends in the incidence of diseases. Vast collections of medical record information are stored all over the world, and sorting through the data can be a very expensive and time-consuming process. In addition, the types of data that can be obtained from these records are only as good as the information that they contain, and often the information is scanty or impossible to verify. Sources of information commonly used in epidemiological studies include medical records, registries, and death certificates.

An epidemiological study can never prove causation; that is, it cannot prove that a specific risk factor actually caused the disease being studied. Epidemiological evidence can only show that this risk factor is associated (correlated) with a higher incidence of disease in the population exposed to that risk factor. The higher the correlation is, the more certain the association is; however, it can never prove the causation.

A prime example of this is the link between smoking and lung cancer. The discovery of the link was based on comparisons of lung cancer rates in smokers and nonsmokers. The percentage of lung cancer was much higher in smokers than in nonsmokers. Did this prove that cigarette smoking causes lung cancer? No. In order to prove that cigarette smoking is the factor causing this increase in lung cancer, it was necessary to expose animals to tobacco smoke and tobacco smoke extracts. This was done under highly controlled conditions where the only difference between the controls (animals not exposed to smoke) and treated animals was the exposure to smoke. These laboratory studies proved the causal association between smoking and increased risk of cancer.

Types of Epidemiology

There are many fields of study within epidemiology. These include study of aging; cancer; chronic disease; injury epidemiology; clinical trials; environmental epidemiology; infectious disease; genetic epidemiology; physical activity; psychiatric epidemiology; reproductive, perinatal, and pediatric epidemiology; telecommunications and public health; women's health; and forensic epidemiology. Some of these subspecialties are briefly described next.

Aging Epidemiology

The epidemiology of aging focuses on two primary areas: (1) etiological research related to important health problems of older adults, and (2) research on methods to promote healthy active aging. Evaluation of potentially disease preventive methods and the interaction of genetic and environmental factors that may influence the progression of "aging" are examined. Primary research focuses on cardiovascular disease, stroke, falls, frailty, physical activity, osteoporosis, arthritis, Alzheimer's disease, and cancer. The goal of aging epidemiology is to optimize health in older adults by emphasizing and promoting disease prevention, healthy aging, longevity, and prevention of disability. Students interested in this field are educated in biology and physiology of aging; epidemiology of aging; epidemiology of cardiovascular diseases; cancer epidemiology; methodological issues in behavioral lifestyle intervention; introduction to molecular epidemiology; human genetics; dimensions of aging, culture, and health; and research methods in aging.

Cancer Epidemiology and Cancer Control and Prevention Programs

Cancer epidemiology and prevention specialists require multidisciplinary training. Cancer prevention requires three basic tools: (1) knowledge of etiology, host response, and malignant processes; (2) the ability to measure risk at the individual and population levels; and (3) effective intervention methods. The ability to succeed within any one of the three conceptual domains requires a complete knowledge base, including relevant biology and special methodological skills. The goals of the program include (1) understanding the molecular and genetic bases of cancer, including the laboratory techniques involved; (2) having a working knowledge of the variety of disciplines concerned with disease prevention and control; (3) possessing the analytic skills required to develop and test hypotheses in cancer etiology, prevention, and control; and (4) know how to measure and modify behavioral risk factors.

Graduates serve in a variety of positions, from academic institutions to state and local health departments to clinical practice. The program emphasizes the importance of understanding disease etiology and identifying risk factors as critical components in devising successful prevention programs as well as in reducing the morbidity and mortality associated with cancer.

Cardiovascular/Diabetes (Chronic Disease) Epidemiology

The major emphasis in this field is the investigation of the etiology of chronic diseases, especially diabetes, coronary heart disease, and cancer; evaluating the effects of intervention on key risk factors; the translation of clinical trial findings into clinical practice; and the pursuit of community studies. Research examines the etiology and natural history of types of diabetes and methods of preventing the complications associated with the disease. The study of the risks of cardiovascular disease focuses on early identification of individuals at risk and the development of effective strategies for prevention.

Environmental Epidemiology

Environmental epidemiology studies provide expertise in the special problems associated with conducting epidemiological research into the health effects of environmental pollution. Students receive training in epidemiological research methods and in aspects of environmental measurements. Current interests include health effects of low-level radiation, noise, chemical contamination, environment, trace elements, and disease.

Infectious Disease Epidemiology

This field is designed to prepare health professionals (e.g., physicians, nurses, and nurse practitioners) for infectious disease surveillance, investigation, prevention, control, quality assurance, and research activities in the hospital, health department, or general community. Students in the program are typically collaborating and conducting joint training/research between the graduate school and Division of Infectious Diseases of the Departments of Medicine and Pathology of the School of Medicine, and the local county health department. Research interests include the epidemiology of HIV, human T-lymphotropic virus type I, and tuberculosis; the epidemiology of meningitis and other invasive bacterial infections in the United States; outbreak investigation; molecular epidemiology; and the genetic susceptibility and progression of hepatitis C virus infection. Students are exposed to epidemiology of infectious diseases, public health statistics, introduction to database management systems, health program evaluation, community health assessment, health survey methods, geographic information systems and spatial data analysis, experimental design, data analysis using computer packages, applied regression analysis, and constructing questionnaires and conducting surveys.

Reproductive, Perinatal, and Pediatric Epidemiology

These epidemiologists are trained to understand the patterns, risk factors, and interventions that might improve reproductive, perinatal, and pediatric health. Their education includes an integration of advanced epidemiologic training with coursework and experiences in obstetrics, gynecology, neonatology, pediatrics, psychiatry, adolescent medicine, and the basic sciences of genetics, molecular biology, and developmental biology.

The goals of reproductive, perinatal, and pediatric epidemiology are to:

- develop skills in epidemiology and biostatistics with particular emphasis on the application of methods needed to address important research questions in reproductive epidemiology;
- understand the pathophysiologic, genetic, behavioral, and environmental determinants of important diseases and disorders of pregnant women and children, emphasizing normative reproductive and developmental physiology, as well as subclinical aberrations on the way to clinical onset of disease;
- understand the domains of exposure, such as infection and inflammation, environmental toxicants, nutrition, injury, mood, substance use and abuse, and genetic susceptibility;
- comprehend the intersections of reproductive, perinatal, and pediatric outcomes such as fertility, preterm birth, growth restriction, fetal death, pre-eclampsia, and diseases of childhood and adolescence; and
- integrate the many different disciplines of science to develop cutting-edge approaches to the etiology, prevention, and treatment of diseases relating to pregnancy and childhood.

Students study reproductive epidemiology; epidemiology of women's health; analysis of cohort studies, epidemiology, and health services; public health genetics; and behavioral factors in disease.

Injury Epidemiology

In the early 1980s, the field of injury epidemiology was born. The field specializes in understanding injuries and their occurrence, outcome, and prevention. Academic curricula illustrate and emphasize the multidisciplinary nature of injuries, including the biomedical, behavioral, social, and risk sciences. Areas of research include the risk factors associated with falls among the elderly, the role of medication, assessments of violence, poisoning, highway safety, child maltreatment, traumatic brain injury, and outcomes from the acute care of injuries.

Genetic Epidemiology

In the late 1960s, genetic epidemiology became a separate field to examine the intertwined role of genetics and disease. Curricula include understanding the interaction between the individual's genetic predisposition and disease, the role of inheritance and prevention, and the interaction between genetics and environmental risk factors. Areas of research training in genetic epidemiology include aging, cancer, cardiovascular disease, diabetes obesity, and osteoporosis.

Psychiatric Epidemiology

This program provides advanced training in psychiatric epidemiology by emphasizing the use of epidemiologic methods and techniques to explore risk factors and the dissemination of psychiatric disorders. Students typically gain experience by working in a local psychiatric institution or clinic. Research opportunities include projects in depression, schizophrenia, geriatric psychiatry, substance use disorders, social and community psychiatry, behavioral medicine, antisocial behavior, delinquency, and assessment in psychiatry. Students are exposed to psychiatric epidemiology, assessment techniques in psychiatric epidemiology, epidemiology of children's psychiatric disorders, and behavioral factors in disease.

Physical Activity Epidemiology

The physical activity epidemiology track is one of the first to be offered within a U.S. school of public health. It is designed for students who already have training in exercise physiology (or a similar discipline) and are seeking an epidemiology graduate degree (master's or doctoral) with an emphasis in physical activity assessment and intervention research. Students are provided with the opportunity to work with a variety of local, national, and international studies examining the role of physical inactivity in the development of chronic diseases and/or the benefits of activity intervention in prevention efforts. A special emphasis in this program is placed on activity assessment and intervention efforts pertaining to minority populations.

Forensic Epidemiology

The most recent field to emerge is forensic epidemiology. This is the application of the basic scientific methods of epidemiology to the science of forensics. A detailed examination of this field is covered in later chapters.

Epidemiology: Education and Experience

The fundamentals of forensic epidemiology are deeply rooted in the principles of the science of epidemiology. Those interested in becoming forensic epidemiologists must first be educated and trained in the basic principles of epidemiology because practicing forensic epidemiologists use the epidemiological model to conduct their investigations of death and other criminal behaviors.

Schools of public health throughout the United States offer programs in the basic science of epidemiology and in some of its subspecialties. Students first receive a master of science (MS) or master of public health (MPH) degree in epidemiology. All students in the MPH program receive the foundational scientific principles of epidemiology. Students may then choose to continue their education and receive a PhD in a specialized area of study; each specialty has its own specific requirements. Those interested in pursuing a PhD in forensic epidemiology should attempt to conduct research at a medical examiner's or coroner's office. Ideally, they could volunteer as death investigators and follow the path of the evidence without the different laboratories to gain a more thorough understanding of the methods of analysis. In addition, exposure to forensic autopsies will offer much real-life training.

Forensic Epidemiology 2

Introduction

The field of forensic epidemiology is the newest area within the study of epidemiology. It merges two scientific fields: epidemiology and forensics. This chapter will provide a brief history of forensic science, the development of the field of forensic epidemiology, and an overview of careers within the field of forensic epidemiology.

Brief History of Forensic Science

The term "forensics" in general means the application of science to law. In other words, applying scientific methods or principles to a legal issue is forensic science. When the principles of physics can determine the trajectory of a fatal bullet, that is forensic science; when DNA recovered from the stamp on a ransom letter can be matched to the estranged husband, that is forensic science; when the chemical breakdown of a paint chip is used to determine the make and model of the hit-and-run vehicle, that is forensic science; and when a chemical test can spot a fake $20 bill, that is forensic science. Forensics is the investigation and establishment of fact or evidence by applying the knowledge and technology of the basic sciences to issues of the law. Forensic sciences are used in both criminal and civil courtrooms. The principles of scientific crime-detection methods such as serology, fingerprinting, firearm identification, and questionable documents were first popularized by Arthur Conan Doyle's fictional character Sherlock Holmes.

The fundamental fields of forensic science include forensic medicine, forensic toxicology, forensic photography, fingerprints, serology, chemistry, trace, ballistics, and document examination. With the development of the microscope, the field of trace evidence developed. In the late 1980s, DNA profiling was being perfected. Table 2.1 shows the chronology of inventions or discoveries critical to the history of forensic science. In 1959, the medical field of forensic pathology was established. Other fields include forensic anthropology, forensic entomology, forensic odontology, forensic psychiatry, forensic accounting, forensic engineering, and forensic epidemiology.

Table 2.1 Key Dates in the History of Forensic Science

	Chronology of the history of forensic science
1591	First practical microscope designed
1804	Discovery of the ultraviolet ray used to detect documents that have been erased
1814	*The Classification of Poisons* published by Mathieu Orfila, also known as the father of toxicology
1822	Reliable photographs possible
1835	Earliest method of comparing between striations on the bullet and the rifle barrel established
1836	Toxicological methods to detect trace amounts of poisons developed
1850	Development of the spectrograph
1858	Introduction of the science of fingerprinting
1876	Beginning of the x-ray
1882	Anthropomeny system developed for the criminal classification system based on body measurements
1893	Publication of a paper titled "Hanbuch fur Untersuchungsrichter als System der Kriminalistik" on the scientific investigation of a crime
1901	First system of grouping blood developed by Landsteiner into the ABO system; system developed to distinguish human from animal blood
1912	Development of tool mark identification
1921	Polygraph machine made portable
1925	Comparison microscope developed
1932	Method of measuring ethyl alcohol in the blood as an indicator of intoxication developed
1959	Field of forensic pathology established
1965	Development of the scanning electron microscope
1984	DNA profiling established

Development of Forensic Epidemiology

In the past, law enforcement and public health authorities did not interact much when they conducted examinations. The classic health inspector would examine a restaurant and had the power to fine or even close the establishment without involvement of the police. In the early days, the risk to public health was mainly from food contamination due to improper storage, cross-contamination, or poor hygiene practices. However, in today's society, the threat of deliberate contamination of water, food, air, or land as an act of bioterrorism is very real. Working alone, law enforcement would not recognize the bioterrorism threat; the same holds true for public health personnel. The problem is that law enforcement personnel are not trained to spot these types of crimes. An unusual or off-season increase in a particular type of virus would not raise suspicion among police officers, but it would be alarming to those in the public health setting. In turn, public health personnel are not trained in the legal methods and procedures of collection and documentation of evidence and other legal structures required to bring a case to trial.

Beginning in the 1970s and 1980s, law enforcement and public health authorities conducted joint investigations. These investigations centered on health problems suspected to have been intentionally caused or crimes that had potentially significant public health consequences. Examples include intentionally caused food-borne outbreaks or the "angel of mercy" syndrome, where health-care providers intentionally assisted patient deaths by administering lethal doses of drugs to patients.

In the late 1990s, the term "forensic epidemiologist" typically referred to epidemiologists that functioned as expert witnesses in civil trials. They were testifying as to the methodology of the study, number of subjects, length of the study, meaning of the results, and any limitations. They were frequently used to resolve such suppositions as whether exposure to certain chemicals related to a birth defect or performing a task repeatedly could cause carpal tunnel syndrome.

The term "forensic epidemiology" was first associated with bioterrorism in 1999 when it was used by the former chief deputy of the USSR bio-weapon program, Dr. Ken Alibek. Forensic epidemiology was defined then as the activity that would help distinguish natural from man-made epidemics. After anthrax-laced letters were mailed in September and October of 2001, Dr. Julie Gerberding, a senior official with the National Center for Infectious Disease of the Centers for Disease Control (CDC) and Prevention, defined forensic epidemiology as an epidemiologist trained to respond to bioterrorism attacks as well as other public health emergencies.

In 2002 several definitions of forensic epidemiology emerged. They included:

- the use of epidemiological methods as part of an ongoing investigation of a health problem for which there are suspicions or evidence regarding possible intentional acts or criminal behavior as factors contributing to the health problem; and
- the use of epidemiological and other public health methods in conjunction with or as an adjunct to an ongoing criminal investigation.

The events of September and October 2001 underscored the need for law enforcement and public health personnel to work together in conducting joint investigations—especially those centered around a possible bioterrorism event. "Forensic Epidemiology: Joint Training for Law Enforcement and Public Health Officials on Investigation Reponses to Bioterrorism" was developed by the CDC in 2002. A joint collaboration between the CDC and FBI resulted in the *Criminal and Epidemiological Investigation Handbook*. In Kentucky, the Department of Criminal Justice Training (DOCJT) designed a course specifically to aid law enforcement officers to operate closely and more effectively with public health officers when investigating a public health problem that may have been intentionally caused or crimes that had a public health consequence. This is accomplished by familiarizing officers with the basic principles of public health and epidemiological approaches to investigation.

Roles of Forensic Epidemiologists

The field of forensic epidemiology, while initially developed to focus on acts of bioterrorism, can also be used to investigate other types of crimes. A forensic epidemiologist can play a vital role in many other types of health emergencies and further threats to public health. He or she can examine a number of diverse crimes ranging from environmental to food-borne illness. Some examples include:

- environmental crimes, such as the improper disposal of hazardous waste that may result in human illness (cancer) or death;
- food-borne disease outbreaks caused by a food-processing plant that intentionally ignores safety protocols;
- automobile repair shops that use inferior parts to save money, resulting in an increase of motor vehicle accidents; and
- natural and non-natural deaths investigated by the medical examiner's or coroner's office.

Individuals trained in forensic epidemiology have the potential of working in a medical examiner's or coroner's office, local or state health department, public health sector, schools of public health, private organizations, as private consultants, and as expert witnesses. This book will primarily focus of the role of the forensic epidemiologist examining deaths investigated by the medical examiner's or coroner's office.

Medical Examiner's or Coroner's Office

The role of the forensic epidemiologist within a medical examiner's or coroner's office is diverse. The major role is to code the vast amount of incoming forensic data systematically. Additionally, he or she will conduct data analysis and provide basic data summaries of the deaths that can be understood and used by the public, news media, law enforcement, and public health officers. The forensic epidemiologist also assists in academic and research studies and the resulting publications. Chapter 3 describes in great detail the role of the forensic epidemiologist operating in a medical examiner's or coroner's office.

Health Department

Health departments employ forensic epidemiologists at the state and local levels. Their traditional function is to collect data regarding the births and deaths of the residents using their access to birth records and fetal and non-fetal death certificates. From these, vital statistics reports are created that include live births and mortality data regarding their specific area, region, or state. The mortality data include a detailed listing of the cause of death, differentiating each type of death (natural and non-natural) by age, sex, and race and also based on international classification of disease.

By examining several years' worth of vital statistics data, researchers can gain a picture of the changes, pattern, and magnitude of the causes of death within a specific region or an entire state. This trend analysis is critical to highlight changes in death patterns, emerging trends in specific areas, and possibly areas for crime prevention.

Public and Private Organizations

Many organizations require mortality data in order to gain funding for their particular study. These organizations employ forensic epidemiologists to locate, collect, and analyze the data using scientific methodology. Grant or funding agencies typically require a forensic epidemiologist on the project if it involves forensic data analyses. Some current examples of using a forensic epidemiologist in studies include investigation of SIDS deaths, providing forensic data for drug prevention programs, and acting as private consultants and expert witnesses.

SIDS Deaths

Suppose that an organization is applying for funding to implement an intervention program with the goal of lowering the number of sudden infant death syndrome (SIDS) deaths in a specific region. The forensic epidemiologist's role would be first to obtain copies of all SIDS deaths in that region over the past 5 years. This would establish a baseline number of annual deaths from SIDS. Next, a profile would be constructed of the characteristics of the SIDS deaths and the intervention protocol would be reviewed. The number and circumstances of SIDS deaths during the intervention period would be monitored. At the conclusion of the study, the numbers and rates of SIDS deaths before and after the intervention period would be compared in order to prove any effect on the number of deaths statistically and, more importantly, any decrease associated with the intervention or some other variable.

Drug Prevention Programs for Middle and High School Students

An organization is interested in obtaining funding to implement a drug prevention program targeting students in high school and middle school. The first step is to determine the magnitude of the drug abuse problem in that age group. This involves the collection and review of all forensic data from all deaths between the ages of 12 and 18 years old examined at the medical examiner's or coroner's office. The deaths would further be scrutinized to reveal deaths caused by a drug overdose, motor vehicle accident involving alcohol or drugs, suicide with a high level of drug detected in the blood, or homicides directly related to dealing or buying of drugs—all of which are related to the drug abuse problem. From these statistics, the forensic epidemiologist will then provide an overview of the drug problem, develop a profile of the typical victim of drug abuse, and, most importantly, provide information on the target population for the prevention program in order to obtain the most significant outcome.

Private Consultant

Forensic epidemiologists can function as forensic consultants. They are normally hired by families and attorneys to review and evaluate medical records, autopsy reports, police reports, technical data, level of investigation, and level and type of testing and then to provide a written report indicating their findings, which will assist in the determination of how to proceed with the case.

Families typically contact a forensic consultant when they refuse to accept the cause of death listed on the death certificate (usually death by suicide); they feel a poor death investigation was conducted or that a private forensic autopsy is warranted. Forensic consultants are also hired by law firms or individual attorneys to advise them; answer questions regarding medical, scientific, or forensic investigation procedures; or explain the meaning of test or study results. They typically produce a written report that often provides an opinion for future actions. This activity is conducted outside the courtroom. See Chapter 13 for a more detailed discussion of the role of the forensic consultant.

Expert Witness

Forensic epidemiologists are playing an ever increasing role as expert witnesses in the courtroom. An expert witness, in contrast to a forensic consultant, is hired to testify in a court of law and express his or her opinions regarding a particular aspect of a case. The role of a forensic epidemiologist functioning as an expert and the rules governing an individual testifying as an expert witness are covered in detail in Chapter 13.

3 The Role of the Forensic Epidemiologist in the Medical Examiner's or Coroner's Office

Introduction

Forensic epidemiologists can function in many settings. This chapter will describe their roles in a medical examiner's or coroner's (ME/C) office. Their primary function is the collection, analysis, and interpretation of the forensic data. In addition, they interact with outside agencies, participate on death review boards, present research results at conferences, create publications, and mentor and teach forensic epidemiological techniques at the undergraduate and graduate levels.

Role of a Forensic Epidemiologist in a Medical Examiner's or Coroner's Office

The main function of a forensic epidemiologist within an ME/C office is to collect raw forensic data, conduct data analysis, and provide an interpretation of the analysis and its limitations. The forensic epidemiologist must be able to collect data typically scattered over several departments or divisions and often within databases that cannot relate to each other, in a manner that can be useful to the office, forensic community, law enforcement, public health officers, and researchers. The data can be separated into three broad categories: *death investigation data, forensic medicine data,* and *crime laboratory data*.

Death Investigation Data

All deaths reported to the ME/C office are investigated by death investigators. Depending on the type of case, the amount of data collected and the level of field investigation carried out vary. In all cases, some basic data are collected that include name; age; data of birth; sex; race; occupation; place of residence; date, time, and place of the incident; time, date, and place of death; reporting agency; next of kin; and funeral home. The forensic epidemiologist will use the basic demographics of age, sex, and race as the starting point of any forensic epidemiological data presentation. He or she will then build on it with information provided by the forensic medical autopsy and later layer the data of the crime laboratory results.

Depending upon the type of death, the length and level of detail vary. The circumstances of the death will determine whether the death falls under the jurisdiction of the ME/C office as well as whether the office will conduct some level of investigation. Deaths called into the ME/C can be classified as *no jurisdiction* cases, *morgue* cases, or *office will issue* (OWI) cases.

A "no jurisdiction" case includes death cases called in by physicians inquiring whether they have the authority to issue the death certificate (DC). The ME/C office records the information for its records but no further investigation into the death is conducted. In a morgue case, the body is brought to the ME/C office. Morgue cases are the main focus of most forensic epidemiological data analysis.

A classification as an OWI case occurs when only medical records are subpoenaed into the office and the body is released directly to the funeral home. In morgue and OWI cases, the basic demographic data plus a detailed narrative of the circumstances of the death will be generated. The detail of this report is covered in Chapter 4. In almost all ME/C offices, this report follows a certain format, is several pages long, and is completed on a typewriter or a computer. The information within these reports is typically not coded; however, the role of the forensic epidemiologist is to create abstract forms for each manner of death as well as each subcategory. (The abstracted data for the different types of death are described in later chapters.)

Forensic Medicine Data

The second type of data available for the forensic epidemiologist to use as research is the *forensic medicine data*. The forensic medicine legal investigation involves the detailed examination of the body through a forensic autopsy. The goal of the autopsy is to determine the cause of death, the mechanism, and the manner of death. The forensic pathologist will first determine the type of autopsy to be conducted. There are two types: an external-only examination and a complete autopsy (described in Chapter 4).

Once the forensic autopsy is complete, the cases may be separated into one of the five manners of death: *natural, suicide, accident, homicide,* and *undetermined*. The deaths within each manner are then further subdivided into the specific subcategories shown in Table 3.1:

- Natural includes subcategories of natural and SIDS.
- Accidents are grouped into drug overdose (OD), industrial, motor vehicle-related, falls, medical misadventure, fire, exposure, and death due to asphyxiation.

The Role of the Forensic Epidemiologist

Table 3.1 The Five Manners of Death and Their Subcategories

Manner of death	Subcategory
Natural	Natural
	SIDS
	Drug OD
Accident	Industrial
	Motor vehicle related
	Falls
	Medical misadventure
	Fire
	Exposure
	Asphyxiation
Suicide	Suicide
Homicide	Homicide
	Homicide by vehicle
Undetermined	Undetermined

- Suicide includes suicide only.
- Homicide includes homicide and homicide by vehicle.
- Undetermined is when the specific cause cannot be conclusively determined.

Once the first two steps have been completed, the third step is the autopsy (Table 3.2). The cases will be divided into autopsy types of external-only or complete examination. This information is important because it affects the level of data available regarding internal organs and the toxicological analysis. An external autopsy has less information and the complete autopsy will provide much more data. The data collected from complete autopsies include the following: features of the body (weight and height), the external and internal trauma, and the internal organs and their weights. This will also facilitate the calculation of the number of cases undergoing a complete versus an external-only examination by subcategories. Knowing this permits the forensic epidemiologist to use statements such as the following in presentations or to media: "Among the individuals who fall and whose deaths are investigated by the ME/C office, only 45% undergo a complete autopsy examination."

The last of the steps to separate morgue death cases is to determine mechanism of death. Within each subcategory specific data are noted. (This is discussed in Chapters 6 through 9 in detail under "data collected by type of death.") For example, the numbers and types of vehicles, use of seatbelts, and the speeds of vehicles are collected in motor vehicle accidents. The results of the forensic examination allow for the determination of the mechanism of

Table 3.2 Steps to Separate Morgue Death Cases

Step	Operation	Separation
1	Manner of death	Natural, suicide, accident, homicide, and undetermined
2	Subcategory within each manner	See Table 3.1
3	Autopsy	External-only and complete
4	Mechanism of death	Specific cause of death:
		Natural—disease: organism, virus, bacterial
		Trauma—blunt force trauma, stabbing or bullet wounds
		Chemical—drug overdose
		Environment—exposure, asphyxiation

death such as a specific disease, organism, type of injury, or exposure that resulted in death. Examples of mechanism include pneumonia, cirrhosis, blunt force trauma, burns, hypothermia, asphyxiation, and gunshot wound.

The last type of separation within each subcategory is by mechanism of death. Some examples for each category of the mechanisms include:

- natural death: restriction of blood flow to the heart due to occlusions of the right coronary artery;
- drug overdose death: lethal ingestion of a prescription medication;
- fire death: inhalation of toxic gases incapable of exchanging oxygen for carbon monoxide at the biochemical level; and
- homicide: gunshot wound to the head that destroyed the brain stem.

Crime Laboratory Data

The last of the categories to gather information is the *crime laboratory data*. The forensic epidemiologist must understand the function of each division within the crime laboratory and the role that it plays in the investigation. He or she must also understand the types of evidence each division handles, the methods used to analyze and process that evidence, the information generated, and the significance of the results in each type of death.

The typical crime laboratory is made up of the following divisions: forensic toxicology, forensic photography, fingerprints, forensic serology, drug chemistry, trace, ballistics, tool marks, and document examination. Data come most frequently from the drug chemistry division—charged with analysis of the evidence collected from the crime scene, on the body, and in body fluids (blood, urine, bile, and eye fluid) collected during the autopsy—and the ballistics division, which provides data on the type and make of the firearm and the distance between the actor and victim; the trace evidence division describes the hair and fibers discovered on the victim. The level of involvement of the crime laboratory in the death investigation depends on the type of case.

Outside Agencies

The forensic epidemiologist also functions as an information officer between the ME/C office and outside agencies such as the local and national news media, Drug Enforcement Administration (DEA), Centers for Disease Control (CDC), Federal Bureau of Investigation (FBI), Drug Abuse Warning Network (DAWN), and private and public organizations.

Local and National News Agencies

Local and national news agencies, including television and print, often consult with the ME/C staff forensic epidemiologist when requesting up-to-date information. Most frequently requested are statistical data regarding deaths from homicides, overdoses, and motor vehicle accidents. On occasion, in-depth analysis of the data explaining trends and emerging or possibly expiring patterns is also shared with the media.

Drug Enforcement Administration

Forensic epidemiologists often work closely with the DEA to assess detailed drug overdose and death data. The DEA is responsible for enforcement of the controlled substances laws and regulations of the United States and brings charges to the U.S. criminal and civil justice systems. Table 3.3 highlights the other primary responsibilities of the DEA.

Drug Abuse Warning Network

Forensic epidemiologists operating in a large ME/C office may become involved in providing detailed drug information to DAWN and become the DAWN reporting office for that ME/C. DAWN is managed by the Office of Applied Studies (OAS), a component of the Substance Abuse and Mental Health Services Administration (SAMHSA) within the U.S. Department of Health and Human Services. The purpose of DAWN is to quantify the extent of the nation's drug problem, assess the effectiveness of local antidrug efforts, guide resource allocation, conduct surveillance of local area drug trends, and

Table 3.3 Primary Responsibilities of the DEA

Investigation and preparation for the prosecution of major violators of controlled substance laws operating at interstate and international levels

Investigation and preparation for prosecution of criminals and drug gangs who perpetrate violence in our communities and terrorize citizens through fear and intimidation

Management of a national drug intelligence program in cooperation with federal, state, local, and foreign officials to collect, analyze, and disseminate strategic and operational drug intelligence information

Seizure and forfeiture of assets derived from, traceable to, or intended to be used for illicit drug trafficking

Enforcement of the provisions of the Controlled Substances Act as they pertain to the manufacture, distribution, and dispensing of legally produced controlled substances

Coordination and cooperation with federal, state, and local law enforcement officials on mutual drug enforcement efforts and enhancement of such efforts through exploitation of potential interstate and international investigations beyond local or limited federal jurisdictions and resources

Coordination and cooperation with federal, state, and local agencies, and with foreign governments, in programs designed to reduce the availability of illicit abuse-type drugs on the U.S. market through nonenforcement methods such as crop eradication, crop substitution, and training of foreign officials

Responsibility, under the policy guidance of the secretary of state and U.S. ambassadors, for all programs associated with drug law enforcement counterparts in foreign countries

Liaison with the United Nations, Interpol, and other organizations on matters relating to international drug control programs

---

serve as a data source for academic research on drug abuse. DAWN obtains data from drug-related visits to emergency rooms and drug-related deaths examined by ME/C offices. The role of the forensic epidemiologist is to review and report to DAWN all drug-related deaths, including accidents, suicides, and undetermined manner of death and provide the following data: age, sex, race, county of death, place of death, manner of death, and a list of all the drugs associated with the death.

Law Enforcement

Local law enforcement agencies frequently contact forensic epidemiologists to obtain homicide data. The police are interested in all relevant data associated with a homicide that may create a pattern. These include the time and day of the week when homicides occur, the locations; the characteristics of the victims; the relationship between the actor and the victim; and the method of death. The forensic epidemiologist provides data about changes in criminal activity by age, sex, type, and mechanism, and also highlights areas with increasing crime. This information is important in reallocating resources to areas that are seeing a rapid increase in criminal activity.

Death Review Boards

Health departments that service a population of over a million individuals will organize and facilitate death review boards—multidisciplinary, multi-agency boards that examine the circumstances surrounding deaths within the jurisdiction of a particular health department. The goals of these boards are to describe trends and patterns of death, develop prevention strategies, and improve the flow of information and communication between various agencies. The two most frequent types are child death review boards and suicide death review boards; in some areas, elderly death review boards are created.

- Child death review boards investigate all deaths (natural and non-natural) among individuals under the age of 18 who died within the jurisdiction of the health department, including premature deaths (deaths prior to 38–40 weeks gestation).
- Suicide death review boards investigate all deaths listed as suicide by the ME/C office. The circumstances surrounding the suicide, past attempts, and access to the psychological community are examined.
- In some areas, elderly death review boards have been formed to investigate all deaths (natural and non-natural) among individuals age 65 and over.

Review Boards are composed of individuals representing the ME/C office, health department, police departments, emergency room physicians, advocate groups, Child Youth Services (CYS), and school administrations.

All death review boards function principally in a similar manner. The director of the board, typically an individual from the health department, composes a list of cases for review from DCs issued within that county. This list is then forwarded to all members of the board. The list contains cases by name and data of death. Local and/or state legislation provides authority for members of the board to obtain all records relating to the death. Each member of the board then reviews the records and prepares a summary of his or her involvement with the case. The ME/C office representative, either a forensic epidemiologist or a forensic pathologist, presents cases examined by the ME/C office, providing a summary of the circumstances leading to the death, the results of the death investigation, toxicological results, and the cause and manner of the death for each case. Cases presented include homicides, suicides, accidents, and some natural deaths, depending on the type of death review board. Cases not examined by the ME/C office (such as natural childhood deaths) are presented by the health department officer or physician where the child was treated.

Next, because the board comprises a cross section of different agencies, information from the other agencies provides supplementary information about the victim. These other agencies typically have access to information not available to the ME/C office. For example, board members from the law enforcement agencies present whether the victim had a criminal history, was associated with local gangs, or involved with the sale of drugs. Members from the schools will provide information about whether the victim had problems in school, such as poor grades, absenteeism, or bullying. Typically, the ME/C office does not have access to school records. Individuals from CYS can provide information as to whether they were ever called to investigate the home environment, the number of times CYS was called to the residence, and if the children were ever removed from the home. The medical treatment the victim received would be presented by physicians on the board who review the hospital records prior to the meeting.

The goal of these review boards is threefold. First, they create a summary report of the deaths presented during the review. These annual reports typically originate from the local health department. Second, they ascertain whether any of the deaths could have been prevented. Research here includes examples such as whether an admitting diagnosis might have been missed, a different treatment regimen would have altered the outcome, or warning signs to alert CYS to remove vulnerable children from a dangerous environment were missed. Finally, recommendations are made to prevent future deaths. For example, if the board examines a large number of deaths associated with drowning in small koi ponds, it would recommend that stronger warning signs be created or public service announcements produced.

Mentoring

Individuals interested in a career in the field of forensic epidemiology should contact their local ME/C office to inquire whether it has a mentoring or internship program. These programs are designed to allow graduate students to get hands-on experience in the fields of forensics science and forensic epidemiology.

These programs allow the student to understand the flow of the death investigation from the death investigators, death scene investigation, autopsy procedure, role of the forensic pathologist, and, finally, role of the forensic epidemiologist. They will gain an understanding of the process of a death call, what types of death are examined by the ME/C office, and what information is collected. The intern will ride along with the death investigators and witness the processing of a crime scene and the methods of evidence collection. At the morgue, interns can watch and possibly assist with the autopsy. They will gain an understanding of the pathology of natural and non-natural causes of death along with the anatomical data collected. The final part of the internship is to understand how all the data collected from the death investigations, autopsy, toxicology analysis, and the death certificate can be used in forensic research.

Teaching

Forensic epidemiologists are often employed at universities and graduate schools of public health to instruct and train future forensic epidemiologists. They are also instructors at law schools to expose law students to the science of forensic epidemiology and how they forensic epidemiologists can assist them in a trial.

Conferences

Conferences are annual meetings of professionals to exchange ideas and learn from the experience of others. Forensic epidemiologists attend these conferences to present their own research and to set up collaborations for future studies. These presentations can be in the form of an abstract or an oral presentation. Conferences of interest for forensic epidemiologists include those sponsored by the National Medical Examiner Association (NMEA), the American Academy of Forensic Sciences, and the National Center for Injury Prevention and Control. Additional related conferences include those held by the International Association of Forensic Nursing, Food and Drug Administration, National Conference on Science and the Law, and United States and Canadian Academy of Pathology.

Research and Publication

The forensic epidemiologist plays an important role in conducting and publishing research studies. Because he or she reviews all the deaths examined by the ME/C office, the forensic epidemiologist is in an ideal position to identify deaths that are unique, rare, or significant in terms of the findings and to write and publish these in a peer-reviewed journal.

However, before an article·(called a case report; see Chapter 13 for more information) is written, a literature review must first be conducted. The main system used to conduct a literature search of published articles is PubMed®. A literature review has three main purposes. The first is to determine the number of published articles that are similar to the proposed article. For example, a PubMed search of published papers may indicate that, in the past 2 years, 55 papers with similar titles concerning death by ethyl glycol (antifreeze) were published. The chances are slim that another paper on this topic will be published. On the other hand, if only seven articles have been published, the likelihood of publication is greater. The purpose of writing an article is to get published. To increase the chances of publication, a forensic epidemiologist should try examining a specific population that has not been thoroughly examined or using some unique angle of examining the data.

The second purpose of a literature review is to provide previous background information. Once the previously published article copies have been obtained, they will provide background information, a description of other cases, and the methods used to investigate such deaths. In the case of the ethyl glycol-poisoning article, a review of past articles will provide background data about the mechanism of death by ethyl glycol ingestion, the number of reported deaths in the literature, the description of the method of analysis, and the findings.

The final reason for a literature review is to avoid the pitfalls encountered by others because not all studies are fully successful. In the discussion section of a paper, most authors highlight the study's strengths, weaknesses, and limitations. After a thorough review, the forensic epidemiologist consults with a forensic pathologist to determine whether the case is significant enough to spend the time, sometimes significant, to write and submit a manuscript for publication. It is typically the role of the forensic epidemiologist to write and format the manuscript properly for submission. Once the manuscript is complete, the next step is to locate a peer-reviewed journal with focus objectives that match the manuscript's topic. Table 3.4 shows the major forensic journals and the focus of each.

The forensic epidemiologist with access to all the raw data within the ME/C office is often involved with research studies. He understands the methods involved in conducting scientific research, the type and level of detail of the information, and the limitation of the data collected. These studies can be initiated by the forensic epidemiologist, by a research question raised by a forensic pathologist, or in collaboration with an outside agency or group.

Peer-Reviewed Journals

Because of their education, experience, and knowledge of the scientific method, forensic epidemiologists are often asked by journals to be peer reviewers. Journals take two forms: peer-reviewed publications and non-peer-reviewed journals. All professional medical research work will be published in peer-reviewed journals where, after an author submits the manuscript, it undergoes a review process by experts in the field. An editor conducts a rapid review of the submission to determine whether the topic conforms to the scope of the journal and whether it is formatted correctly. Then the manuscript is sent to three or more reviewers who are experts in the field addressed in the paper. A more detailed examination of the peer-review procedure is presented in Chapter 12.

Table 3.4 Major Forensic Journals and Their Focus

Journal	Focus
Journal of Forensic Sciences	Original investigation, observations, case reports, and reviews in various branches of forensic sciences (forensic pathology, toxicology, psychiatry, immunology, odontology, jurisprudence, criminalistics, questionable documents, and engineering)
The American Journal of Forensic Medicine and Pathology	Features original articles on new examination and documentation procedures, as well as provocative discussions of the forensic pathologist's expanding role in human rights protection, suicide and drug abuse prevention, occupational and environmental health, and other key areas. Unique special features include case reports, technical notes on new examination devices, and reports of medicolegal practices worldwide
Journal of Forensic and Legal Medicine	Topical articles on all clinical aspects of forensic medicine and related specialties
Forensic Science International	Applications of medicine and science in the administration of justice
Forensic Science, Medicine, and Pathology	Encompasses all aspects of forensics, including pathology, science, toxicology, human identification, mass disasters/war graves, nursing, police surgeons/scene of crime, entomology, biology, and DNA. Balanced to reflect modern advances in the subjects through peer-reviewed papers, short communications and meeting proceedings, and case reports; provides coverage on the full international spectrum of forensic science, not concentrating on the sole practice of a single country or becoming top heavy with a particular scientific advancement
Clinical Forensic Medicine	Topical articles on all clinical aspects of forensic medicine and related specialties
Journal of Forensic Nursing	Makes forensic nursing science available to clinicians, educators, administrators, and researchers. Presents scholarly manuscripts to expand empirical evidence important to the practice of forensic nursing worldwide

The Operations of a Medical Examiner's or Coroner's Office

4

Introduction

It is important for a forensic epidemiologist working in an office of a medical examiner or coroner (ME/C) or utilizing data generated from an ME/C office to conduct research to have a good understanding of the general operations of such offices. This chapter will explain the origin of the current coroner system, examine the differences between a medical examination office and that of a coroner, and provide a definition of an ME/C case—the step-by-step procedures after someone dies, a general understanding of the key personnel and their roles in the forensic investigations, the reports generated by the death investigations, and the forensic pathologist's final report. Detailed types of information collected in various manners of death are covered in Chapters 6–9.

Death Investigation Systems in the United States

Over time, two types of forensic investigative systems have come to be in place in the United States: the medical examiner's office and the coroner's office. Figure 4.1 shows the jurisdiction of ME/C offices in the United States.

The Coroner's Office

The majority of small counties have a coroner system, which is mainly dictated by economics and workload. The qualifications of a coroner are governed by the bylaws and statutes of each county. In general, this is an elected position of a 4-year term open to all individuals over 18 years old and living in that county. Typically, the individual has no or limited medical training. Recently, however, most areas require that the coroner receives some training and continuing education. The coroner typically appoints deputy coroners to investigate deaths and hires or contracts with a nearby forensic pathologist on a part-time basis to handle complicated death investigations. The role of the coroner is to determine positive identification and the cause and manner of death.

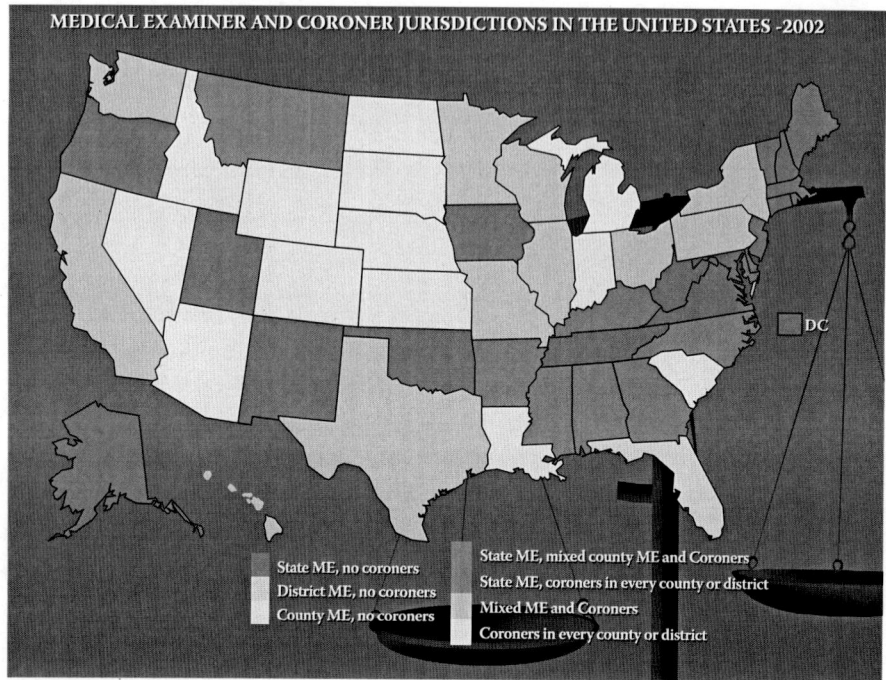

Figure 4.1 Medical examiners' and coroners' jurisdictions in the United States in 2002.

The Medical Examiner's Office

The ME system has been steadily replacing the older coroner's system in many areas. The medical examiner is appointed, typically for a 5-year term. The individual must be an MD with 4 additional years of forensic pathology specialty training, including anatomy and clinical pathology. Forensic pathology became a subspecialty of medicine in 1959. The role of the medical examiner is identical to that of the coroner: the determination of the cause and manner of death and positive identification of the victim.

The Death Call

All forensic death investigations begin with a "death call" to the ME/C office. These calls reporting a death are made by a police officer, paramedic, physician, emergency room (ER) staff, or family member. The calls are transferred to the Death Investigative Division staffed 24 hours a day, 7 days a week by specially trained investigators who are often called death investigators, forensic investigators, or deputy coroners. During this initial telephone conversation, the investigator first ascertains whether the death falls under one of the categories of reportable deaths (see next section). The main factors that a death investigator considers to determine whether the death is an ME/C case include:

- the specific circumstances surrounding the death;
- whether the death was unexpected, suspicious, or traumatic in nature;
- whether a physician will sign a death certificate (DC) citing a natural death; and
- the office's specific protocol as to the types of cases that will be investigated.

A large number of death calls are simply inquiries by physicians because they are unsure if they are permitted to sign the DC. People who die natural, expected deaths under the care of a treating physician willing to sign the DC typically go directly to the funeral home. However, if the victim has no physician or the physician does not feel comfortable or refuses to sign the DC, the body comes under the jurisdiction of the ME/C office. Some ME/C offices that serve a large metropolitan area with a large number of homicides or drug overdose deaths may not investigate motor vehicle accidents, but rather will allow state police to investigate such deaths.

Once the death is determined to fall under the jurisdiction of the ME/C office, the death investigation begins. The death investigator collects preliminary information and then determines the level of investigation and the types of criminalists required to process the scene, or the death investigator determines that obtaining the medical records is sufficient for the death investigation.

What Constitutes a Reportable Death in an ME/C Case?

Not every death constitutes an ME/C case. In most jurisdictions, death investigators are trained to identify the types of deaths that fall under the jurisdiction of the ME/C mandate. In general, deaths that are sudden, unexpected, unexplained, or traumatic, as well as medically unattended deaths, are investigated by the ME/C office. The following is a general list of reportable deaths:

- all sudden deaths not caused by readily recognizable disease or wherein the cause of death cannot be properly certified by a physician on the basis of prior (recent) medical attendance;

- all deaths occurring under suspicious circumstances, including but not limited to those in which alcohol, drugs, or other toxic substances may have had a direct bearing on the outcome;
- all deaths occurring as a result of violence or trauma, whether apparently homicidal, suicidal, or accidental, including but not limited to those due to mechanical, thermal, chemical, electrical or radiation injuries; drowning; and cave-ins and/or subsidence, regardless of the time elapsing between the time of the injury and death;
- any stillbirth or infant death occurring within 24 hours of birth where the mother has not been under the care of a physician or the mother has suffered trauma at the hand of another person;
- all criminal abortions, regardless of the gestational age of the fetus;
- all hospital deaths that occur as a result of accidental injury during diagnostic or therapeutic procedures, including but not limited to surgical procedures; all deaths following the accidental administration of excessive amounts of a drug, including but not limited to blood or blood products. In addition; all operative, perioperative, and postoperative deaths in which the death is not readily and clearly explainable on the basis of prior disease;
- deaths of all persons while in legal detention, jails, or police custody, including any prisoner who is a patient in a hospital, regardless of the duration of hospital confinement;
- deaths due to disease, injury, or toxic agent that occur during active employment;
- any death wherein the body is unidentified or unclaimed; and
- any death in which there is uncertainty as to whether it should be reported.

Number of Cases Investigated by ME/C Offices

Not all deaths are investigated by the ME/C office. In fact, only a small percentage of all deaths undergo a formal forensic investigation. Table 4.1 illustrates the number of deaths in a large metropolitan city with a population of 1.3 million served by an ME office that undergo a forensic investigation.

Table 4.1 Total Number of Deaths Investigated by the ME/C Office

	Number	Percentage
Total population	1,300,000	—
Number of deaths annually	15,000	100
Number of cases investigated by the ME/C office	1,750	11.7
Number that receive no forensic investigation	13,250	88.3

Among the 15,000 annual deaths, 11.7% undergo some form of forensic investigation while over 88% receive no form of investigation.

ME/C Death Cases

Once a death is determined to fall under the jurisdiction of the ME/C office, a formal death investigation begins. The role of the death investigator is threefold: obtain detailed information about the circumstances surrounding the death, collect forensic evidence at the scene and from the body and surrounding environment, and create a *death investigation report*. This report is an official written report recording the personal observation of the death investigator; a summary of statements obtained through interviews with the next of kin (NOK), family, friends, and police; a review of outside agency reports (emergency medical services [EMS], hospital, and police reports); a description of the evidence that was collected; and basic epidemiological data about the victim.

The death investigator begins by collecting initial information about the death, some of which is the same basic epidemiological information about the victim: name, age, date of birth, sex, race, marital status, residence address, social security number, and contact information of the NOK. Next, the investigator obtains a brief summary of the possible type of death and the location where the event occurred and where the body is now. A death can occur virtually anywhere, but we will generalize the location to residence, hospital, or scene.

Death at a Residence

When an individual is discovered unresponsive in a residence, EMS is called to the scene. Depending on the location, this may be emergency medical technicians (EMTs), paramedics, police, or fire personnel. In cases where the individual is dead on arrival (DOA), the EMS personnel typically attach a three-lead electrocardiograph (EKG) to the chest to verify asystole (no cardiac activity). This EKG strip is sent electronically to the ER physician, who confirms that the individual is dead and pronounces him or her dead. This protocol varies from state to state. Individuals who are permitted to pronounce an individual dead vary greatly from state to state and even within each state.

At this point, either the body is released from the residence directly to the funeral home or the death becomes an ME/C case. The EMS personnel at the residence will collect medical history, contact the ME/C office, and report the death and the specific circumstances surrounding the death. Based on the information provided, the ME/C will determine what will happen to the body. Factors contributing to this determination include whether the death was witnessed, circumstances surrounding the death, whether there is any reason to suspect foul play, signs of trauma, the deceased's personal medical history (PMH), and information provided by the victim's physician and his or her willingness to sign the DC. A few examples that best illustrate the differences follow.

Example 4.1

A wife comes home to find her 87-year-old husband unresponsive on the couch. She calls 911 and the responding paramedics determine that he had expired several hours earlier. The wife informs the paramedics that he had three prior heart attacks and is on digoxin. The body does not exhibit any signs of trauma and no foul play is suspected. The family physician is comfortable completing the DC with the immediate cause of death as myocardial infarction (MI) and the manner of death as natural. In this illustration, the ME/C would be contacted and would permit the body to be released directly to the funeral home.

Example 4.2

A man arrives home at 3:45 a.m. and discovers his 17-year-old roommate unresponsive on the living room floor. When paramedics arrive, they determine that the victim is beyond medical treatment. The residence is very messy, littered with beer bottles and pizza boxes. A white powdery residue is noticed on the coffee table. The roommate is unable to provide a PMH or the name of a physician. The paramedics contact the police and ME/C about the suspicious death. At this point, the role of the police or medics is to secure the scene until the ME/C personnel arrive at the residence to collect evidence and remove and transport the body to the morgue.

Example 4.3

An apartment superintendent receives calls from residents about a strong odor coming from apartment 305. Using his passkey, he enters and discovers a badly decomposed body and a large number of flies. He immediately locks the door and calls 911. A quick look by the responding policeman determines the victim is dead and he seals the apartment until the ME/C personnel arrive. During the interview with the super, the death investigators learn that the apartment was rented by a single 56-year-old white male who worked for an airline. The ME has jurisdiction over this body for several reasons. First, a positive identification must be made but, due to the advanced decomposition, other methods such as dental records or fingerprints will be required. Second, to determine the cause of death, the body must undergo a complete forensic autopsy. Finally, the body represents a biological hazard and cannot be left at the apartment.

Death in a Hospital

Not all deaths occur in a residence, even though the precipitating event occurred there. Individuals can initially be alive and transported to the emergency room or cardiopulmonary resuscitation (CPR) may have been initiated by a family member and then continued by emergency personnel en route to the ER. They can die shortly after arrival, be admitted into an intensive care unit (ICU); they may die weeks later from the injuries or from complications associated with the injuries or in a long-term-care facility years after the event.

The reporting of an individual's death in a hospital depends on the circumstance. Reportable deaths include those listed previously, with special emphasis on those that occurred as a result of accidental injury during diagnostic or therapeutic procedures, including but not limited to surgical procedures, and all deaths following the accidental administration of excessive amounts of a drug, including but not limited to blood or blood products. In addition, all operative, perioperative, and postoperative deaths in which the death is not readily and clearly explainable on the basis of prior disease are reported.

Death at a Nonresidence

Deaths outside the residence or hospital are typically not witnessed and receive the highest level of investigation. Examples include the discovery of a dead individual in a park or a vehicle that collided with a tree. Because these types of deaths are not witnessed, the sequence of events leading to the death must be reconstructed based on forensic death investigation techniques.

Regardless of where the death occurred, the date, time, and the person who reported the death to the ME/C office are collected for the report. The time, date, and location of the incident and the time, date, and location of death are presented next. The next section is entitled "Circumstance of Death." This is a detailed narrative of the events surrounding the death. The death investigators take the information from all the various sources (police reports; statements by family, friends and witnesses; hospital reports) and their individual observation of the death scene to write this in-depth description of the events that occurred prior to death, the death itself, and the actions taken after the event. If outside agencies such as emergency response teams, police, and firemen responded to the scene, the names, badge numbers, and/or company numbers are also included in the report. The report contains the address and phone number of the funeral home handling the arrangements.

The death scene and the location of the body may not be the same. For example, consider an individual who is shot in his home and then transported to the ER, where he dies. The ER is not the crime scene but rather the place of pronouncement of death. Death investigators will contact local police agencies to secure the crime scene while they recover the body. At the hospital, they also collect any effects such as the clothing worn by the victim, all medical records from the hospital including x-rays and CAT scans, and any body fluids collected. Once the body is placed in the morgue cooler, they process the scene. The forensic investigation can take two forms: office will issue or a morgue case.

Office Will Issue (OWI)

A large number of deaths are never brought into the ME/C office for a forensic examination or have a death scene investigation. They are classified as "office will issue" (OWI). These cases are typically natural deaths or accidental falls. The forensic pathologist will order all medical records and review the data and then complete the DC based on information contained within the medical records. The body is transferred directly to the funeral home.

Morgue Cases

A morgue case is a death that falls under the jurisdiction of the ME/C office and undergoes a full forensic investigation. A death investigation, in brief, involves sending death investigators to the scene and place of pronouncement of death. The location of the death can be at a residence, hospital, or other scene (e.g., a highway or coal mine). The type of incident dictates the number and type of personnel required to process the scene.

The death investigator collects the following basic information: identity of the victim, if possible; age; sex; race; marital status; permanent home address; the time, date, and location where the incident occurred; and the time, date, place of death, and the NOK information. The categories of identification are listed in Table 4.2.

After the scene has been processed, which includes photographs and evidence collection, the body is put on a white sheet, placed in a body bag, and then transported to the morgue. Upon arrival, the body is placed on a flat gurney and a head block is put under the victim's head to prevent a large amount of blood from collecting (pooling) in the face. The body is placed in a cooler kept at 40°F. At this temperature, the decomposition process is slowed down but not stopped.

When the death investigator returns to the office, he or she works on creating the death investigation report. This report includes downloading digital images taken at the scene and, if warranted, subpoenaing medical records, EMS trip sheets, and police reports.

The death investigator writes a summary of events report that contains a detailed narrative of the events leading up to the death and the observations

Table 4.2 Level of Identification

Categories of identification	Methods used
Positive	Next of kin, family, photo ID, fingerprints, dental records, DNA
Tentative	Clothing, jewelry, position with vehicle
Unknown	Body no. 1, body no. 2, etc.

of the death investigators at the scene, plus names and IDs of police, EMS, and fire personnel at the scene. It also contains a list of evidence collected from the scene.

Prior to the start of the autopsy, the forensic pathologist reviews the death investigation report, the scene pictures, and medical records, and he or she may contact the investigating police officers. This is done to (1) determine the type of autopsy to perform, (2) determine whether additional information is required, (3) notify the crime laboratory that special tests are required, and (4) notify other forensic specialists (odontologists, anthropologists, entomologists) that their services will be required during the autopsy. Additionally, the forensic pathologist must inquire whether police officers or homicide detectives are requesting to be present during the autopsy.

Direct Release to the Funeral Home

Bodies can be released directly to the funeral home from the residence or hospital when the individual's physician is willing to sign a DC as natural or after the ME/C has reviewed the circumstance of the death and/or provided sufficient past medical history to allow the physician to sign the DC or the office to issue the DC (OWI) as a natural death. This serves as an unofficial safety system to prevent cases that should have undergone a forensic investigation from not going through it. Most funeral home personnel have a great understanding of what types of cases qualify as ME/C cases. Therefore, if a body is released directly to the funeral home from a residence or nursing home and personnel observe bruising or other evidence of trauma, they will contact the ME/C.

Forensic Examinations

The forensic epidemiologist must understand the different types of forensic examinations of the dead and the advantages and limitations of each type. The body can undergo two types of forensic examinations: an external-only examination or a complete examination. The type is determined by the forensic pathologist.

External Examination

The purpose of an external examination is to document and describe how the body appeared when it arrived at the morgue. This examination consists of six phases: (1) photographing the body, (2) description of the clothing, (3) detailed head-to-toe examination documenting the physical description of the body, (4) identification and collection of evidence, (5) collection of body fluids, and (6) review of medical records. An external examination is conducted on all bodies brought into the morgue.

Photographing
Autopsy technicians place the body on an examination table, where it is photographed by an autopsy forensic photographer. The body is photographed following a set protocol. It is first photographed head to toe in the exact condition in which it arrived at the morgue. Next, close-up shots of the face are taken. Then the body is rolled over and overall pictures are taken. If there is forensic evidence on the body or the clothing, that evidence is photographed and then collected prior to removal of the clothing. After all the trace evidence is recovered, the clothing is removed. The body is then photographed again. The body is then washed in cool water and the entire body is photographed again. Several methods are used to document the appearance of the body as it arrived: photographs, handwritten notes by the forensic pathologist, and, in some agencies, use of tape recordings or video recordings.

Clothing
After the body is photographed, the clothing is described by the forensic pathologist. The examination and description of the clothing include noting the condition, such as wet, dry, dirty, or odoriferous, as well as noting tears and/or holes. The clothing is removed layer by layer, and each layer is described in terms of the type of clothing, color, and condition; each piece is then placed on a white sheet. The pants and shirt pockets are searched for evidence by the autopsy technicians. In cases of homicide, the clothing is wrapped up in white paper sheets and taken to a forensic crime lab for processing. If the death is not suspicious, the clothing is placed in a brown paper bag and given to the funeral director when the body is picked up.

The External Body Examination
The now naked body is first described by the forensic pathologist in terms of body development, state of preservation, body temperature, level of rigidity, presence of unfixed and fixed lividity, and the level of nutrition. Body development refers to the state in which the body size should be for that stated age. Terms used to describe these features include "underdeveloped," "well nourished," "well developed," etc. The level of nutrition is described as "adequately nourished," "well nourished," "obese," or "morbidly obese." "Underdeveloped" refers to a body that may be receiving insufficient nutrition due to a poor diet or deliberate starvation. The level of obesity is also noted.

The preservation of the body would be described as "good," "early decomposition," "putrid," or "skeletonized," and any areas of skin slippage are noted. Skin slippage occurs when the outer layer of skin comes off the body when pulled; it is often seen on bodies in advanced stages of decomposition (2–3 weeks after death). The body temperature is documented in general terms such as "warm," "cool," "frozen," or "cold to the touch." The rigor, livor, and algor displayed by the body are described next. Rigor is the chemical changes within the muscle fibers that cause them to be rigid. Livor is the setting of blood due to gravity, which causes a purplish discoloration. Algor is the cooling of body.

The process then continues with a meticulous head-to-toe examination. Starting at the head, the hair is described by color, length (short, medium, long), and grooming. If a moustache or beard is present, its color and length are noted and described. The eyelids are opened and the eye color and pupil size are documented. Signs of petechial hemorrhage are also looked for on and around the eyes and face. Petechial hemorrhages are small, pin-head-sized collections of blood caused by an acute increase in venous pressure that in turn causes rupture of the thin-walled venules. The presence of petechial hemorrhages is a classic sign of death from asphyxia, compression of the neck, or strangulation. However, they can be seen in some natural deaths.

The nose is examined for fractures and foreign bodies. The lips are examined externally and internally for recent trauma and then pulled back to expose and examine the teeth. The upper and lower dentures are described in terms of natural teeth or dentures, overall condition, and the state of repairs. The oral cavity is examined for foreign material such as food or, in the case of young children, toys and the presence of trauma to the tongue. The head is manually examined in order to detect lumps, deformity, and areas of trauma that may be visually obscured by the hair.

The neck region is examined next for symmetry, deformity, fractures, or other signs of injury or trauma. The pathologist then moves to the chest region, where signs of asymmetry, old and recent scars (from surgery), bruises, and other signs of trauma are noted. Normally, the chest is symmetrical (i.e., the right and left sides are the same). However, if one side is distended, it may be a sign of a tension pneumothorax, which occurs when there is damage to the lungs caused by trauma; air is allowed to enter the chest cavity with each breath but cannot escape, causing the distension.

The pathologist then moves to the abdominal region, again looking for distention, bulging, and masses by palpation and observation. Abdominal distention can be a sign of gas production, whereas a mass could be a possible tumor or a hernia. The pelvic region and external genitals are examined next, and any trauma is noted and described in detail. Bruises discovered during the examination may have a major impact regarding the course and type of further examination. A bruise is an injury caused by blunt-force trauma

(BFT) that causes hemorrhage into the skin and the tissue underneath. Dating a bruise by its color is an inaccurate method.

The extremities are examined next, starting with the shoulders and working down to the fingers. Any evidence of trauma or injury is noted. The fingernails are specifically examined. The nails are described in terms of cleanliness, length, presence of debris, and presence of polish. In addition, broken or missing fingernails are also noted. Next, the legs and toenails are examined in the same manner as that used for the arms and fingernails. The location, length, and age (recent or remote) of all scars are noted.

In cases where a firearm was involved, the hands of the victim should have been placed in paper bags and secured at the scene. At the autopsy, the bags are removed, and the hands will be carefully examined. When a firearm is discharged, the burned and unburned powder can deposit on the hands of the individual firing the firearm, his or her clothing, individuals in close proximity to the firearm when it is discharged, and among individuals that handle a fired firearm. The test for the presence of these fine particles is carried out with an atomic absorption analysis kit.

This kit is used to detect primer elements—barium and antimony—on the hands. This residue is removed by swabbing the back and palm of the right hand and back and palm of the left hand, using a small cotton swab saturated with 5% nitric acid. These cotton tips are further analyzed for the presence or absence of these compounds.

The next item noted is evidence of recent medical or surgical treatment. This includes things like endotracheal tubes, electrocardiogram electrodes, and intravenous catheters. In some cases, the forensic pathologist allows the removal (recovery) of organs and tissues for the purpose of transplants prior to arrival at the morgue. The organs (eyes, heart valves) or tissues (long bone or skin) that are removed must be specifically designated and reports should be requested from the tissue transplant team recording their condition.

Special Processing of the Body

In certain cases, the examination requires special processing. If the victim suffered a self-inflicted gunshot wound, the region may be x-rayed. The reason is to document that the projectile (bullet) went through the body, to show the location of fractures and the bones involved, and for the presence and location of any residual foreign materials.

Types of Complete Forensic Examinations

The external examination described earlier is conducted on all bodies that are brought into the ME/C office. This can be followed by what is called a "complete forensic autopsy." This involves the examination of the internal organs. There are basically two methods of conducting a complete forensic examination: the Virchow technique (described later), where the organs are removed from the body one by one, and the Rokitansky technique, which involves the dissection of the internal organs as a block.

The Complete Examination (Virchow Technique)

After the external examination, the internal examination begins with a Y-shaped incision to the chest. This extends from the upper left chest region near the shoulder and angles downward toward the tip of the sternum. A similar incision is made on the right side. These two incisions intersect at the xyphoid process located at the end of the sternum. From there, the incision extends downward in the midline of the body to the pelvic region (symphysis pubis), curving slightly around the umbilicus (belly button). Care needs to be taken not to injure the underlying organs. These three folds of skin and subcutaneous adipose tissue are dissected from the underlying musculoskeletal structure, exposing the chest plate and the internal abdominal organs. There is very little bleeding because there is no blood pressure. The fat pad is measured in centimeters at the umbilicus. The ribs and sternum are now exposed and examined for fractures and any deformity.

It is not uncommon, especially among the elderly, for the ribs and the sternum to have been fractured as a result of administering potentially life-saving CPR. The position of the diaphragm is noted. The diaphragm is the muscle that divides the chest (thoracic) cavity organs from those of the abdominal cavity. Normally, the diaphragm is positioned at the level of the fifth rib. Rib cutters are used to free and remove the ribs and sternum to expose the heart, lungs, liver, and stomach.

The internal organs are usually examined in the following order: heart, lungs, liver, pancreas, spleen, kidneys, prostate, and brain.

Heart

The first internal organ examined is the heart, which is located beneath the chest plate (sternum) and enclosed by a thin membrane called the pericardium. Normally, the pericardium contains a few cubic centimeters of fluid. However, excess fluid or blood within this space will place pressure on the heart and prevent its proper functioning. The pericardial space is examined by making a small incision into the pericardium to determine the amount of fluid within the space. Then the pericardium is opened, exposing the heart. A large bore syringe is inserted into the aorta to collect blood for analysis. The heart is examined *in situ* (as it is situated within the body). The heart is then removed by cutting the aorta, superior and inferior vena cava, and pulmonary arteries and veins, and it is then weighed. (Appendix A shows the normal weight of the male heart.)

The weight of the heart can offer clues as to the cause of death. An enlarged heart may be a marker of myocardial disease such as hypertension, valvular heart disease, or ischemic heart disease. The forensic pathologist examines the four chambers of the heart (right atrium, right ventricle, left atrium, and left ventricle). The color (dark red or cherry red) and amount of clotted blood within the chambers are noted. The thicknesses of the left and right ventricles are measured. In an average sized individual, the normal right ventricle is 0.3–0.4 cm thick, and the left is 1.5–1.8 cm thick. Thickening of the ventricles or hypertrophy may be a cause of heart failure. The heart contains four valves (tricuspid, pulmonic, mitral, and aortic), whose circumferences are measured; each one is examined for evidence of thrombi. A thrombus is a solid mass composed of blood, platelets, fibrin, and red and white blood cells formed due to inflammation.

The heart muscle receives its blood supply from three coronary arteries (right coronary artery, left coronary artery, circumflex artery). Normally, the heart beats 70 times a minute and pumps 5 quarts of blood. It takes 20 seconds for blood to circulate throughout the entire vascular system. These arteries are examined by multiple cross sectioning of the arteries (i.e., cutting it like a loaf of bread). The pathologist is looking for evidence of pathological changes, which include the degree of atherosclerosis, luminal narrowing, or calcification. The most common pathology of the heart is atherosclerosis, a disease of the arteries characterized by the formation of plaques composed of lipids, collagen, and calcium. The pathologist makes cross sections of each of the three coronary arteries and estimates the percentage of blockage or luminal narrowing. He or she ranks the percentage of narrowing into minimal (less then 20%), moderate (20–50%), or severe (over 50%). The myocardium (heart muscle) is described in terms of consistency, color, and any gross signs of scarring.

Lungs

The lungs are examined next. The respiratory system begins at the nasal and oral cavities that lead to the pharynx, past the larynx (vocal cords), and down the trachea (windpipe), which then divides into the right and left bronchi that enter the lungs. The primary function of the lungs is to exchange gases (i.e., eliminate carbon dioxide and supply blood cells with oxygen). This takes place in the alveolar (air sac) capillaries, takes 0.25 seconds, and is referred to as the blood–gas exchange. The surface area of the lungs is 80 m^2 and contains a total of 300 million alveoli.

The lungs are first examined *in situ*. The forensic pathologist runs his hand along the perimeter of the lungs searching for adhesions (when the lungs stick to the internal walls of the chest), which can be caused by prior surgery or tumors. The lungs should be free floating. The surface of the lungs is described in terms of its color. Lungs are normally pink to light reddish tan to purple in color. They are separated by cutting at the primary bronchial attachments and then weighed. (Appendix A shows the normal weight of the male lungs.)

Weight can offer clues to the pathology of the lungs. Diseases causing chronic obstructive pulmonary disease (COPD), or emphysema, result in lungs below the normal range, while pulmonary infection such as pneumonia produces heavier than normal lungs. The interior of the lungs is examined first by cutting along the path of the bronchioles to expose the smaller airways. Then, cuts are made along the long axis of the lung to expose the maximal amount of surface area. Each lung is sectioned from top to bottom across the organ and examined for congestion, tumors, infarcts (a localized area of dead tissue due to a lack of blood supply), infections, and edema (swelling). Representative samples from the different lobes of the lung are placed in formaldehyde and later sent to histology for preparation.

Liver

The examination then focuses on the liver, the largest internal organ. The functions of the liver are (1) fuel management, (2) nitrogen excretion, (3) water balance, and (4) detoxification. The liver manages the three main fuels of the body: carbohydrates, fat, and protein. This is the only organ capable of removing nitrogen from the body. The liver controls the distribution of water among the blood, cells, and tissue and it has the ability to alter and break down toxins. The external surface is described in terms of contour (smooth, glistening) and color (brown, yellow, reddish-brown). The liver is lifted *in situ* to expose the gallbladder, where bile is collected for analysis. Then the liver is removed and weighed. (Appendix A shows the normal weight of the male liver.) It is placed on the examination table in a facedown position to expose the gallbladder, dissected, and examined for evidence of fatty change, cirrhosis, and infection. The gallbladder is opened and the fluid inside is collected and the amount measured. If it contains stones, the number and size are noted.

Pancreas

When the liver is removed, the oblong-shaped pancreas is exposed. The pancreas's primary function is to secrete hormones and digestive enzymes. The most important hormone released is insulin, which is used to regulate blood sugar levels. These digestive enzymes are released into the duodenum. The most common disease associated with the pancreas is diabetes, which cannot be diagnosed based on the gross examination of the organ. The morphological changes associated with this diseased state can only be seen microscopically. The pancreas is removed and weighed. (Appendix A shows the normal weight of the male pancreas.) Examination is made by making multiple cross sections.

Kidneys

The kidneys are located in the small of the back near the vertebral column. The primary functions are to separate urea, mineral salts, toxins, and other waste products from the blood. In addition, they conserve water, salt, and electrolytes. An individual can live with one functioning kidney. The right and left kidneys are removed, weighed, and examined for disease. (Appendix A shows the normal weight of the male kidney.)

Spleen

Located in the left side of the abdomen is the spleen. The primary functions are the creation of lymphocytes and serving as a reservoir of blood. The spleen is first examined within the body and the presence and number of accessory spleens are noted. Accessory spleens are small circular structures functionally similar to the normal spleen. The spleen is then removed and weighed. (Appendix A shows the normal weight of the male spleen.)

Other Internal Organs

Other internal organs, such as the prostates of males and reproductive organs of females, are removed and examined.

Gastrointestinal Tract

The stomach and small and large intestines are the last internal organs examined and removed from the abdominal cavity.

Stomach Contents

The stomach lies directly under the diaphragm in the left region of the upper abdomen. It is connected to the mouth via the esophagus. The stomach contains recently digested food at a low pH environment. The stomach is removed below the esophagus and at the duodenum. It is opened and the contents are emptied into a shallow container and examined. The contents are described and an estimate of the weight and amount of fluid, food, and other materials is noted. In cases of deaths from ingested drugs, the stomach is examined to recover the tablets. This may aid the pathologist in ascertaining whether the death was an accident or suicide. For example, a large number of pills recovered from the stomach is a strong indication of a deliberate suicide attempt as opposed to an accident. The examination of the stomach contents can also offer an estimate of the time of death (see Chapter 4) and may be used to corroborate or dispute an alibi.

The small and large intestines are examined externally for tumors, ulcers, obstructions, and gangrene. The intestines are opened using special intestinal scissors. The pathologist looks for evidence of any abnormalities.

Central Nervous System (CNS)

Brain

The brain uses 20% of the body's energy and contains over 100 billion neurons. It is composed of 77–78% water, 10–12% lipids, 8% protein, 1–2% soluble organics, and 1% inorganic salts. Once the organs of the chest and abdomen have been removed, attention is focused on the CNS, specifically the brain and spinal cord. A head block is used in order to raise the head above the shoulders. The autopsy technician stands above the head of the body. An incision is made starting behind the right ear, encircling the back of the head and ending behind the left ear. The skin of the scalp is then peeled forward toward the front of the head and the lower portion is reflected down toward the neck to expose the skull. The skull is carefully examined by the pathologist for any signs of blunt-force trauma. If the victim has thick hair, trauma to the head may not be seen during the external examination. A special vibrating circular saw is used to cut the skull and expose the brain with the dura mater in place. The saw is designed to cut bone but not soft tissue. The brain is first examined *in situ*.

The pathologist looks for signs of infection or hemorrhage. The most common nervous system infectious disease is meningitis. Grossly (visible to the naked eye), the subarachnoid space will contain a viscous exudate. Hemorrhage can be caused spontaneously (nontraumatic), due to hypertension or from an aneurysm (rupture of a thinned walled artery), or from BFT to the head. The technician then removes the brain by cutting it away from the brain stem and weighs it. (Appendix A shows the normal weight of the male brain.)

After the dura mater lining the inside of the skull is removed, the skull is examined for signs of old and new injuries and fractures. When the brain is removed, it is relatively soft, having the consistency of jello. The brains of infants are the most fragile, as are the brains of individuals with numerous cerebrovascular accidents (cerebrovascular accidents/strokes) or neuorogenic disease such as Alzheimer's. Therefore, the brain is suspended by a string upside down in a bucket of formaldehyde for 10–14 days. This process is called "fixing the brain" and causes it to become harder and easier to dissect (cut) into cross sections.

Spinal Cord

There are two methods for removal of the spinal cord; each offers specific advantages and limitations.

The *posterior method* has the advantage of allowing complete exposure of the spinal cord *in situ*, including the spinal canal, and the roots and ganglia of the spinal nerves. In brief, the body is placed face down on the table. An incision is made in the midline of the back from the base of the skull to the sacrum (tail bone), and the muscles surrounding the spine are cut away. Then a saw is used to cut on both sides of the vertebrae. The vertebrae are removed, exposing the spinal cord surrounded by the dura mater. A three-step process is used to remove the spinal cord: (1) cut the dura mater, (2) cut the projecting spinal nerves projecting from both sides of the spinal cord, and (3) free the cord by cutting at the top and base of the cord.

The *anterior approach* is the second method. After the internal organs have been removed, the vertebral column is cut with a saw. The blade enters the column at a 30° angle starting at the neck region and running the length of the column to the pelvic region. This is then repeated on the other side of the column. At the two ends, a cut is made across the column. To free the column, a broad chisel is wedged under it. Now the dura mater, nerve roots, and ganglia are exposed. For removal, the dura mater is incised, exposing the spinal cord. The spinal nerves projecting from the spinal cord are cut on both sides of the cord. This method is less labor intensive and does not require an additional skin incision. The only minor limitation is the inability to obtain the nerve roots of the thoracic vertebrae.

Skeletal System

The adult skeleton consists of 206 bones. The major bones of the body include the arms, legs, head (skull, upper/lower jaw, and nose), ribs, sternum, pelvis, and vertebral column. The body is examined for gross deformities, fractures, dislocations, and compressions. The sites and types of bone fractures can offer the pathologist an indication of the type of injury. There are several types of fractures:

- complete—the bone is broken into two pieces;
- partial—the fracture is not all the way through the bone;
- closed—the broken bone does not break through the skin; and
- open—the broken bone protrudes through the skin.

For example, consider an individual who is found dead on the sidewalk. There were no witnesses to the events that led to this man's death. Possible causes include a massive heart attack or some other natural conditions. However, the x-rays and detailed examination of the legs suggest a different explanation. The x-ray shows a fracture of the right tibia bone. The examination of the lower leg shows several impact marks, one at 15 inches and another 13 inches above the ground level. These findings indicated to the pathologist that these are bumper injuries. The man was the victim of a hit and run. Each car manufacturer keeps a detailed record of the profile for the front end of each car it produces that includes the top and bottom heights of the bumper, lights, and grill. Based on the measurements from the body, the model of the car involved can be narrowed down and eventually traced.

Final Pathological Diagnosis Report

After the forensic pathologist has completed the autopsy of the body, it is cleaned, sewn up, and released to the funeral home. Tissue sections from each organ collected during the autopsy are sent to the histology department, where they are cut, mounted, and stained to allow the pathologist to examine them microscopically. The body fluids collected during the autopsy have been sent to the toxicology department, where they underwent analytic analysis to determine the number and levels of compounds in the fluids. The forensic pathologist writes the *final autopsy report* after the microscopic slides and the results of the toxicology report have been reviewed. This report contains the final pathological diagnosis, a detailed description of all the external injures to the body, a detailed description of all the internal organs, the opinion as to the cause of death, and the manner of death. The forensic pathologist completes parts I and II of item 27 and items 28–31 of the DC. Table 4.3 shows how the final pathological diagnosis appears on the final autopsy report and how that information is transferred to the final DC.

Table 4.3 Comparison between Final Pathological Diagnosis and Death Certificate

	Final pathological diagnosis	Death certificate
1.	Asphyxiation due to compression of the trunk	Part I
	Congestion of the upper chest and face	Asphyxiation
	Fractured sternum	Compression of the trunk
	Fractured rib, bilateral	
	Fractured pelvis	
	Laceration of the spleen	
2.	Arteriosclerosis cardiovascular disease	
	Marked atherosclerosis of the left anterior descending coronary artery with ~75 luminal narrowing	
	Moderate atherosclerosis of the right coronary artery	
	Opinion: Died as a result of asphyxiation due to compression of the trunk when the lawn mower he was driving rolled over and crushed his trunk	
	Manner: accident	Accident

The Death Certificate 5

Introduction

One of the functions of a physician or a forensic pathologist is completion of the death certificate (DC). This chapter will define a DC, delineate its multiple functions, explain who can complete it, list the information within the parts of standard and medicolegal DCs, describe the path DC data follow from the physician to the national level, and discuss the advantages and limitations of the DC.

Definition

The death certificate is an official permanent government record documenting the facts of a death. It contains personal information about the decedent, the circumstances of the death, and the cause and manner of death.

Functions of the Death Certificate

The DC has several functions:

- It serves as a legal document certifying the fact of a death.
- This document is required for obtaining a cremation or burial permit. The survivors cannot bury or otherwise dispose of a corpse until a physician or ME/C signs a permanent DC. After a DC has been signed, local authorities issue a certificate of disposition of remains, which is also called a burial or cremation permit.
- The DC allows the next of kin the authority to settle life insurance claims, family pensions, distribution of movable and immovable property of the deceased, and to obtain any bequeathed inheritance. A DC is required to delete the decedent's name from property such as homes, stocks, or businesses. In addition, a DC must be presented if there are any legal claims involving an accidental death.
- A death certificate provides family members with closure. Although a funeral service typically functions as the final farewell by loved ones, in some situations the remains cannot be returned to the next

of kin, so the DC is tangible evidence that the individual is in fact dead.
- The DC provides a documented opinion as to the cause and manner of an individual's death; however, these are not legally binding for any other agency or any other individual. Therefore, the DC does not mandate, prevent, or preclude any other type of action, such as further investigation, independent review of the conclusions, and reexamination of the body, by any other individual, agency, or public office. In other words, the cause and manner of death section in the medicolegal certification represents an opinion. It sets forth the best effort of the medicolegal officer to reduce to a few words a synopsis of the cause of death and a reasonable opinion as to the manner of death. The ME/C office should use reasonable medical probability in the formulation of opinions and in the certification of death in the same way that clinicians make diagnoses and plans for treatment. The death certificate is a civil law document, rather than a medical or scientific document.
- A death certificate is also a useful tool in genealogical research. The information found there can be used to trace one's lineage or discover the occupation of distant relatives.
- The final function of the DC is to serve as a source of fatality data for biostatistics and epidemiological research at the local, state, national, and international levels. Mortality data provide the only sources of information about the causes of death and illness preceding death. A copy of every completed DC is provided to the state's vital records office, which transfers the data to the National Center for Health Statistics (NCHS). The NCHS, a division of the Centers for Disease Control (CDC) and Prevention, uses these collected data to document the health statutes of the general population and subpopulation by generating tables of the total number of deaths by age, sex, race, and location (state and county); by disease; and by manner of death. The data are also used to monitor trends, identify health problems, determine life expectancies, and provide research for biochemical and health studies. In addition, the data are used to compare mortality in the United States to that in other countries.

Completion of the DC

Determination of who is legally authorized to complete a DC is dictated by the possible manner of the death. The DC can be completed by a licensed physician if the manner of death is natural. Any physician with a clear

The Death Certificate

understanding of the past medical history of the patient can complete a DC as long as the cause of death is natural.

All deaths that appear to be unnatural in nature or manner fall under the jurisdiction of the ME/C. This includes deaths from suicides, accidents, and homicides and deaths where the cause and manner are listed as undetermined. *Under these circumstances, the DC can be completed only by a forensic pathologist and issued by an ME/C office.* Natural deaths can also be certified by the ME/C office. Typically, DCs for deaths from natural conditions are issued by a physician; however, in three circumstances the ME/C will issue a natural DC: (1) in cases where the family physician has not seen the individual for a significant period of time and does not feel comfortable signing the DC, (2) when the physician refuses to issue a DC, and (3) when the individual does not have a regular physician.

Death certificates listing trauma or injuries and signed by a physician (not a forensic pathologist) will be returned by the state and must be reissued by the ME/C office.

Types of Death Certificates

In the United States three types of DCs are used: a *standard certificate of death, a death certificate for fetal and stillborn deaths,* and *a certificate of death for medicolegal cases.* The standard DC is used for deaths caused by a well documented disease process and is completed by a physician. The medicolegal DC is used if the death is undergoing a forensic investigation and it is completed by a forensic pathologist. A DC for fetal deaths is required if the fetus was 20 weeks gestation or older.

Anatomy of the Standard Certificate of Death

The parts of a standard certificate of death are described next. Figure 5.1 shows a standard certificate of death.

Parts of the Death Certificate

Part	Title	Contains
1	Decedent's legal name	First, middle, and last name of the decedent
2	Sex	Male or female
3	Social security number	The number assigned at the time of birth by the government
4a	Age	If the individual is over 1 year old, the age at the last birthday is entered
4b	Under 1 year	If the individual is less than 1 year old, the age is listed by months and days

Parts of the Death Certificate (continued)

Part	Title	Contains
4c	Under 1 day	If the individual is less then 24 hours old, the age is entered in hours and minutes
5	Date of birth	Entered by month, day, and year
6	Birthplace	The city and state or foreign country
7a	Residence—state	The state where the individual lived
7b	County	The county where the individual lived
7c	City or town	The city or town where the individual lived
7d	Street and number	The exact mailing address for a home
7e	Apartment number	In cases of an apartment, the exact number
7f	Zip code	The nine-digit zip code
7g	Inside city limits	Was the location of the home inside the city's boundary: yes/no
8	Ever in Armed Forces?	Did the individual ever serve in the Army, Navy, Air Force, Coast Guard or Reserves?

9	Marital status at time of death	Choose from one of the following:
		  Married
		  Married but separated or widowed
		  Divorced
		  Never married
		  Unknown

10	Surviving spouse's name	If it is a wife, list the name prior to last marriage
11	Father's name	Enter the first, middle, and last name
12	Mother's name	Enter the mother's first, middle, and last name using mother's name prior to the first marriage
13a	Informant's name	The name of the individual providing the funeral director with the information contained on the DC
13b	Relationship to decedent	The relationship to the decedent: wife, husband, brother, sister, etc.
13c	Mailing address	The exact mailing address of the informant
14	Place of death	If death occurred in a hospital: check from one of the following: inpatient, emergency room/outpatient, or dead on arrival
		If death occurred somewhere other than a hospital: check one of the following: hospice facility, nursing home/long term care facility, decedent's home, other (specify)
15	Facility name	If not an institution such as a hospital or nursing home, provide the exact house mailing address
16	City or town, state, and zip code	The location of the place of death

The Death Certificate 55

Parts of the Death Certificate (continued)

Part	Title	Contains
17	County of death	List the county where the death occurred
18	Method of disposal	Check one of the following: burial, cremation, donation, entombment, removal from state, other (specify)
19	Place of disposal	Name of facility: cemetery or crematory
20	Location—city, town, and state	Where the remains will be placed to rest
21	Name and complete address of funeral faculty	The exact mailing address of the funeral home
22	Signature of funeral service licensee or other agent	Signature required
23	License number	List physician's license number
24	Date pronounced dead	The month, day, and year that the decedent was pronounced dead. This is the date the decedent was legally pronounced dead. If the death was not witnessed, this is the time the body was located and death was pronounced by the ME/C office
25	Time pronounced dead	Use military time
26	Signature of person pronouncing death	This section lists the possible individuals that can pronounce an individual dead. The following individuals are allowed to pronounce an individual dead: first responders such as emergency medical technicians (EMTs), paramedics, and police; nurses; and physicians
27	License number	List physician's license number
28	Date signed	The month, day, and year
29	Actual or presumed date of death	The month, day, and year that the decedent was determined to have died
30	Actual or presumed time of death	Use military time
31	Was medical examiner or coroner contacted?	Yes or no
32	Cause of death	The cause of death is defined as the pathological condition (disease) or injury responsible for initiating the chronology of events, acute or prolonged, that produced death. This section contains two major areas. Part 32 is composed of two parts: part I, the immediate cause of death and underlying cause of death; and part II, the conditions contributing to death. See the following for more specific details

U.S. Standard Certificate of Death

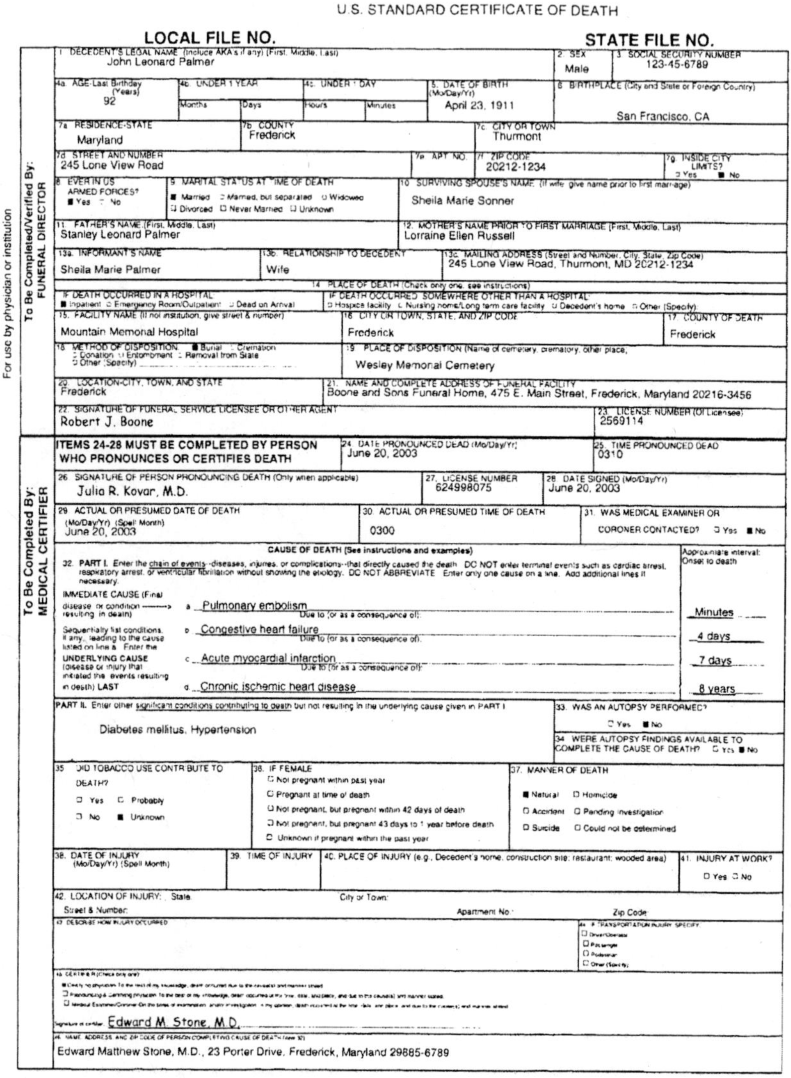
U.S. STANDARD CERTIFICATE OF DEATH

LOCAL FILE NO. STATE FILE NO.

To Be Completed/Verified By: FUNERAL DIRECTOR

1. DECEDENT'S LEGAL NAME (Include AKA's if any) (First, Middle, Last): John Leonard Palmer
2. SEX: Male
3. SOCIAL SECURITY NUMBER: 123-45-6789
4a. AGE-Last Birthday (Years): 92
4b. UNDER 1 YEAR: Months / Days
4c. UNDER 1 DAY: Hours / Minutes
5. DATE OF BIRTH (Mo/Day/Yr): April 23, 1911
6. BIRTHPLACE (City and State or Foreign Country): San Francisco, CA
7a. RESIDENCE-STATE: Maryland
7b. COUNTY: Frederick
7c. CITY OR TOWN: Thurmont
7d. STREET AND NUMBER: 245 Lone View Road
7e. APT. NO.
7f. ZIP CODE: 20212-1234
7g. INSIDE CITY LIMITS? ☐ Yes ■ No
8. EVER IN US ARMED FORCES? ■ Yes ☐ No
9. MARITAL STATUS AT TIME OF DEATH: ■ Married ☐ Married, but separated ☐ Widowed ☐ Divorced ☐ Never Married ☐ Unknown
10. SURVIVING SPOUSE'S NAME (If wife, give name prior to first marriage): Sheila Marie Sonner
11. FATHER'S NAME (First, Middle, Last): Stanley Leonard Palmer
12. MOTHER'S NAME PRIOR TO FIRST MARRIAGE (First, Middle, Last): Lorraine Ellen Russell
13a. INFORMANT'S NAME: Sheila Marie Palmer
13b. RELATIONSHIP TO DECEDENT: Wife
13c. MAILING ADDRESS (Street and Number, City, State, Zip Code): 245 Lone View Road, Thurmont, MD 20212-1234
14. PLACE OF DEATH (Check only one; see instructions)
IF DEATH OCCURRED IN A HOSPITAL: ■ Inpatient ☐ Emergency Room/Outpatient ☐ Dead on Arrival
IF DEATH OCCURRED SOMEWHERE OTHER THAN A HOSPITAL: ☐ Hospice facility ☐ Nursing home/Long term care facility ☐ Decedent's home ☐ Other (Specify):
15. FACILITY NAME (If not institution, give street & number): Mountain Memorial Hospital
16. CITY OR TOWN, STATE, AND ZIP CODE: Frederick
17. COUNTY OF DEATH: Frederick
18. METHOD OF DISPOSITION: ■ Burial ☐ Cremation ☐ Donation ☐ Entombment ☐ Removal from State ☐ Other (Specify):
19. PLACE OF DISPOSITION (Name of cemetery, crematory, other place): Wesley Memorial Cemetery
20. LOCATION-CITY, TOWN, AND STATE: Frederick
21. NAME AND COMPLETE ADDRESS OF FUNERAL FACILITY: Boone and Sons Funeral Home, 475 E. Main Street, Frederick, Maryland 20216-3456
22. SIGNATURE OF FUNERAL SERVICE LICENSEE OR OTHER AGENT: Robert J. Boone
23. LICENSE NUMBER (Of Licensee): 2569114

For use by physician or institution

To Be Completed By: MEDICAL CERTIFIER

ITEMS 24-28 MUST BE COMPLETED BY PERSON WHO PRONOUNCES OR CERTIFIES DEATH
24. DATE PRONOUNCED DEAD (Mo/Day/Yr): June 20, 2003
25. TIME PRONOUNCED DEAD: 0310
26. SIGNATURE OF PERSON PRONOUNCING DEATH (Only when applicable): Julia R. Kovar, M.D.
27. LICENSE NUMBER: 624998075
28. DATE SIGNED (Mo/Day/Yr): June 20, 2003
29. ACTUAL OR PRESUMED DATE OF DEATH (Mo/Day/Yr) (Spell Month): June 20, 2003
30. ACTUAL OR PRESUMED TIME OF DEATH: 0300
31. WAS MEDICAL EXAMINER OR CORONER CONTACTED? ☐ Yes ■ No

CAUSE OF DEATH (See instructions and examples)

32. PART I. Enter the chain of events--diseases, injuries, or complications--that directly caused the death. DO NOT enter terminal events such as cardiac arrest, respiratory arrest, or ventricular fibrillation without showing the etiology. DO NOT ABBREVIATE. Enter only one cause on a line. Add additional lines if necessary.

		Approximate interval: Onset to death
IMMEDIATE CAUSE (Final disease or condition resulting in death)	a. Pulmonary embolism	Minutes
Sequentially list conditions, if any, leading to the cause listed on line a. Enter the UNDERLYING CAUSE (disease or injury that initiated the events resulting in death) LAST	Due to (or as a consequence of): b. Congestive heart failure	4 days
	Due to (or as a consequence of): c. Acute myocardial infarction	7 days
	Due to (or as a consequence of): d. Chronic ischemic heart disease	8 years

PART II. Enter other significant conditions contributing to death but not resulting in the underlying cause given in PART I: Diabetes mellitus, Hypertension
33. WAS AN AUTOPSY PERFORMED? ☐ Yes ■ No
34. WERE AUTOPSY FINDINGS AVAILABLE TO COMPLETE THE CAUSE OF DEATH? ☐ Yes ■ No
35. DID TOBACCO USE CONTRIBUTE TO DEATH? ☐ Yes ☐ Probably ☐ No ■ Unknown
36. IF FEMALE: ☐ Not pregnant within past year ☐ Pregnant at time of death ☐ Not pregnant, but pregnant within 42 days of death ☐ Not pregnant, but pregnant 43 days to 1 year before death ☐ Unknown if pregnant within the past year
37. MANNER OF DEATH: ■ Natural ☐ Homicide ☐ Accident ☐ Pending investigation ☐ Suicide ☐ Could not be determined
38. DATE OF INJURY (Mo/Day/Yr) (Spell Month)
39. TIME OF INJURY
40. PLACE OF INJURY (e.g., Decedent's home; construction site; restaurant; wooded area)
41. INJURY AT WORK? ☐ Yes ☐ No
42. LOCATION OF INJURY: State / City or Town / Street & Number / Apartment No. / Zip Code
43. DESCRIBE HOW INJURY OCCURRED
44. IF TRANSPORTATION INJURY, SPECIFY: ☐ Driver/Operator ☐ Passenger ☐ Pedestrian ☐ Other (Specify)
45. CERTIFIER (Check only one):
■ Certifying physician-To the best of my knowledge, death occurred due to the cause(s) and manner stated.
☐ Pronouncing & Certifying physician-To the best of my knowledge, death occurred at the time, date, and place, and due to the cause(s) and manner stated.
☐ Medical Examiner/Coroner-On the basis of examination, and/or investigation, in my opinion, death occurred at the time, date, and place, and due to the cause(s) and manner stated.
Signature of certifier: Edward M. Stone, M.D.
46. NAME, ADDRESS, AND ZIP CODE OF PERSON COMPLETING CAUSE OF DEATH (Item 32): Edward Matthew Stone, M.D., 23 Porter Drive, Frederick, Maryland 29885-6789

Figure 5.1 Standard certificate of death.

Part 32: Parts I and II

Part I is for reporting the sequence of events leading to the death, proceeding backward from the final disease or condition that resulted in death. It is composed of an immediate cause of death and several underlying (due to or as a consequence of) causes of death. The top line of part I (line *a*) is for the immediate cause of death, which is the final disease, injury, or complication

The Death Certificate

Table 5.1 Basic Structure of Parts I and II (Part 32)

32. Part I Immediate cause:

    a. _____ Most recent condition
    (resulting from b)

    b. _____ Intermediate cause; antecedent
    (older) condition (resulting from c)

    c. _____Underlying cause; first (older,
    original) condition

    d.

32. Part II Significant conditions contributing to death:

directly causing death. Line *a* can be the sole entry in the cause of death section if that condition is the only one causing the death. Only one cause can be entered on each line of part I. See Figure 5.1.

Below the immediate cause of death are the listings for underlying causes of death, which are diseases or injuries that initiated the chain of events that led directly and inevitably to the death. These are listed on the lowest line. Underlying causes of death are listed going backward in time in lines *b*, *c*, and *d*.

Part II of the cause of death section contains conditions contributing to death and reports all other significant diseases, conditions, or injuries that contributed to death, but did not result in the underlying cause of death listed in part I (see Table 5.1).

The following examples illustrate how parts I and II are completed.

Example 5.1

A 55-year-old male was discovered dead in the bathroom by his wife. Blood was seen in his mouth and a moderate pool of blood on the floor by his head. During the interview with the wife, she said he had a long history of alcohol abuse and uncontrolled hypertension. The autopsy revealed a liver with diffuse, small nodules—an anatomical sign of alcoholic cirrhosis. The esophagus was lined with blood, and when the stomach was opened, it was filled with a moderate amount of blood. The cirrhosis and portal hypertension caused the veins of the esophagus to dilate (from varices). These findings led the pathologist to the cause of events leading to the death and allowed him to complete the DC: One of the veins within the esophagus ruptured due to the portal hypertension and cirrhosis, which caused blood to flow into the stomach and out of the mouth. Table 5.2 shows part 32, parts I and II, on the DC for this death.

Table 5.2 The Competed DC, Part 32, Parts I and II, for Example 5.1

Part I	Immediate cause:
	a. Upper gastrointestinal hemorrhage
	b. Esophageal varices
	c. Cirrhosis of liver
	d. Chronic alcohol use
Part II	Significant conditions contributing to death:

Example 5.2

A 27-year-old welder received second- and third-degree burns over 75% of his body surface following an industrial accident. He was immediately transferred to a burn center. After several weeks, he developed renal failure, pneumonia, and, finally, sepsis from the infected wounds. He died 5 days after the accident. Table 5.3 shows part 32, parts I and II, of the DC for this death.

Table 5.3 The Competed DC, Part 32, Parts I and II, for Example 5.2

Part I	Immediate cause:
	a. Sepsis
	b. Pneumonia
	c. Thermal burns
	d.
Part II	Significant conditions contributing to death:

Example 5.3

A 70-year-old female was admitted to the ICU with dyspnea and chest pain that were not relived with nitroglycerin. Her PMH included obesity, non-insulin-dependent diabetes mellitus, hypertension, and angina pectoris. Enzyme levels confirmed an acute myocardial infarction. A temporary pacemaker was installed to control type II second-degree atrioventricular block. Over time she developed dyspnea with fluid retention and cardiomegaly confirmed by radiograph. While in the hospital, she suddenly experienced chest pain and increased dyspnea, became unresponsive, and expired. Table 5.4 shows part 32, parts I and II, of the DC for this death.

The Death Certificate

Table 5.4 The Competed DC, Part 32, Parts I and II, for Example 5.3

Part I	Immediate cause:
	a. Pulmonary embolism
	b. Acute myocardial infarction
	c. Chronic ischemic heart disease
	d.
Part II	Significant conditions contributing to death:
	Non-insulin-dependent diabetes mellitus, obesity, hypertension

Example 5.4

A 27-year-old white male was discovered unresponsive on the floor in a backyard shed by his wife. A large amount of blood was noted around the head and a small handgun was located near the body. He was pronounced dead at the scene. During the death scene investigation, it was learned that the victim had recently been diagnosed with lung cancer. A suicide note was also located in the bedroom. The autopsy revealed a single through-and-through gunshot wound to the right temporal region. Table 5.5 shows part 32, parts I and II, of the DC for this death.

Table 5.5 The Completed DC for Part 32, Parts I and II, for Example 5.4

Part I	Immediate cause:
	a. Gunshot wound, head
	b.
	c.
	d.
Part II	Conditions contributing to death:

Example 5.5

A 56-year-old black male was discovered unresponsive in his bed at a long-term care facility. He has been a resident for the past 40 years after being shot in the back at the C4 level, resulting in his becoming a quadriplegic. Prior to death, he had been battling pneumonia for the past few years. Table 5.6 shows part 32, parts I and II, of the DC for this death.

Table 5.6 The Competed DC for Part 32, Parts I and II, for Example 5.5

Part I	Immediate cause:
	a. Pneumonia
	b. Quadriplegia
	c. GSW to C4
	d.
Part II	Conditions contributing to death:

Parts of the Death Certificate (Continued)

Part	Title	Contains
33	Was an autopsy performed?	Yes or no. Yes indicates that either a partial or complete autopsy was performed
34	Were autopsy findings available to complete the cause of death?	Yes or no
35	Did tobacco use contribute to death?	Check from one of the following: yes, no, probably, or unknown. This is one of the newer questions added to the DC. If "yes" is checked, it indicates that, in the opinion of the signing physician, tobacco or tobacco exposure contributed to the death. For example, tobacco use may have contributed to death due to emphysema or lung cancer. Tobacco use may also contribute to heart disease and head and neck cancer. Tobacco use should also be reported in deaths due to fires started by smoking
36	If female:	Check one of the following: Not pregnant within past year Pregnant at time of death Not pregnant, but pregnant within 42 days of death Not pregnant, but pregnant 43 days to 1 year before death Unknown whether pregnant within the past year This is another one of the newer questions added to the DC. If the woman is too old or too young, check "not pregnant within past year." Leave the part blank if the decedent is male
37	Manner of death	The manner of death is defined as the manner in which the cause of death came to be. There are five classifications of manner of death: natural, accident, suicide, homicide, and cannot be determined or undetermined. In addition, there is also one temporary manner of death called pending investigation or simply pending.

The Death Certificate

Part 37: Manner of Death

The manner of death is defined as the fashion in which the cause of death came to be. There are five classifications of manner of death: natural, accident, suicide, homicide, and cannot be determined or undetermined. In addition, there is also one temporary manner of death called pending investigation or simply pending.

- *Natural deaths* are those caused from naturally occurring disease processes without trauma. Examples include cancer, heart disease, liver disease, etc. If the death is ruled natural, there is no criminal investigation needed. However, a thorough examination of the facts leading to the natural manner of death must be undertaken.
- *Accidental deaths* are those that occur as a result of behavior or actions that unintentionally end in death. In the United States, accidental death is the number one cause of death among individuals 1–34 years old. The most frequently encountered accidental deaths are from drug overdose, followed by motor vehicle accidents, falls, and fires. Most people taking illegal drugs are not trying to commit suicide. An accidental death ruling may result in a continuation of the investigation, but in a different direction. There may be civil liability, and the coroner or medical examiner may be called to testify in civil court. The amount of time devoted to this extended investigation will vary from one jurisdiction to another.
- A *suicide* is defined as the deliberate termination of one's own life. The most common methods of suicide vary by sex; males typically use firearms, while females typically overdose on pills. The manner of suicide will need a thorough confirmation. In most cases that are ruled suicide, the determination will stand; however, occasionally new evidence brought out by an in-depth investigation will change the coroner's or medical examiner's mind.
- *Homicide* is defined as the action of taking the life of another person. Based on this definition, all police shootings and all executions are homicides. The determination of first degree, second degree, third degree, and other types of homicide is made by a court rather than by the ME/C. Chapter 9 provides a detailed explanation of the different types of homicides.
- *Undetermined* is used when, after all avenues of investigation have been explored, a valid conclusion cannot be reached.
- *Pending* simply means that further testing or investigation is warranted before a definitive manner can be declared. Most states require that the death certificate must be issued within 72 hours after the discovery of the body, even if the cause of death is unknown. If the

cause of death cannot be established with reasonable certainty after the autopsy, the ME/C office will issue a certificate of death with the cause of death designated as "pending further action" or simply "pending." In most cases, the pathologist is awaiting results of toxicological analysis, supplementary police reports, or histology slides. Once the determination of the cause and manner of death is made, the ME/C will issue a replacement DC. The cause of death can be undetermined, but the manner of death must be changed from pending to one of the five other manners of death.

Parts of the Death Certificate (Continued)

Part	Title	Contains
38	Date of injury	The month, date, and year when the injury occurred
39	Time of injury	Use military time
40	Place of injury	Describe in terms of residence, restaurant, hospital, work, construction site, or wooded area where the injury occurred

41	Injury at work?	Yes or no. Work is defined as being on the clock and conducting activity related to the job.
		Examples of injury at work:
		    Injured while working for pay or compensation
		    Injured while working as a volunteer law enforcement officer or fireman
		    Injured while traveling on business
		Examples of injury not at work:
		    Injured while engaging in personal recreational activity on work premises
		    Injured as a homemaker working at homemaking activity
		    Commuting to or from work
		    Conducting illegal activity (drug dealer, prostitute)

42	Location of injury	Provide the exact address of the place where the injury occurred
43	Describe how injury occurred	Provide a concise summary of how the individual received the injuries (e.g., fell off ladder while painting room, hit by train, shot at bar)

44	If transportation injury, specify	Check from one of the following:
		    Driver/operator
		    Passenger
		    Pedestrian
		    Other (specify).
		Specify the role of the decedent (driver, passenger, or pedestrian). If vehicle was other than a motor vehicle, it should be described (e.g., bicycle)

The Death Certificate

Parts of the Death Certificate (Continued)

Part	Title	Contains
45	Certifying	Check from one of the following:
		Certifying physician: "To the best of my knowledge, death occurred due to the cause(s) and manner stated"
		Pronouncing and certifying physicians: "To the best of my knowledge, death occurred at the time, date, and place, and due to the cause(s) and manner stated"
		Medical examiner/coroner: "On the basis of examination and/or investigation, in my opinion, death occurred at the time, date, place, and due to the cause(s) and manner stated"
46	Name, address, and zip code of person completing cause of death	This is the same individual that completed part 32
47	Title of certifier MD	
48	License number	
49	Date certified	Month, day, and year
50	For registrar only, date filed	
51	Decedent's education	Check from one of the following:
		8th grade or less
		9th–12th grade: no diploma
		High school graduate or GED completed
		Some college credits: no degree
		Associate degree (AA, AS)
		Bachelor's degree (BA, AB, BS)
		Master's degree (MA, MS, MEng, Med, MSW, MBA)
		Doctorate (PhD, EdD, MD, DDS, DVM, LLB, JD)
		Check the box that describes the highest level of education completed at the time of death
52	Decedent of Hispanic origin?	Check from one of the following:
		No, not Spanish/Hispanic/Latino
		Yes, Mexican, Mexican American, Chicano
		Yes, Puerto Rican
		Yes, Cuban
		Yes, other Spanish/Hispanic/Latino (specify)
53	Decedent's race	Check from one of the following:
		White
		Black or African American

Parts of the Death Certificate (Continued)

Part	Title	Contains
		American Indian or Alaska native
		Name of tribe_____
		Asian Indian
		Chinese
		Filipino
		Japanese
		Korean
		Vietnamese
		Other Asian (specify)_____
		Native Hawaiian
		Guamanian or Chamorro
		Samoan
		Other Pacific Islander (specify)_____
		Other (specify)_____
54	Decedent's usual occupation	Indicate the type of work done during most of the individual's working life. Do not list retired
55	Kind of business/industry	

Anatomy of the Medicolegal Death Certificate

The parts of a *medicolegal certificate* of death are described next. Figure 5.2 shows a standard medicolegal certificate of death. Note the difference between the two types of DCs in Figures 5.1 and 5.2.

Parts of the Medicolegal Death Certificate

Part	Title	Contains
1	Decedent's legal name	First, middle, and last name of the decedent
2	Sex	Male or female
3	Social security number	The number assigned at the time of birth by the government
4	Date of death	Enter by month, day, and year
5	Age	Date of death: entered by month, day, and year
6	Age: under 1 year	If the individual is less than 1 year old, the age is listed by months and. If the individual is less then 24 hours old, the age is entered in hours and minutes
7	Date of birth	Entered by month, day, and year
8	Birthplace	The city and state or foreign country

The Death Certificate

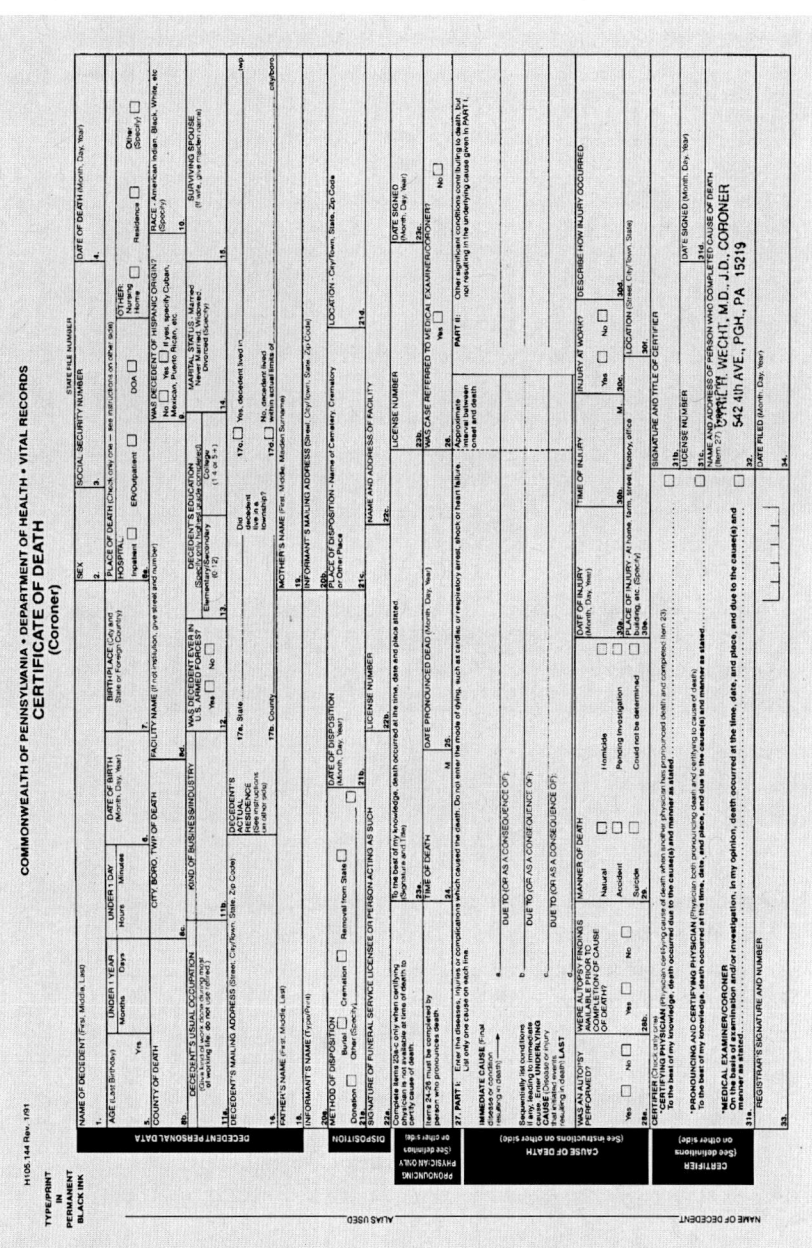

Figure 5.2 Medicolegal death certificate.

Parts of the Medicolegal Death Certificate (continued)

Part	Title	Contains
8a	Place of death	If death occurred in a hospital: check from one of the following: inpatient, emergency room/outpatient, or dead on arrival
		If death occurred somewhere other than a hospital: check one of the following: hospice facility, nursing home/long-term care facility, decedent's home, other (specify)
8b	County of death	The county where the individual lived
8c	City, borough, town of death	The city or town where the individual lived
8d	Facility name	If not an institution, provide the complete street address
9	Was decedent of Hispanic origin?	No or yes. If yes, specify: Cuban, Mexican, Puerto Rican, etc.
10	Race	Specify white, black, American Indian, etc.
11	Decedent's usual occupation	Indicate the type of work done during most of the individual's working life. Do not list retired. Indicate the kind of business/industry
12	Was decedent ever in the U.S. Armed Forces?	Yes or no. Did the individual ever serve in the Army, Navy, Air Force, Coast Guard, or reserves?
13	Decedent's education	Specify only highest grade completed: elementary/secondary (0–12) or college (1–4 or 5+)
14	Marital status at time of death	Choose from one of the following: Married Married but separated or widowed Divorced Never married Unknown
14	Surviving spouse's name	If wife, give maiden name
16	Decedent's mailing address	The exact mailing address of the decedent
17a	Decedent's actual residence	List state
17b	Decedent's actual residence	List county
17c	If decedent lived in a township	List the township the decedent lived in
17d	If decedent did not live in a township	List the actual limits of the city or borough that the decedent lived in
18	Father's name	Enter the first, middle, and last name
19	Mother's name	Enter the mother's first, middle, and last name (maiden or surname)

The Death Certificate

Parts of the Medicolegal Death Certificate (continued)

Part	Title	Contains
20a	Informant's name	The name of the individual providing information to the ME/C office
20b	Informant's mailing address	The exact mailing address of the informant
21a	Method of disposal	Check one of the following: burial, cremation, donation, entombment, removal from state, other (specify)
21b	Date of disposal	The month, day, and year
21c	Place of disposal	Name of facility: cemetery or crematory
21d	Location—city, town, and state	The location where the remains will be placed to rest
22a	Signature of funeral service licensee or other agent	Signature required
22b	License number	List license number of the funeral home
22c	Name and complete address of funeral facility	The exact mailing address of the funeral home
23a	To the best of my knowledge, death occurred at the time, date and place stated (signature and title)	The exact mailing address of the funeral home
23b	License number	License number
23c	Date signed	The month, day, and year
23a–c		These items are only completed when a certifying physician is not available at time of death to certify cause of death
24	Time of death	Use 12-hour clock with a.m. and p.m.
25	Date pronounced dead	The month, day, and year that the decedent was pronounced dead. This is the date the decedent was legally pronounced dead. If the death was not witnessed, this is the time the body was located and death was pronounced by the ME/C office
26	Was case referred to a medical examiner/coroner?	Yes or no
27	Cause of death	The cause of death is defined as the pathological condition (disease) or injury responsible for initiating the chronology of events, acute or prolonged, that produced death. This section contains two major areas: part I, the immediate cause of death and underlying cause of death, and part II, the conditions contributing to death

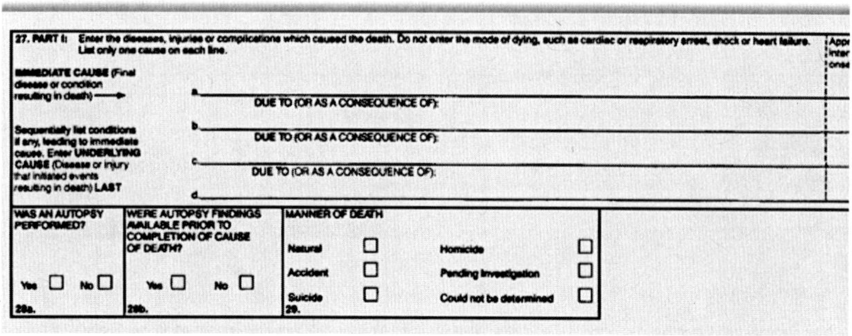
27. PART I: Enter the diseases, injuries or complications which caused the death. Do not enter the mode of dying, such as cardiac or respiratory arrest, shock or heart failure. List only one cause on each line.

IMMEDIATE CAUSE (Final disease or condition resulting in death) → a. ______

DUE TO (OR AS A CONSEQUENCE OF):

Sequentially list conditions if any, leading to immediate cause. Enter UNDERLYING CAUSE (Disease or injury that initiated events resulting in death) LAST

b. ______

DUE TO (OR AS A CONSEQUENCE OF):

c. ______

DUE TO (OR AS A CONSEQUENCE OF):

d. ______

WAS AN AUTOPSY PERFORMED? Yes ☐ No ☐ 28a.

WERE AUTOPSY FINDINGS AVAILABLE PRIOR TO COMPLETION OF CAUSE OF DEATH? Yes ☐ No ☐ 28b.

MANNER OF DEATH: Natural ☐ Accident ☐ Suicide ☐ Homicide ☐ Pending investigation ☐ Could not be determined ☐ 29.

Figure 5.3 Part 27, parts I and 28a–29, of the DC.

Part 27: Cause of Death

Part I is for reporting the sequence of events leading to the death, proceeding backward from the final disease or condition that resulted in death (Figure 5.3). It is composed of an immediate cause of death and several underlying (due to or as a consequence of) causes of death. The top line of part I (line *a*) is for the immediate cause of death, which is the final disease, injury, or complication directly causing death. Line *a* can be the sole entry in the cause of death section if that condition is the only one causing the death. Only one cause can be entered on each line of part I.

Below the immediate cause of death are the listings for underlying causes of death, which are diseases or injuries that initiated the chain of events that led directly and inevitably to the death. These are listed on the lowest line. Underlying causes of death are listed going backward in time in lines *b, c,* and *d*.

Part II of the cause of death section contains conditions contributing to death and reports all other significant diseases, conditions, or injuries that contributed to death, but did not result in the underlying cause of death listed in part I (Figure 5.4).

Parts of the Medicolegal Death Certificate (Continued)

Part	Title	Contains
28	Did tobacco use contribute to death?	Check from one of the following: yes, no, probably, or unknown. This is one of the newer questions added to the DC. If "yes" is checked, it indicates that, in the opinion of the signing physician, tobacco or tobacco exposure contributed to the death. For example, tobacco use may have contributed to deaths due to emphysema or lung cancer. Tobacco use may also contribute to heart disease and head and neck cancer. Tobacco use should also be reported in deaths due to fires starting by smoking
29	If female:	Check one of the following:

The Death Certificate

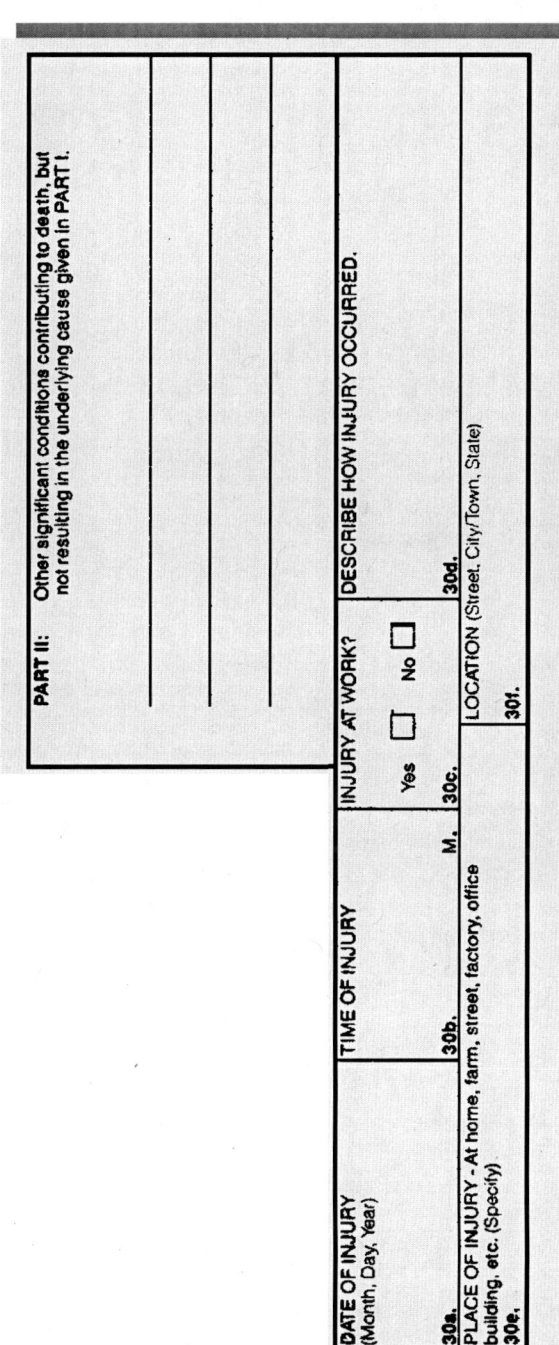

Figure 5.4 Part 27, parts II and 30a–30f, of the DC.

Parts of the Medicolegal Death Certificate (Continued)

Part	Title	Contains
		Not pregnant within past year
		Pregnant at time of death
		Not pregnant, but pregnant within 42 days of death
		Not pregnant, but pregnant 43 days to 1 year before death
		Unknown if pregnant within the past year
		This is another one of the newer questions added to the DC. If the woman is too old or too young, check "not pregnant within past year." Leave this part blank if decedent is male
30	Was an autopsy performed? Yes or no	Yes indicates that a partial or complete autopsy performed
30b	Were autopsy findings available to complete the cause of death?	Yes or no
31	Manner of death	The manner of death is defined as the manner in which the cause of death came to be. There are five classifications of manner of death: natural, accident, suicide, homicide, and cannot be determined or undetermined. In addition, there is also one temporary manner of death called pending investigation or simply pending
32a	Date of injury	The month, day, and year when the injury occurred
32b	Describe how injury occurred	Provide a cryptic summary of how the individual received the injuries (e.g., fell off ladder while painting room, hit by train, shot at bar)
32c	Place of injury	Describe in terms of residence, restaurant, hospital, work, construction site, or wooded area where the injury occurred
32d	Time of injury	Use 12-hour clock with a.m. and p.m.
32e	Injury at work? Yes or no	Work is defined as being on the clock and conducting activity related to the job

32f	If transportation injury, specify	Check one of the following:
		    Driver/operator
		    Passenger
		    Pedestrian
		    Other (specify)
		Specify the role of the decedent (driver, passenger, or pedestrian). If vehicle was other then a motor vehicle, it should be described (e.g., bicycle)

32g	Location	The exact address (street, city, town, state) where injury occurred

The Death Certificate

Parts of the Medicolegal Death Certificate (Continued)

Part	Title	Contains
33a	Certifying	Check one of the following:
		Certifying physician (physician certifying cause of death when another physician has pronounced death and completed part 23): "To the best of my knowledge, death occurred due to the cause(s) and manner as stated"
		Pronouncing and certifying physician (physician pronouncing death and certifying to cause of death): "To the best of my knowledge, death occurred at the time, date, and place, and due to the cause(s) and manner as stated"
		Medical examiner/coroner: "On the basis of examination and/or investigation, in my opinion, death occurred at the time, date, place, and due to the cause(s) and manner as stated"
33b	Signature and title of certifier	Signature required
33c	License number	List licensed number
33d	Date signed	Month, day, and year
34	Name and address of person completing cause of death	This is the same individual that completed part 27
35	Registrar's signature and district number	
36	Date files	Month, day, and year

Pathway of the DC

The official DC issued by an attending physician or the ME/C office is sent to the funeral home handling the arrangements. DCs are incomplete and the funeral home must make entries in order to complete them. This occurs when information is received from a physician; the physician completes parts 24–50 and the funeral home completes parts 1–23 and 51–55. The same holds true when the DC is received from the ME/C. An official DC will be provided to the next of kin in order for them to collect insurance and other benefits, sell property, and settle other estate issuers. The now completed death certificate will be copied to the local, city, or county health department; state government offices (vital statistics); and the CDC and NCHS.

A copy of every completed DC is provided to the local county health department. At this level, the completeness and accuracy are verified. The DC is sent from the local level to the state's vital records office. The state agency responsible for compiling the vital statistics for that state provides statistical summaries and detailed information that are then forwarded to the federal level: CDC, NCHS, and the National Vital Statistics Division of the Public Health Service. The NCHS, a division of the CDC, uses these collected data to document the health statistics of the general population and subpopulation by generating tables of the total number of deaths by age, sex, race, and location (state and county); by disease; and by manner of death. The data are also used to monitor trends, identify health problems, determine life expectancies, and provide research for biochemical and health studies as well as to compare mortality in the United States to other countries. Table 5.7 shows the path of the death certificate and the roles of individuals or agencies at each step.

The cause of death listed on the DC is coded in accordance with the *International Classification of Disease, Tenth Revision* (ICD-10). The *ICD* also codes the underlying cause of death. The tabulations of cause-of-death statistics are all based solely on the underlying cause of death, which is defined by the World Health Organization (WHO) as the disease or injury that initiated the train of events leading directly to death, or the circumstances of the accident or violence that produced the fatal injury. The *ICD* provides the basic guidance used by almost every county to code and classify causes of death. The *ICD* classification has undergone several revisions: the sixth revision covered 1949–1957, the seventh covered 1958–1967, the eighth covered 1968–1978, and the ninth revision covered 1979–1998. Changes due to

Table 5.7 Path of the Death Certificate and the Roles of Individuals or Agencies at Each Step

Responsible individual or agency	Path of the death certificate
Physician	Complete only deaths from natural causes
Complete cause of death and manner part of DC	
Send to the funeral director	
Medical examiner's or coroner's office	Complete deaths from natural causes and all death from non-natural causes
Complete cause of death and manner part of DC	
Send to the funeral director	
Funeral director	Complete personnel part of DC
Send certificate to local office or state office	
Local office (local registrars, city or county health department)	Send certificate to state registrars
State registrar, Office of Vital Statistics	Send certificate to National Center for Health Statistics

revisions in the classification may result in discontinuities when comparing different years that overlap revision periods.

Advantages of Using the DC

The main advantage of the DC is that it is the only source of information about the causes of death and illness completed on every individual in a standard manner. The DC is also a very useful document to obtain critical features of the death—namely, the cause and manner of death plus some basic demographic information. The information contained on the DC is a public record. The other advantage is that the information within the DC has already been coded and is easily accessible at national, state, and local levels. Table 5.8 shows the basic data available from the DC.

Table 5.8 Data Available from the Death Certificate by Manner of Death

Manner of death	Data obtained in the DC
Natural	Demographic characteristics
Cause of death	
Accident: MVA	Demographic characteristics
Location of the occupant within the vehicle	
Number of vehicles involved	
Cause of death	
Accident: OD	Demographic characteristics
Drugs that contributed to the death	
Cause of death	
Accident: falls	Demographic characteristics
Type of fall	
Cause of death	
Accident: fires	Demographic characteristics
Cause of death	
Accident: medical misadventure	Demographic characteristics
Medical procedure involved	
Organ affected	
Cause of death	
Homicide	Demographic characteristics
Some characteristics of the actor	
Cause of death	
Suicide	Demographic characteristics
Cause of death	

Disadvantage of Using the DC

Those using only DC data for research or forensic investigation must be aware of the limitations. The DC does not contain all the important information about the death. The information contained on the DC from natural deaths may be the most limited. In cases of deaths from common heart disease, such as atherosclerotic cardiovascular disease, which causes death from occlusion of the main coronary arteries, the coronary arteries and percentages of occlusion are typically not noted. Deaths involving a firearm do not contain the following data: caliber of bullets, number of times shot, location of entrance, path, level of damage to the internal organs, location of exit wound, and the characteristics of the shooter. This information is contained within the final anatomical pathology report. The police report, if there is an arrest, will contain features of the shooter.

In cases of suicide, the DC does not provide information as to whether the victim had prior suicide attempts, if a suicide note was left, and the reason for the suicide. The death investigation report contains the history of previous attempts and the methods used. A copy of the suicide note is kept in the case file. If the death involved drugs, the concentration of the drugs and method of ingestion are not listed on the DC. The toxicology report lists all the drugs tested for and the concentration of each drug. The method that the drugs were taken into the body is contained in the death investigation report. Deaths involving a motor vehicle accident do not contain the following data: type or speed of the vehicle, road and weather conditions, and the past medical history of the victim. In deaths involving a fall, the DC does not indicate the height of the fall, role of drugs or alcohol, and past medical history. In fire deaths, the carbon monoxide level, cause of the fire, and whether smoke detectors were operational during the fire are not contained in the DC.

Studies ascertaining the accuracy of the DC have reported that 29% of DCs erroneously reported the cause of death, age of the deceased, and where an autopsy was conducted. These studies, however, reported that less error was seen in listing the marital status, race, and place of birth. Overall, more errors were cited among minority groups.

Natural Deaths

6

Introduction

A death by natural causes is not always easy to identify. The most tranquil scene, such as the discovery of an elderly man lying dead in his bed, could be hiding an unspeakable murder; however, a man found lying on a bloody bathroom floor can later be ruled a natural death. Forensic epidemiologists examining natural deaths must have a deep understanding of how natural deaths are investigated, why certain natural deaths receive a forensic investigation and others do not, and the type of data available for analysis.

This chapter will define a natural death, the annual number of natural fatalities in the United States, criteria used by the ME/C office to determine the level of investigation of a natural death, the basics of a natural death investigation, types of natural deaths and the anatomical information collected, and the role of the forensic epidemiologist investigating natural deaths. The strengths and weaknesses associated with studying natural deaths from ME/C and DC data will be discussed. Then this chapter will highlight how forensic epidemiological studies of sudden infant death syndrome (SIDS) played a key role in dramatically reducing such deaths.

Definition

Natural deaths are those due to a spontaneous or naturally occurring disease or a degenerative process. If the death has been ruled natural, there is no evidence of trauma or any indication of foul play. Examples of natural deaths include cancer, heart disease, stroke, and liver disease.

Fatalities

In 2005, a total of 2,448,017 deaths occurred in the United States, with natural deaths accounting for over 1,800,000 deaths. Table 6.1 shows a select number of natural deaths by their cause of death and their corresponding ICD-10 code by sex and race. In 2005, there were 559,312 deaths from neoplasm (C00–C97), 75,119 from diabetes mellitus (E10–E14), 19,544 from

Table 6.1 Number of Deaths by Sex and Race for a Selected Number of Natural Deaths in 2005

Cause of death	ICD-10 Code	Total number	Male	Female	White	Black
Malignant neoplasm	C00-C97	559,312	290,422	268,890	482,132	63,165
Diabetes mellitus	E10-E14	75,119	36,538	38,581	59,755	12,970
Parkinson's disease	G20-G21	19,544	11,247	8,297	18,496	711
Alzheimer's disease	G30	71,599	20,559	51,040	66,191	4,620
Major cardiovascular diseases	I00-I73	856,030	405,780	450,250	737,248	100,099
Influenza and pneumonia	J10-J18	63,001	28,052	34,949	55,540	5,780
Chronic liver disease and cirrhosis	K70, K73+K74	27,530	17,937	9,593	24,003	2,530

Parkinson's disease (G20–G21), 71,599 from Alzheimer's disease (G30), 856,030 from major cardiovascular diseases (I00–I78), 63,001 from influenza and pneumonia (J10–J18), and 27,530 from chronic liver disease and cirrhosis (K70, K73, K74). These numbers were generated from DCs submitted by each state to the CDC. At the CDC, the information on the DC is coded and the underlying causes of death are calculated to create these statistics. (See Chapter 5 for a more detailed explanation of the ICD-10 coding process.)

Natural Deaths Not Reported to the ME/C Office

The vast majority of natural deaths are never reported to or investigated by the ME/C office. These deaths are not unexpected; their etiology is well documented in medical records and the patients are well known to their physicians. Upon patient's death, the physician completes the death certificate based on his detailed knowledge of the patient's past medical history. It is important to note that any physician can sign a DC as long as he or she lists a natural condition or disease as the cause of death and indicates that the manner is natural. It is important to note that no personal physician can sign a DC with a cause or manner other than natural. Only the ME/C office is allowed by legislation to certify a DC with a non-natural manner of death. If a physician does issue a DC with a non-natural condition listed as the cause of death or with a manner other than natural, it will be returned to the issuing physician to change it to a natural condition and resubmit it or to refer the death to the ME/C to investigate and issue a non-natural DC.

Natural Deaths

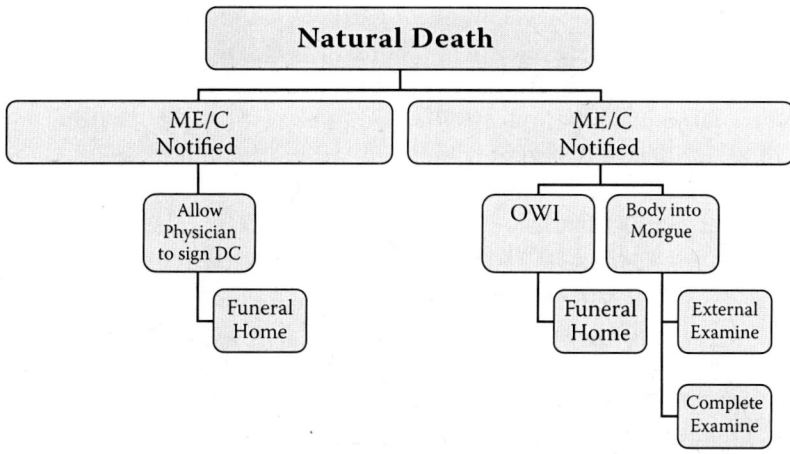

Figure 6.1 The flow of the body of a natural death victim through the ME/C system.

Natural Deaths Investigated by ME/C Office

Chapter 4 outlined the types of deaths that can be reported to the ME/C office. However, individual ME/C offices, based on their manpower, budget, and facilities, can set up their own protocols on how they choose to handle deaths from natural causes. The body of an individual who died a natural death and was reported to the ME/C office can take several paths after pronouncement of death (Figure 6.1). The ME/C can notify the physician that he or she is clear to complete the DC and release the body directly from the residence or hospital to the funeral home. The ME/C can take jurisdiction of the body. In this case, the body can take one of three paths: (1) the ME/C can issue the DC without bringing the body to the morgue for an examination, referenced office will issue (OWI) the DC; (2) the body can be ordered into the morgue, where it will undergo an external-only examination; or (3) the body brought into the morgue will receive a complete forensic examination.

Table 6.2 Number of Natural Deaths by Level of Investigation and Examination Type 2005

Type	1999	2000	2001	2002	2003	2004	2005
Total	751	752	725	758	766	749	696
OWI	282	232	240	250	198	196	193
Morgue:	469	520	485	508	568	553	503
Complete	368	393	378	384	429	414	365
External	101	127	107	124	139	139	138

Note: Total = OWI number + morgue number. Morgue number = complete number + external number.

Table 6.2 shows the level of investigation conducted among the natural deaths referred to the ME/C office. For example, in 2005 a grand total of 696 natural deaths were initially investigated by the ME/C office; of these, 194 were issued as OWI cases; 503 bodies were brought into morgue, of which 365 underwent a complete examination and 138 received an external-only examination.

Natural deaths usually fall under the jurisdiction of the ME/C for a number of reasons: (1) the death was sudden or unexpected, (2) no physician had sufficient knowledge or awareness of the decedent's medical condition to sign the DC, (3) the physician refused to sign the DC because he or she had not seen the patient in years, (4) past medical history was insufficient to issue a DC, or (5) the circumstances surrounding the death aroused suspicion.

Although the majority of natural deaths are not reported to the ME/C, a review of the workload shows that natural deaths composed a significant number of the cases investigated by an ME/C office. Table 6.3 shows the number of deaths investigated by an ME office by manner of death.

Forensic Investigation of Natural Deaths

All forensic investigations are initiated by a "death call" to the ME/C office. Based on the information provided to the death investigator and the protocol of that office, three outcomes can occur:

- Based on information provided by the physician or other medical personnel reporting the death, the death investigator is satisfied that the death is natural, that medical records sufficiently document past medical history to support the cause of death, and that no trauma or foul play is suspected.
- The physician will issue the DC and the body is released to the funeral home. In this case, the individual had significant and well documented medical conditions, but the physician will not or

Table 6.3 Number of Deaths by Manner of Death, 1999–2005

Manner of death	1999	2000	2001	2002	2003	2004	2005
Natural	751	752	725	758	766	749	696
Accident	493	591	682	711	741	749	740
Suicide	157	157	149	144	163	171	168
Homicide	100	73	98	89	130	90	96
Homicide by vehicle	16	13	14	11	9	13	16
Pending/under investigation	3	19	4	84	—	11	10
Undetermined	22	25	32	31	39	23	26
Total	1549	1630	1709	1768	1848	1812	1752

cannot issue the DC. The ME/C office would in this case order only the medical records for that individual to be brought into the office for review by a forensic pathologist. The body is transported directly from the residence, nursing home, or hospital to the funeral home. The forensic pathologist will complete the DC based solely on the information contained within the medical records. In this case, the DC issued is OWI.

- During the death call, either documented medical information provided to the death investigator was insufficient to assign a cause of death or some level of suspicion was raised requiring that the body and all relevant medical records be transported to the morgue. The death investigator would go to the scene (residence, hospital, or long-term nursing home) and collect information from the medical staff and next of kin. The ME/C office will order that copies of all medical records be sent to the ME/C office for review. In this scenario, the body can undergo one of two types of examination: an external-only examination or a complete postmortem examination.

Prior to the examination of the body, the forensic pathologist will review the death investigation report and all the medical records in order to determine which type of examination is required. A discussion to conduct an external-only examination is predicated on the ability to ascertain the cause of death from information contained within the medical records. The external examination is a safeguard procedure to ensure that the body does not exhibit any signs of trauma that may warrant further investigation because they were not documented within the medical records, communicated by the medical staff to the death investigator, or were inconsistent with statements provided by the next of kin. If, for example, a review of the medical records documents that the deceased had had double bypass surgery, had suffered several cardiac events (heart attacks), and was complaining of chest pain prior to death, this would be sufficient for the forensic pathologist to issue the DC as atherosclerosis cardiovascular disease (ASCVD) without conducting a complete autopsy.

Remember that the role of the postmortem examination is to determine the cause and manner of death. The forensic pathologist could also decide to conduct a complete autopsy. This is typically done if there is a lack of significant past medical history, no medical history at all, or the death was sudden or unexpected.

Upon completion of an autopsy, the forensic pathologist completes the final pathology report described in detail in Chapter 4. Contained within this report are the anatomical findings of the external and internal examination of the body and its organs. Forensic epidemiologists must become familiar with the layout and type of information it contains.

Types of Natural Deaths

The role of the forensic autopsy in a natural death is to determine which organ or organ system has failed and attempt to determine if it was due to age, disease, or abuse resulting in death. Natural deaths investigated by the ME/C office can be categorized into the following systems: cardiovascular, respiratory, hepatobiliary, gastrointestinal, renal, lymphatic, endocrine, pancreatic, reproductive, neurological, infectious, metabolic, congenital, and immunological, as well as psychiatric disorders and sudden infant death syndrome (SIDS). The forensic epidemiologist must have some basic anatomical understanding of the function of each organ, the normal weights of the internal organs, and the common pathological diseases encountered within each organ.

The amount of anatomical data available depends on the type of autopsy preformed and the level of description and documentation by the forensic pathologist. A complete autopsy will provide the greatest amount of anatomical data and the level of disease of each organ. However, the level of detail of the gross and microscopic examinations carried out by the forensic pathologist will vary greatly. In contrast, an external-only examination provides no anatomical or disease state data and provides only a regurgitation of the information contained within the medical documents.

Next is a brief overview of the major internal systems examined during a complete autopsy and the types of data available to the forensic epidemiologist within each system.

Cardiovascular System

The cardiovascular system consists of the heart and blood vessels (arteries and veins) throughout the body. A complete autopsy will provide the forensic epidemiologist with the following data on the heart: weight, percentage of occlusions of the three main coronary arteries (right coronary, left coronary, and circumflex arteries), thickness of the left ventricle, location and size of scarring, and documentation of medical interventions (stents, bypass, etc.). Deaths caused by an aneurysm, the localized abnormal dilation of a vessel, and the type, location and size will be noted.

In cases where the forensic pathologist bases his determination of the cause of death after reviewing the information in the medical record review of an OWI case or conducted external-only type examination, no anatomical and pathological data are available. Caution should be taken in deaths certified as natural when the immediate cause of death is listed as cardiovascular in nature but did not receive a complete forensic examination. These diagnoses are only as accurate as the physician's ability at diagnosis and the level of instrumentations available for that diagnosis. Remember that only a small percentage of the total number of natural deaths reaches the ME/C office. The vast majority of the DCs for natural deaths is completed by family physicians, who rarely request that a hospital autopsy be performed to confirm their diagnosis.

Forensic epidemiological investigation of the collected cardiovascular data can study a number of associations, such as the relationship of body mass index (BMI) to the weight of the heart; the location and percentage of occlusions and damage to the heart muscle, precipitating events leading to death; survival time, and the type and effectiveness of medical treatment. Microscopic sections of the heart can be examined and small changes due to disease progression noted.

Respiratory System

The respiratory system includes the nasal and oral cavities, pharynx, larynx, trachea, right and left bronchi, right and left lungs, and the alveoli. A complete autopsy will provide the forensic epidemiologist with the following data: weight of the right and left lungs, specific identification of the organism causing the diseases, and location, size, and degree of disease involvement within the lung. Common diseases of the lung include chronic obstructive pulmonary disease (COPD), pneumonia, emphysema, and occupationally related diseases. Recently, some DC forms have been changed in order to collect data on smoking history.

Forensic epidemiologists investigating respiratory data can study the usefulness of the weight of the lungs as an indicator of the degree of involvement of the disease, the percentage of lung diseases to years of exposure to cigarettes or exposure to hazardous materials, and the effects of a reduced lung capacity on the profusion of other organs.

Hepatobiliary System

The hepatobiliary system includes the liver and the biliary tract. A complete autopsy will provide the forensic epidemiologist with the weight of the liver and the disease state (fatty liver, fibrosis, cirrhosis, cancer). Forensic epidemiologists focusing on the diseases of the liver could study the relationship between alcohol consumption history and the pathology of the liver and how liver disease affects other organ systems.

Nervous System

The nervous system includes the brain and the spinal cord. A complete autopsy will provide the forensic epidemiologist with the following data: weight of brain; locations and sizes of hemorrhages (epidural, subdural, subarachnoid, and intracerebral); sizes and locations of aneurysms; types, sizes, and locations of tumors; level of degenerative diseases (Alzheimer's disease), and diseases of the spinal cord. In cases of a cerebral event, names and locations of the vessels involved and the specific area of the brain affected are collected. However, some natural conditions do not leave anatomical or physical evidence and the diagnosis is based on the behaviors exhibited by the victim and documented within the death investigation report. These conditions include several types of seizures and epilepsy.

Forensic epidemiologists focusing on neurological diseases could study the specific locations of hemorrhage and its relationship to other diseases, the size and location of aneurysms, and the microscopic structure of the surrounding vessels.

Organ Weights

The weights of the internal organs recovered during the autopsy must be compared to the organs' normal weights. Appendix A presents the weights, standard deviation, and range of the main internal organs for males; in general, the organs of females are 10% lighter. The forensic epidemiologist should not examine the anatomical data in isolation but in context with the information within the death investigation report, events leading up to the death, important past medical history, and medical response to the event.

Stored Tissue and Microscopic Slides

During an autopsy, large sections of each organ are placed in storage jars filled with formaldehyde. Smaller sections of each organ are placed in smaller jars that will be sent to the histology division, where the organs will be cut, mounted on glass slides, and stained. These will be reviewed by the forensic pathologist and are typically stored forever, therefore enabling retrospective or future studies. In addition, the larger sections of organs are retained and stored for 5 years (this storage varies by ME/C office).

Forensic Epidemiological Investigation of Natural Deaths

The role of the forensic epidemiologist in investigation of natural deaths is first to describe the basic epidemiological characteristics of the victim and to

Natural Deaths

Table 6.4 Basic Data Collected on Natural Deaths

Characteristics	Variables
Basic epidemiological features	Age
	Sex
	Race
Residence	Exact address
Incident: location	Residence
	Hospital
	Other
Incident: time/date	Time
	Day of the week
	Month
Place of death	Scene
	Residence
	Hospital
Death: time/date/location	
Number and level of drugs detected	
Primary organ or system involved	
Organ weights	
List of prescription medications	
Past medical history	

conduct a detailed examination of the affected organ or organ systems and to present these data in a manner that can be used by emergency medicine personnel, individuals in the health field, and researchers. The basic information that should be collected in a forensic epidemiological investigation of natural death is listed in Table 6.4.

The basic epidemiological profile is important to show the characteristics of the individuals at most risk of dying from a natural disease. The basic epidemiological profile includes the total number of deaths, separated into number by age, sex, and race. These types of data can be abstracted from the death investigation report or the DC. This information is important to identify the population most at risk in that specific region. In addition, these data can serve as baseline data that can be used to evaluate the general health of the region. Table 6.5 shows the number of natural deaths by sex and race examined by the ME/C office covering an 8-year period. The table shows that the majority of deaths occurred among white males and the yearly distribution remained relatively stable during the study period. Questions that should be asked include: Did the population's sex and race distribution remain stable as well? Would this distribution remain similar if the natural deaths not examined by the ME/C were added to this table?

Table 6.5 Demographic Characteristics of Natural Deaths, 1998–2005

Race/sex	1998 Number (%)	1999 Number (%)	2000 Number (%)	2001 Number (%)	2002 Number (%)	2003 Number (%)	2004 Number (%)	2005 Number (%)
White/male	277 (57.5)	226 (49.7)	268 (52.5)	265 (54.1)	262 (51.5)	313 (55.1)	294 (53.2)	260 (52.2)
White/female	101 (21.0)	112 (24.6)	108 (21.2)	119 (24.5)	128 (25.2)	138 (24.3)	130 (23.5)	127 (25.5)
Black/male	61 (12.6)	78 (17.1)	85 (16.7)	59 (12.2)	76 (14.9)	67 (11.8)	84 (15.2)	67 (13.4)
Black/female	40 (8.3)	31 (6.8)	47 (9.2)	41 (8.4)	39 (7.7)	47 (8.3)	44 (7.9)	42 (8.4)
Other	3 (0.6)	7 (1.5)	2 (0.4)	1 (0.2)	3 (0.6)	3 (0.5)	1 (0.2)	2 (0.4)
Total	482	454	510	485	508	568	553	498

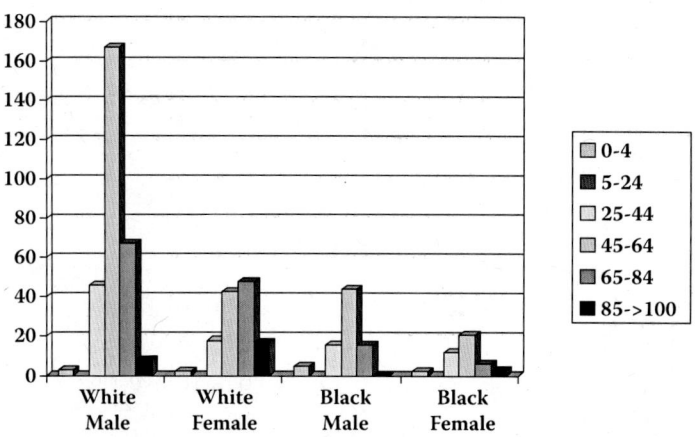

Figure 6.2 Natural deaths by age, sex and race, 2005.

The age distribution of the natural deaths should be examined next. One would expect that deaths from natural conditions would affect the older segment of the population. Figure 6.2 shows the natural deaths examined at the ME/C office grouped by age, sex, and race in 2005. In looking at this table, all indications show that the majority of natural deaths in that region occurred among fairly young individuals (45–64 years old). The forensic epidemiologist must remember that only a small percentage of natural deaths receive an investigation by the ME/C office. Those over 85 years old typically are under the care of a physician that will sign the DC. It more important to state that, among the natural deaths investigated by the ME/C, the majority occurred in individuals

Natural Deaths

between the ages of 45 and 64, the deaths were most likely unexpected, and the decedents were not under the care of a physician at the time of death.

In order to obtain a complete picture of the causes of natural deaths in an area, the forensic epidemiologist must combine the deaths investigated by the ME/C with those issued by a physician. The questions to ask regarding these cases is why these natural deaths required a forensic investigation to determine the cause of death. Death among those under age 45 may be sudden and unexpected and warrant an investigation; however, one would expect that individuals over 65 would comprise a population with a well documented past medical history and under the care of a physician. By the age grouping, the forensic epidemiologist should delineate the reason why the death was investigated by the ME/C office. These reasons could include the following: lack of a physician, physician did not have significant medical documentation to warrant signing the DC, or the physician refused to sign the DC.

The next level of forensic epidemiological investigation would be to obtain the final pathological diagnosis (see Chapter 4 for a detailed

Table 6.6 Number of Deaths by Organ/System, 2000–2005

Organ/system	Total number of deaths					
	2000	2001	2002	2003	2004	2005
Heart-related deaths	369	358	369	412	400	380
Vascular system-related death	4	13	—	—	—	—
Respiratory system-related death	45	38	40	35	44	37
Hepatobiliary system-related death	19	13	18	20	24	24
Gastrointestinal tract-related death	9	14	12	17	15	8
Pancreatic disorder-related death	1	2	1	—	1	1
Lymphatic system-related death	2	1	—	—	—	—
Renal system-related death	2	—	2	4	3	4
Female reproductive system-related death	6	4	4	1	—	—
Endocrine system-related death	5	6	9	8	7	6
Nervous system-related death	29	21	33	49	40	20
Congenitally related death	—	1	—	—	—	—
Infection-related death	—	2	8	11	5	3
Cancer-related death	5	1	3	3	1	2
Immunological disorder-related death	1	—	1	1	2	—
Connective tissue-related death	—	—	—	—	—	—
Psychiatrically related death	—	—	—	—	3	1
Systemically related death	—	—	—	—	2	1
Blood-related death	—	—	—	—	—	2
Sudden infant death syndrome	13	11	8	7	6	9
Total deaths	510	485	508	568	553	498

Table 6.7 Cause of Death by Subcategories among 498 Natural Deaths in 2005

Causes of death	Number of cases
Cardiovascular disease-related deaths	
Atherosclerotic cardiovascular disease (ASCVD)	207
Hypertensive heart disease	36
Atherosclerotic cardiovascular disease/hypertensive heart disease	30
Arteriosclerotic/hypertensive CVD	23
Arteriosclerotic/valvular heart disease	1
Cardiomyopathy (primary/dilated/hypertrophic)	18
Cardiomegaly	7
Hypertensive/valvular heart disease	2
Cardiac tamponade	17
Cardiac dysrhythmia (arrhythmia)	3
Arrhythmogenic right ventricular dysplasia	1
Valvular heart disease	2
Sudden death (suspected cardiac arrhythmia)	1
Myocardial fibrosis	4
Myocardial infarction	3
Hypoplastic CAD	2
Thrombosis RCA	3
Tunneling LAD coronary artery	1
Congestive heart failure	4
Dissection: aortic	1
Dissection: coronary artery	1
Ruptured aneurysm: AAA	3
Thoracic AA	2
Left ventral artery	1
Congenital anomaly LCA	1
Transposition of great vessels	1
Aortic stenosis	1
Anomalous origin LCA	1
Congenital	1
Systemic Sjogren vasculitis	1
Total number of cardiovascular disease-related deaths	**379**
Respiratory system-related deaths	
Pulmonary embolism (PE) and infarction	12
Pneumonia (acute/bronchopneumonia/hemorrhagic)	12
Bronchitis	1
Chronic obstructive pulmonary disease (COPD)	5
Asthma	2
Pulmonary thrombosis	1
Carcinoma of the Lungs	2

Table 6.7 Cause of Death by Subcategories among 498 Natural Deaths in 2005 (continued)

Causes of death	Number of cases
Respiratory system-related deaths	
Suppurative pleuritis	1
Invasive squamous cell carcinoma	1
Total number of respiratory system-related deaths	**37**
Hepatobiliary system-related deaths	
Liver cirrhosis	15
Fatty liver	6
Steatosis of liver	1
End-stage liver disease	1
Liver cancer	1
Total number of hepatobiliary system-related deaths	**24**
Gastrointestinal tract-related deaths	
Gastrointestinal hemorrhage	4
Megacolon	1
Strangulation of small intestine	1
Chronic inflammatory bowel disease	1
Colon cancer	1
Total number of gastrointestinal tract-related deaths	**8**
Renal disorder-related deaths	
Renal failure	3
Renal cancer	1
Total number of renal disorder-related deaths	**4**
Systematic-related deaths	
Lupus	1
Total number of systematic-related deaths	**1**
Blood disease-related deaths	
Anemia	1
Myeloma	1
Total number of blood disease-related deaths	**2**
Endocrine system-related deaths	
Diabetes mellitus/diabetic ketoacidosis	5
Hypoglycemic coma	1
Total number of endocrine system-related deaths	**6**
Pancreatic disorder-related deaths	
Pancreatitis	1
Total number of pancreatic-disorder related deaths	**1**
Nervous system-related deaths	
Intercerebral (intracranial) hemorrhage	3

Table 6.7 Cause of Death by Subcategories among 498 Natural Deaths in 2005 (continued)

Causes of death	Number of cases
Nervous system-related deaths	
Subarachnoid hemorrhage (Berry aneurysm)	1
Seizure disorder	12
Epilepsy	1
Sudden unexplained death—epilepsy	1
Cortical infarction	1
Diffusely infiltrating ganglin–glioma spinal cord	1
Total number of nervous system-related deaths	**20**
Psychiatrically related deaths	
Sudden unexpected death in schizophrenia	1
Total number of psychiatrically related deaths	**1**
Infection-related deaths	
Sepsis (septicemia)	1
Staphylococcal	2
Total number of infection-related deaths	**3**
Cancer-related deaths	
Ovarian	1
Breast	1
Total number of cancer-related deaths	**2**
Total number of sudden infant death syndrome (SIDS) deaths	**9**

description of this diagnosis), which provides a detailed explanation of the cause of death that can be grouped into broad organ or system categories. Table 6.6 shows one possible method of dividing these deaths. The forensic epidemiologist must have a firm understanding of the organs or systems affected among natural deaths. The table shows that the majority of natural deaths investigated by the ME/C are related to the cardiovascular system.

The next phase would be to break down each general grouping to the specific disease condition or organism that caused the death. Table 6.7 presents a detailed breakdown within each category. After that, the next step would be to create a profile of the demographic features (age, sex, and race), location of death, and level of treatment within each subcategory. For example, what was the average age of victims that died from a cardiac tamponade? Did these individuals die in their residence, emergency room, or operating room and was their diagnosis upon admission correct?

Natural Deaths

Strengths and Weaknesses of ME/C Natural Death Data

The major strengths of forensic data collected on natural deaths are found among those undergoing a complete autopsy, thus allowing for the following: (1) confirmation of documented medical information or diagnosis, (2) investigation of changes to the internal organs over time and by diseases, (3) examination of the effects of internal organs' exposure to different compounds at the gross and microscopic levels, and (4) better understanding of how a diseased organ affects other organs.

The autopsy is the last opportunity to examine the body before burial or cremation to determine if the diagnosis of cancer, cirrhosis, or an enlarged heart made during life was correct. An ME/C office examines a large number of natural deaths and collects information on the anatomy of the organs covering a wide age range and both sexes. The weights of the internal organs can be documented over a life span to determine the normal range of each organ. Diseases at different stages of progression can be studied by the effect they have on the weight and functional level of the internal organs. The effects of exposure to compounds such as tobacco or alcohol can be examined. The availability of the gross and microscopic slides allows for a better understanding of the effect that the disease state of one organ has on another.

One of the major weaknesses of forensically investigating natural deaths is that they do not represent the entire population of natural deaths in that area. Only a small fraction of natural deaths receives a forensic investigation and, of those investigated, only a small fraction undergoes a complete autopsy. Therefore, caution should be taken before making generalizations about the general population based on the information obtained by reviewing the natural deaths examined by the ME/C office. Another weakness is the high number of external-only examinations. Although the external examination does locate a small number of non-natural deaths that would have been signed out as natural—mostly from blunt force trauma (BFT)—it offers no tangible anatomical data about the mechanism that caused the death.

Natural Death and the DC

Forensic epidemiologists investigating natural deaths that have access only to the DC data must understand the weakness of such data. Death certificates can be completed by family physicians who have very little training or understanding of the meaning of "immediate cause of death" and "contributory causes of death." In all their years of training, physicians receive virtually no instructions as to the proper method of completing a DC. Even among those completed by the ME/C, the methods and level of detail vary greatly. Although there are some guidelines, most forensic pathologists are allowed great liberty in completing a DC. Therefore, the level of information transferred from the final pathology report to the DC varies. Two identical types of death can be reported on the DC in different ways by different forensic pathologists. Some examples include the following:

1. One may sign the DC with the immediate cause of death as ASCVD; another may complete it with the immediate cause of death as ASCVD due to 75% occlusion of the right coronary artery.
2. The immediate cause of death may be simple COPD; in another case, the immediate cause of death may be COPD due to smoking.
3. The immediate cause of death may be simple cirrhosis of the liver; in another case, immediate cause of death may be cirrhosis of the liver due to acute alcohol toxicities.

The DC also has the limitation that it contains no weights of the internal organs. When death was caused by cardiomegaly—an enlarged heart (hearts weighing more than 500 g)—the actual weight of the heart, although noted in the final pathology report, will not appear on the DC.

Sudden Infant Death Syndrome (SIDS)

Introduction

One of the most challenging types of investigations conducted by ME/C offices is that of a previously normal, healthy infant who dies suddenly and unexpectedly. Typically, these infants are discovered dead by the parents in the morning hours. These cases are challenging because of the high emotional cost to the family, the intense level of investigation required, and the end result failure to provide a clearly identifiable cause and manner of death.

Definition

Sudden infant death syndrome (SIDS) is an idiopathic condition that typically affects infants during their first year of life. SIDS involves (1) the sudden and unexpected death of an infant under 1 year of age who was relatively healthy prior to death; (2) an infant death that remains unexplained even after the performance of a complete postmortem examination, including toxicological and genetic testing; (3) a death scene investigation; and (4) a review of the infant's and mother's medical histories. The diagnosis of SIDS on a DC can only be used if these four conditions have all been met. A diagnosis of SIDS is one of exclusion; therefore, only after all other possible causes have been eliminated should the medical examiner or coroner conducting

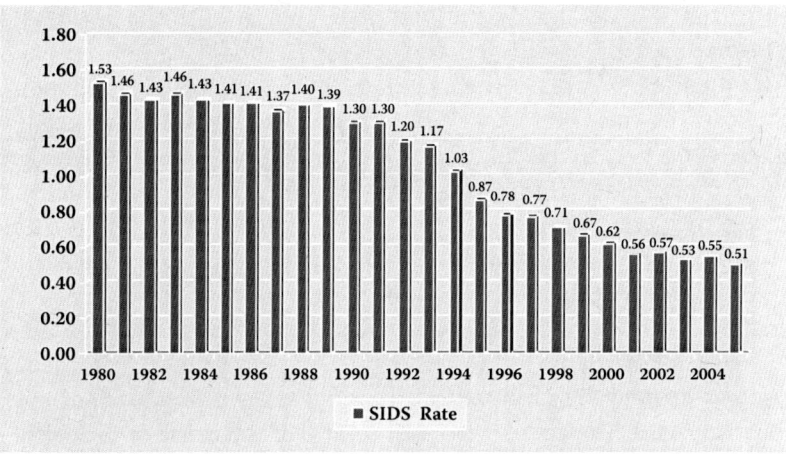

Figure 6.3 U.S. annual SIDS rate per 1,000 live births, 1980–2004.

Table 6.8 Deaths from SIDS by Sex and Race among 2005 Deaths

Cause of death	Total number	Male	Female	White	Black
SIDS	2,230	N/A	N/A	1,493	663

the investigation sign the cause of death as SIDS. Although infants over 1 year of age are still susceptible to SIDS, this occurs very rarely. SIDS deaths in the older literature were referred to as "crib deaths" because the deaths typically occurred in the baby's crib.

Fatalities

The national numbers of SIDS has been declining since 1980 (Figure 6.3). In 2005, SIDS deaths (ICD-10 code: R95) in the United States numbered 2,230 (Table 6.8).

Foundations of SIDS

In a typical SIDS case, the parents put their previously healthy infant to sleep at around 11:00 p.m. They hear nothing unusual during the night. The next morning they discover the infant unresponsive in the crib. The infants are frequently cold to the touch, blue in color, and stiff. The parents immediately call 911 and often initiate CPR. Based on the protocol of the responding EMS, the infant is either transferred to the ER or pronouncement of death is made at the residence. Once the infant is pronounced dead, the ME/C office is notified and takes jurisdiction and begins its investigation. The death is typically investigated by both the police and the ME/C office.

The theories to explain the causes of SIDS have varied over the years. Theories during the 1940s and 1950s were focused on suffocation caused by blankets, clothing, or the mattress. During the 1970s and 1980s, theories included prolonged QT intervals, immunopathogenesis, unstable homeostatic controls, and prolonged sleep apnea. The focus shifted to anatomical examinations of SIDS during the 1990s. Microscopic examination of the brains of infants that died of SIDS showed them to have fewer CO^2 receptors when compared to the non-SIDS deaths of infants. Supporting the theory is the fact that SIDS infants fail to respond to high levels of CO^2 in the microatmosphere around their mouths. There is currently no evidence of a genetic etiology for SIDS. The current understanding of the cause of SIDS is a syndrome composed of a heterogeneous group of disease processes rather than a single entity.

Forensic Investigation of a SIDS Death

The ME/C office investigation of a possible SIDS death is conducted identically to that of any other type of death, consisting of a scene investigation, a complete autopsy, and laboratory studies. The main difference is that, in other types of deaths, the forensic pathologist has the ability to determine if a complete or external examination is sufficient to determine the cause and manner of death; however, in the case of a possible SIDS death, this option is removed, and a complete autopsy is required.

The death scene investigation involves a detailed examination and photographing of the location where the infant was discovered dead. If the infant has been moved from the original position, an anatomically correct doll is used to show the exact position in which the infant was put to sleep and the position the infant was in when discovered. Information collected about the sleeping environment includes room temperature and type of bed; if the bed is a crib, then the condition, type, number and types of blankets, sleeping surface, and list of items within the crib are noted. The investigator questions the parents as to the circumstances leading up to and surrounding the death and ascertain the time of the last feeding, the position the infant was placed in to sleep, the time the infant was last seen alive, the time at which and position in which the infant was discovered, and who discovered the dead infant. All medical records pertaining to the mother and infant should be obtained from the hospital.

The SIDS forensic autopsy is similar to an adult autopsy. The laboratory examination includes toxicological analysis of the body fluids and atmospheric testing of the sleeping environment for the presence of any toxic substances. Samples of the blood are tested for metabolic disorders as well as any genetic disorders. In most investigations, the police conduct a parallel investigation. They conduct interviews with individuals that had interactions with the infant immediately prior to and after discovery, including parents, babysitters, or day-care workers. In some cases, polygraph examinations are conducted. The results of their investigation are forwarded to the ME/C office.

Methods of Investigation

The investigation of a possible SIDS death can be divided into seven interrelated areas: prebirth factors, the birth, postbirth environment, postbirth parental behaviors, infant characteristics, and death scene reports.

Prebirth Factors

The behavior of the mother during pregnancy can have grave effects upon the fetus. During pregnancy, the fetus shares the blood supply of the mother. The mother's consuming legal or illegal drugs (including alcohol) or smoking tobacco exposes the fetus to these same compounds. The mother should also have regular health-care prenatal visits during the pregnancy. The investigator should obtain a behavior history of the mother prior to the birth such as the interval between pregnancies, the date at which she last gave birth, history of drug, alcohol, or tobacco use, and the number of prenatal visits.

Birth Factors

Information regarding the birth can be obtained by interviewing the mother and/or a review of the medical records. The ME/C office has the authority to order copies of all medical records surrounding the infant's birth. Medical data collected include the length of gestation (number of weeks), type of birth (vaginal, C-section), birth weight and height, APGAR scores, complications surrounding the birth, and the results of the newborn screening for metabolic disorders.

Postbirth Environment

The investigation of the infant's environment involves making a detailed examination of the sleeping environment. The location where the infant typically slept is described and photographed. If the infant slept in a crib, the following data are collected: the size of the crib, size of the mattress, number of layers, and a list of objects within the crib (stuffed animals, etc.). The type of heat and the temperature of the infant's room are also collected. If the infant slept in something other than a crib, that location is described in great detail and photographed.

Postbirth Parental Behaviors

The behaviors of the parents (caregivers) prior to the death must be considered. These factors include the number of smokers in close proximity to the infant and the parents' frequency of alcohol and drug use. How often the parents slept with the infant in the adult bed is noted.

Infant Characteristics

Characteristics of the infant include the following: the physical features (height and weight) at the time of death, which is compared to normal growth charts; time of last feeding; dietary history (formula/breast); position placed in to sleep (face up, face down, on the side); position in which found dead; and who discovered the infant. One of the key pieces of information is the location where the infant was sleeping, such as a crib, sofa, or adult bed. In addition, the number of pediatric examinations, vaccine history, illness after birth, and any current medications prescribed for the infant should be ascertained.

Autopsy/Toxicology Investigation A forensic pathologist will conduct a complete forensic examination of the infant. All internal organs will be weighed and examined at gross and microscopic levels. During the autopsy, body fluids (blood, urine, bile, eye fluid, and stomach contents) are sent for analysis and screening.

Death Scene Reports

Once the investigation is completed, the death investigator writes a death investigation report, including a completed CDC-created SIDS data form (available at www.cdc.gov/SIDS/pdf/SUIDSIform.pdf).

Manner: Natural or Undetermined?

The final result of the death investigation, autopsy, toxicological testing, genetic screening, and questioning of the parents is that no environmental, physical, anatomical, or chemical cause for the infant's death was found. In this case, the immediate cause of death should be listed as SIDS.

The manner of death is not so straightforward. Checking the "natural" box implies that some natural process was identified that resulted in the death of the infant; however, SIDS is a diagnosis by exclusion. Calling it natural has a psychological effect of communicating to the parents that they did nothing wrong and the death could not have been predicted. However, some people believe that the manner should be listed as "undetermined." This is a more accurate portrait of the results of the death investigation. The investigation failed to show an anatomical or pathological cause for the death of the infant and therefore the manner is unknown.

Because the diagnosis of SIDS is one of exclusion, a complete autopsy must be conducted before the diagnosis can be made. However, in some jurisdictions, the next of kin are allowed to prevent a complete autopsy on a suspected SIDS case. In these circumstances, the correct cause of death should be listed as "undetermined" and the manner should also be "undetermined."

Multiple SIDS within the same family is rare. In such cases, the first infant death that presents as SIDS should be signed out as SIDS with a manner "natural." The second death to the same mother should be labeled as "undetermined." The reason for labeling the second death as "undetermined" is to mark or flag that particular case. If a third death occurs to the same mother, that infant's death should be ruled as a homicide and the first two deaths should be reinvestigated.

Research

Forensic epidemiological investigations of SIDS deaths have resulted in a dramatic reduction in the number of SIDS cases. Those studying the phenomenon today must be cautious. The forensic epidemiologist should inquire of the ME/C with regard to the protocol for the investigation of possible SIDS deaths. Questions to ask include the level of investigation and the manner of death to which these cases are assigned (natural or undermined). A SIDS diagnosis without an autopsy should be analyzed separately from those that were diagnosed after a thorough forensic investigation.

Application of Forensic Epidemiological Investigation of SIDS

One of the classic examples of forensic epidemiological investigation techniques that have resulted in the reduction of deaths is highlighted by the forensic investigation of SIDS deaths. During the 1960s, SIDS accounted for 10,000 deaths annually in the United States. These deaths were investigated and, although large amounts of epidemiological information were collected, data lay in file cabinets in ME/C offices around the United States and the world. When forensic epidemiologists begin investigating these deaths, they started by compiling the scattered case data. Then they began looking for features (variables) common to the majority of the deaths. They looked at factors such as age, sex, race, time and place of death, diet, the position in which the decedent was placed to sleep and in which decedent was found unresponsive, prenatal care, type of birth, birth order, and environmental factors.

The forensic epidemiological examination of the vast amount of data revealed a unique pattern only seen among infants that died from SIDS.

The data showed (1) a unique death distribution, with the majority of deaths occurring between 2 and 5 months of life and 90% of all SIDS deaths occurring within the first 6 months of life; (2) higher rates among blacks; (3) more frequency among male infants; (4) increased frequency of deaths during the cold winter months; and (5) death, typically unwitnessed, occurring between the hours of midnight and 9 a.m.

In 1994, there were approximately 5,500 SIDS deaths in the United States, with an incidence rate of 2–3 per 1,000 live births. In Western countries, SIDS is among the top three leading causes of postneonatal infant mortality for infants between 1 month and 1 year of life. Based on 2002 national data, over 2,000 infants died from SIDS, resulting in a rate of 50.6 per 100,000 live births. Of these deaths, 1,343 occurred among whites (42.3 per 100,000 live births) and 603 among blacks (102.1 per 100,000 live births).

The research identified several possible risk factors associated with SIDS deaths. Materially related risk factors included smoking, drug use, maternal youth, short intergestational interval, lack of prenatal care, and race. Environmental risk factors included sleeping position, sleeping location, and sleeping surface. Cultural, ethnic, and economic factors each played a role in the behavioral risk factors of the caregivers. The forensic epidemiological investigation highlighted a number of characteristics of SIDS that were considered modifiable, including prenatal care, smoking, sleeping position, proper sleeping environment, and bed sharing.

Researchers are not certain what causes SIDS, though they believe that a dynamic interaction of several factors causes death. One early theory viewed SIDS as a developmental phenomenon in which normal maturation of nervous system control centers failed to occur; another suggested that SIDS was multifactoral and did not depend on a single characteristic, but rather on a dynamic interaction of risk factors. Another study found that infants who died from SIDS had decreased binding of serotonin in the arcuate nucleus and other brain regions that control breathing, heart beat, body temperature, and arousal. These findings may point to a more global biological deficit in SIDS victims, perhaps originating in early fetal life, than researchers previously believed.

Research has proposed a triple-risk hypothesis that SIDS may occur when a predisposed infant experiences an unstable period of homeostatic control along with triggering factors. Triggering factors such as prone sleep position (an infant sleeping on the stomach), bed sharing (an infant sharing an adult bed with others), soft bedding (such as sheepskins, comforters, or quilts), maternal smoking, viral infections, and premature birth are associated with an increased risk of dying of SIDS.

Forensic epidemiological data have shown that the risk for SIDS is greater for babies whose mothers have given birth multiple times, are black or Native American, and are members of lower socioeconomic groups. Forensic epidemiological research has also identified four major triggering modifiable factors that appear to be associated with an infant's increased risk of dying of SIDS. These are discussed in detail next and include (1) sleep position of the baby, (2) use of soft bedding, (3) bed sharing, and (4) cultural factors of socioeconomics and ethnicity.

Sleep Position

International forensic epidemiological studies from New Zealand, Australia, and England have all suggested a link between the prone sleep position (an infant sleeping on the stomach) and SIDS. These studies have led governments to recommend the supine position (sleeping on the back) for infants. Following this recommendation, SIDS rates declined in all three countries.

In 1992, the American Academy of Pediatrics (AAP) Task Force on Sleep Position examined these same studies and recommended policy changes for American babies to be placed on their sides or backs to sleep. Following the AAP recommendation, prone sleep position in the United States decreased from 70% in 1992 to 43% in 1994, and SIDS rates in the United States decreased approximately 20%.

Based on these findings, in June of 1994, the "Back to Sleep" campaign was initiated in the United States through a coalition of the National Institute of Child Health and Human Development, the Maternal and Child Health Bureau, the American Academy of Pediatrics, the SIDS Alliance, and the Association of SIDS and Infant Mortality Programs. This campaign aimed at educating parents, grandparents, caregivers, and members of the medical community about the importance of the supine sleeping position. In 1996, the American Academy of Pediatrics Task Force on Positioning and SIDS updated its recommendation for preferred sleep position to supine, with lateral (side) sleep position as the next preferred position. Hence, by 1998, 56% of U.S. infants were reportedly placed in the supine position and 17% in the prone position.

Soft Bedding

Based on forensic epidemiological analysis of SIDS data, the Consumer Product Safety Commission (CPSC), the American Academy of Pediatrics (AAP), and the National Institute of Child Health and Human Development (NICHD) revised their recommendations for infant sleep environment in an advisory dated April 8, 1999. They recommended that infants under 12 months of age be put to sleep in a crib with no soft bedding on top of or under the baby. The CPSC had previously warned parents of the dangers to sleeping infants associated with the use of adult beds, waterbeds, featherbeds, futons, beanbag cushions, sheepskins, sofa cushions, comforters, pillows and other improvised sleep arrangements not specifically designed for infant use.

Forensic epidemiological research also suggested an increased risk for SIDS if the infants' heads are covered by soft bedding while they are asleep, and as many as 900 infant deaths each year are associated with suffocation in soft bedding. This led the CPSC, AAP, and NICHD to make the following recommendations for safe bedding practices:

1. Place the baby on his or her back on a firm, tight-fitting mattress in a crib that meets current safety standards.
2. Remove pillows, quilts, comforters, sheepskins, stuffed toys, and other soft products from the crib.
3. Consider using a sleeper or other sleep clothing as an alternative to blankets, with no other covering.
4. If a blanket is used, put the baby with feet at the foot of the crib. Tuck a thin blanket around the crib mattress, reaching only as far as the baby's chest.
5. Make sure the baby's head remains uncovered during sleep.
6. Do not place the baby on a waterbed, sofa, soft mattress, pillow, or other soft surface to sleep.

Bed Sharing

Bed sharing is defined as an infant sleeping with others on an adult bed or nontraditional surface. Hazards due to bed sharing include overlying by the parent, sibling, or other adult sharing the bed; entrapment or wedging of the child between the mattress and other objects; head entrapment in bed railings; and suffocation on waterbeds. This is particularly dangerous when the adult is in an altered state of consciousness due to the use of alcohol or other drugs or if the adult is obese.

Bed sharing, especially on sofas with multiple family members, has been found to be a major risk factor for infant death. Studies have also found that soft bedding, such as comforters, pillows, and waterbeds was more common among infants who shared a bed; these infants were more than twice as likely to have been placed in the prone sleeping position. Research has documented that infants that share an adult bed are approximately 40 times more at risk of accidental suffocation than infants who sleep in cribs.

Ethnicity and Socioeconomic Status

Although the rate of SIDS in the United States has been reduced approximately 43–50%, the infant mortality rate has not dropped as dramatically among infants in low-income black families. Overall SIDS rate in the United States declined from 1.2 per 1,000 live births in 1992 to 0.53 per 1,000 births in 2000. Despite this decline, the infant mortality rate for black infants in some areas continues to be almost three times that for white infants.

NICHD studies reveal that black infants consistently have a higher prevalence of prone sleeping than infants in other ethnic groups, and this was found to be a significant risk factor for SIDS in a black urban sample. In 1998, the NICHD National Infant Sleep Position Study demonstrated that 43% of black infants were sleeping prone, as compared to 29% among white infants in the overall study. Also, women less likely to lay their infants in the supine position typically were black, had fewer than 16 years of education, had more than one child, and/or lived in a southern or mid-Atlantic state.

A Consumer Product Safety Commission "Safe Sleep Campaign 2000" survey revealed that only 31% of black parents surveyed put their babies to sleep supine as opposed to 43% of all parents. Moreover, Kemp et al. (2000) found that more than 50% of sudden deaths among black infants occurred during bed sharing, with bed sharing occurring due to the perceived lack of funds to purchase a crib. Further research suggested that higher SIDS rates in low-income and black communities may be attributable to high-risk bed-sharing practices and that education about the risk associated with bed sharing should be coupled with the provision of cribs. The combination of soft bedding and prone sleep position is particularly dangerous, as is infant bed sharing with one or more people.

The significance of the forensic epidemiological investigation of SIDS deaths has been to identify a number of modifiable behaviors that have been shown to reduce the incidence of SIDS. These modifiable behaviors are easy to implement and are low cost. Campaigns such as the "Back to Sleep" campaign in 1994 have resulted in an overall SIDS rate decline. In addition, education efforts to promote a proper and safe infant sleep environment have also resulted in a reduced number of SIDS. Unfortunately, this simple behavioral modification has had a limited impact among black women with a low socioeconomic status. Because the SIDS rate is higher for such families and because of a perceived lack of funds for a crib coupled with the risk associated with a parent's sharing a bed with an infant, the current study assesses the effectiveness of a primary prevention approach to reduce deaths by SIDS.

Forensic Epidemiological Investigation of SIDS

Forensic epidemiological investigation of SIDS deaths, like any investigation, starts by collecting basic epidemiological data. Caution should be taken before the collection and presentation of SIDS data. ME/C office personnel should be spoken to first to ascertain that all cases signed out as SIDS conform to the definition of SIDS stated earlier. Only SIDS that adhered to the definition should be included in the analysis. The basic information that should be collected in a forensic epidemiological investigation of SIDS is listed in Table 6.9.

Table 6.9 Basic Information Collected in a Forensic Epidemiological Investigation of SIDS

Characteristics	Variables
Basic epidemiological features	Age
	Sex
	Race
Incident: location	Residence
	Other family residence
	Friend's residence
	Hotel
Incident: time/date	Time
	Day of the week
	Month
Last feeding	Type of feeding
	Time
Placed down	Position
	Location
	Time
	Layer of clothing
Discovered	Position
	Time
	By whom
Sleeping environment	Describe sleeping surface
	Type of bed: crib, sofa, adult bed (type), other
	If crib: size, number of covers, items in crib
	Air temperature
	Co-sleeping behavior
Mother's features	Number of prenatal visits
	Type of delivery
	Complications
	Smoking and drug history
Infant features	Length of gestation
	Birth weight/height
	Health prior to death
	Vaccination history
	Last visit to doctor

The basic epidemiological characteristics are important to show the profile of infants that die from SIDS. SIDS deaths should first be described by total number of cases and the numbers by sex, race, and age. Table 6.10 shows these featured over a 9-year period. Overall, the SIDS profile displayed in Table 6.11 conforms to the established characteristics cited in most nationwide studies. The majority of SIDS deaths occurred among black males, to

Table 6.10 Total Number of SIDS Deaths by Age, Sex, and Race, 1997–2005

Year	1997 Number (%)	1998 Number (%)	1999 Number (%)	2000 Number (%)	2001 Number (%)	2002 Number (%)	2003 Number (%)	2004 Number (%)	2005 Number (%)
Age (months)									
<1	—	—	—	2 (15.4)	1 (9.1)	—	—	—	—
1–2	3 (27.3)	6 (46.2)	1 (14.3)	5 (38.5)	7 (63.6)	7 (87.5)	3 (42.8)	2 (33.3)	4 (44)
3–4	3 (27.3)	5 (38.5)	3 (42.9)	4 (30.8)	1 (9.1)	—	2 (28.6)	4 (66.6)	3 (33)
5–6	3 (27.3)	1 (7.7)	—	2 (15.4)	2 (18.2)	1 (12.5)	1 (4.3)	—	—
7–8	—	—	1 (14.3)	—	—	—	—	—	2 (22)
9–10	—	1 (7.7)	2 (28.6)	—	—	—	—	—	—
11–12	—	—	—	—	—	—	1 (4.3)	—	—
>12	2 (28.2)	—	—	—	—	—	—	—	—
Total	11	13	7	13	11	8	7	6	9
Race and sex									
White	6 (63.6)	6 (46.1)	5 (71.4)	5 (38.5)	3 (27.3)	2 (25.0)	1 (14.3)	3 (50)	4 (44)
Male	2	5	5	5	1	2	—	2	2
Female	4	1	—	—	2	—	1	1	2
Black	5 (36.4)	6 (46.1)	2 (28.6)	8 (61.5)	8 (72.8)	6 (75.0)	5 (71.4)	3 (50)	5 (55)
Male	3	1	2	5	2	4	1	3	3
Female	2	5	—	3	7	2	4	—	2
Other	—	1 (7.7)	—	—	—	—	1 (14.3)	—	—
Male	—	—	—	—	—	—	—	—	—
Female	—	1	—	—	—	—	1	—	—

infants under the age of 5 months, were discovered during the morning hours, and occurred more frequently during the colder months (Tables 6.10 and 6.11).

Aside from national comparison, comparisons should be made between local results and those of nearby counties or regions with similar population demographics. If there is a major discrepancy, a forensic epidemiological

Table 6.11 Total Number of SIDS Deaths by Time, Day of the Week, and Month of Discovery, 1997–2005

Year	1997 Number (%)	1998 Number (%)	1999 Number (%)	2000 Number (%)	2001 Number (%)	2002 Number (%)	2003 Number (%)	2004 Number (%)	2005 Number (%)
Total number of SIDS deaths	11	13	7	13	11	8	7	6	9
Time of day (hour)									
0000–0400	—	—	2 (28.6)	3 (23.0)	—	—	—	2 (33.3)	1 (11)
0401–0800	1 (9.1)	2 (15.4)	2 (28.6)	2 (15.4)	3 (27.3)	2 (25)	4 (57.1)	2 (33.3)	6 (67)
0801–1200	6 (54.5)	3 (23.1)	1 (14.3)	5 (38.5)	5 (45.5)	4 (50)	2 (28.6)	2 (33.3)	2 (22)
1201–1600	3 (27.3)	6 (46.2)	1 (14.3)	2 (15.4)	2 (18.2)	—	—	—	—
1601–2000	—	—	1 (14.3)	—	1 (9.0)	—	—	—	—
2001–2400	1 (9.1)	2 (15.4)	—	1 (7.7)	—	1 (50)	—	—	—
Day of week									
Monday	1 (9.1)	1 (7.7)	—	1 (7.7)	3 (27.3)	3 (37.5)	—	—	1 (11)
Tuesday	—	1 (7.7)	2 (28.6)	3 (23.1)	3 (27.3)	—	2 (28.6)	1 (16.6)	—
Wednesday	1 (9.1)	—	1 (14.3)	1 (7.7)	—	—	—	1 (16.6)	2 (22)
Thursday	—	2 (15.4)	1 (14.3)	1 (7.7)	1 (9.1)	—	2 (28.6)	2 (33.3)	1 (11)
Friday	3 (27.3)	2 (15.4)	2 (28.6)	2 (15.4)	1 (9.1)	1 (12.5)	—	1 (16.6)	2 (22)
Saturday	4 (36.4)	3 (23.1)	1 (14.3)	4 (30.8)	1 (9.1)	3 (37.5)	2 (28.6)	1 (16.6)	2 (22)
Sunday	2 (18.2)	4 (30.8)	—	1 (7.7)	2 (18.2)	1 (12.5)	—	—	1 (11)
Month of year									
Spring (Mar–May)	3 (27.3)	5 (38.5)	—	5 (38.5)	5 (45.5)	2 (25)	3 (42.8)	2 (33.3)	1 (11)
Summer (June–Aug)	3 (27.3)	—	1 (14.3)	5 (38.5)	1 (9.1)	2 (25)	1 (14.3)	—	3 (33)
Fall (Sep–Nov)	2 (18.2)	3 (23.1)	2 (28.6)	1 (7.7)	1 (9.1)	—	2 (28.6)	2 (33.3)	2 (22)
Winter (Dec–Feb)	3 (27.3)	5 (38.5)	4 (57.1)	2 (15.4)	4 (36.4)	4 (50)	—	2 (33.3)	3 (33)

investigation should be conducted to explain the difference. Factors to consider are the level of forensic investigation, the level of education provided to the mother regarding risk factors associated with SIDS, and the frequency of the risk factors associated with the deaths.

The SIDS cases should then be separated into the main risk factors and determine the percentage of the total that exhibited these characteristics. The cases can be grouped by sleep position (prone, supine, or side), baby's position when discovered dead (prone, supine, or side), age, sex, race, and sleeping environment. Questions to be investigated include: Is one type of sleeping surface associated with a high frequently of rolling over than another? The sleeping locations should be grouped into: crib, sofa, bed (type), playpen, or floor. Then, within each grouping, the number of layers of clothing, number of covers, and number of others in the same bed at the time of the death should be added.

Accidental Deaths 7

Introduction

Accidental deaths encompass a wide range of deaths, including drug overdoses (ODs), motor vehicle accidents, falls, fires, deaths at work or during a medical procedure, and drowning. Each type demands a different level of forensic investigation and some require the mandatory reporting of the event to outside agencies. Among the many types of cases investigated by an ME/C office, accidental deaths as a group represent the largest percentage of the annual workload of most offices. In general, an accidental death is one that occurs from non-natural processes, that is noncriminal, and that is not self-induced. Accidental deaths are those caused by activities conducted in a manner that, according to the individual's reasoning, would not result in death.

This chapter will examine seven types of accidental death: drug overdoses, motor vehicle accidents, falls, fires, industrial accidents, medical misadventure, and asphyxia-related deaths. For each type, the following will be presented: what defines that type of death, the number of fatalities, the CDC ICD-10 code used to classify these deaths, basic forensic foundations, the forensic investigation and mechanisms of death, the types of data collected, and the application of the forensic epidemiological investigation. In addition, medical examiners' data will be used to illustrate some basic methods of presenting and interpreting the data.

Accidental Drug Overdose Deaths

Definition

An accidental drug overdose is defined as taking any drug or chemical at levels beyond the medically recommended dosage or at levels that the individual metabolism cannot detoxify fast enough to avoid death—other than in a deliberate attempt to commit suicide. A fatal overdose can occur by consuming any substance from water to prescription medicines.

Table 7.1 Deaths from Accidental Poisoning or Exposure to Noxious Substances by Sex and Race, 2005

Total deaths	Male	Female	White	Black	Other
23,618	15,884	7,734	20,163	2,986	469

Fatalities

In 2005, a total of 23,618 U.S. deaths were due to accidental poisoning or exposure to noxious substances (ICD-10 codes: X40–X49). Table 7.1 shows the total number of ODs in the United States in 2005 by sex and race.

Fundamentals of Drug Overdose Deaths

Drugs are taken for two main reasons. First, they are taken as a form of treatment for sickness and disease. These drugs can take two forms: those requiring a prescription by a physician and those that do not require a prescription—commonly referred to as over-the-counter (OTC) medications. Medications are prescribed for viral disease such as influenza and psychological disorders like schizophrenia, to reduce suffering from joint disease like arthritis, or to reduce the pain associated with a broken leg. The second reason that drugs are taken is to alter one's mental state and induce a sense of euphoria and well-being, and/or induce hallucinations. The most common drugs to cause these effects include illegal drugs such as cocaine and heroin and the legal drug alcohol. In both cases there is a significant chance of addiction to the drug.

During the 1950s and 1960s there was widespread misuse of drugs and a growing number of people in the United States became addicted to various types of drugs. In response to the growing drug abuse problem, the Misuse of Drugs regulations were developed in 1985. The five classifications of drugs (the five schedules of drugs) and regulations as to which types of physicians were permitted to prescribe which types of drugs were created (Table 7.2).

The pathways to drug abuse can begin by addiction initially to medications prescribed legally or by experimenting with legal and illegal substances in order to get high. The danger of taking any medication or drug is in developing a psychological or physical dependency.

Psychological dependency is when an individual is drawn to repeat the use of the drug because of the sense of pleasure it provides or as a means of relief from personal problems or stress. Drugs such as alcohol, heroin, cocaine, PCP, and barbiturates are typically taken for their psychological effects.

Physical dependence, on the other hand, is when the body's physiological need for the drug brings about its regular use. Once a physical dependency has been established, the sudden discontinuance of the drug will result in "withdrawal sickness" with symptoms such as restlessness, irritability,

Accidental Deaths

Table 7.2 Classifications, Definition, and Examinations of the Five Schedule Drugs

Schedule	Definition	Examples
1	High potential for abuse; no current accepted medical use	Cannabis Heroin LSD
2	High potential for abuse; medical use with severe restrictions	Methadone Amphetamines Barbiturates Pentobarbital
3	Less potential than 1 or 2; currently acceptable use in medicine; low to moderate physical dependence or high psychological dependence	Codeines Steroids
4	Relatively low potential for abuse; currently acceptable use in medicine; may lead to limited dependence	Diazepam Valium Librium Phenobarbital Tranquilizers
5	Low potential for abuse. Currently acceptable use in medicine. Low potential for abuse and low dependence	

tremors, nausea, vomiting, diarrhea, chills, sweating, abdominal cramps, and spasms. In the case of narcotic drugs, the withdrawal symptoms start only 12 hours after the last use.

Drugs can be classified into four main categories: narcotics, depressants, stimulants, and hallucinogens. Table 7.3 lists the four categories of drugs, their effects on the body, and examples of each.

Forensic Investigation of an Accidental Drug Overdose

A possible drug OD death is investigated like any other suspicious death. The majority of victims of a drug OD death are discovered within a residence and are either unresponsive or dead on arrival. Upon notification of a death, investigators from the ME/C office concentrate their investigation on the death scene, examinating the body, and questioning the next of kin, family, and friends. A scene is examined in great detail in an attempt to ascertain the mechanism of death.

However, at drug OD deaths, the scene rarely provides clues to cause of death. The scene is often cleaned up of any drug paraphernalia and the drugs are often disposed of down the toilet before the arrival of the police and ME/C office. The attention is then focused on the body, which is typically located in a bed or on a couch displaying no signs of trauma with the only visible physical characteristics being a white foamy froth around the nose and mouth. When family members and friends are questioned about the circumstances

Table 7.3 The Four Major Drug Categories, Their Effects on the Body, and Examples

Category	Effect	Examples
Narcotics	Inhibit brain activity Dull the senses Relieve pain	Opium Heroin Oxycodone Vicodin Marijuana
Stimulants	Stimulate the CNS Cause euphoria	Amphetamines Cocaine Ephedrine Caffeine Tobacco
Depressants	Inhibit brain activity Reduce bodily functions	Alcohol Barbiturates Benzodiazepines
Hallucinogens	Cause alteration in perception and mood	Ecstasy LSD Cannabis

surrounding the death, they rarely provide death investigators with an accurate representation of the events prior to the death or the victim's past drug use. This type of death represents one of the most labor-intensive investigations by the ME/C office and requires a substantial amount of laboratory analysis time.

At the morgue, the external and internal forensic examinations of the body typically do not present the cause of death. The external examination rarely shows the tell-tale signs of drug abuse such as needle marks or track marks. The examination of the internal organs does not show any pathology signs associated with an acute drug overdose. In some rare cases, the stomach may contain some partially dissolved pills that can aid in the identification of the compound that might have caused the death.

The focus of a drug OD death investigation turns from the forensic pathologist to the forensic toxicologist and the analysis of body fluids (blood, urine, bile, eye fluid) collected during the postmortem examination and, in some cases, antemortem blood collected at the hospital. In cases where the victim survived long enough to be transported to a hospital, blood is collected in the ER (antemortem). This sample is important for the ME/C to obtain because it provides drug levels before any medical treatment was initiated.

The role of the forensic toxicologist is to determine which one or combination of compounds among the literally 10,000+ substances that can be ingested, inhaled, or injected caused the death. The analysis begins by testing for the presence of different classes of drugs and then identifying qualitative and quantitative amounts of the specific drugs within each class. The goal of

Accidental Deaths

Table 7.4 Methods of Drug Intake

Intake	Route	Example
Ingestion	Mouth → gastrointestinal track → blood	Alcohol
Inhalation	Mouth → lungs → blood	Solvents
Injection	Vein or muscle	Heroin
		Cocaine
Skin contact	Direct contact with skin	Organic mercury
Mucous membrane contact	Eyes, ears, mouth, nose, or rectum	Amphetamines
		Cocaine
		Heroin

the analysis of the body fluids is to establish, first, whether drugs played a role in the cause of death and, second, if they did, the number of drugs and the concentration of each.

Mechanism of an Overdose

The mechanism of a drug OD is affected by the route of intake, dose, tolerance, accumulation, and general health. Substances can enter the body in the following ways: ingestion, inhalation, injection, or through contact with the skin or mucous membranes. Table 7.4 shows the typical methods of intake of some common drugs.

The dose of the drug determines the response of the body. This is why medications given to infants or children are prescribed in terms of so many cubic centimeters of medication per weight in kilograms. The dose an individual consumes can be divided into three levels: *therapeutic, toxic,* and *lethal.* Therapeutic levels are levels consistent with taking the medication (prescription and nonprescription) as prescribed by the pharmaceutical company or physician. Toxic levels are when individuals exceed the recommended dosage, resulting in immediate damage to the internal organs. These levels do not cause death; rather they result in severe injury to the organs. Lethal levels are levels of a compound that result in death. The intervals among these three levels vary greatly from drug to drug. Table 7.5 is a list of several compounds and their corresponding levels.

Table 7.5 Therapeutic, Toxic, and Lethal Levels of Drugs

Drug	Therapeutic	Toxic	Lethal
Tylenol	1.2–2.0 mg%	40.0 mg%	150 mg%
Valium	0.05–0.25 µg%	0.5–2.0 µg%	≥2.0 µg%
Oxycodone	1.7–3.6 µg%	20.0–500 µg%	
Mercury	0.0–8.0 µg%	100 µg%	600 µg%

As shown in Table 7.5, Tylenol has a narrow therapeutic range and a toxic level would require taking a number of pills well beyond those necessary for its therapeutic effect; to reach a lethal level requires taking a substantial number of pills. These levels assist in the determination as to whether the death was an accident or a suicide. For example, consider an elderly woman found dead in her apartment. The scene was in order and no suicide note was located. Her next of kin informed the death investigator that she suffered from severe arthritis, for which she took Tylenol. A toxicological analysis of the blood that revealed a Tylenol level of 27.6 mg would be an indication that the individual, due to decreased brain function, forgot the number of pills she had taken; the death would be ruled an accidental drug OD. However, in the same scenario, a level of 158 mg would be an indication that, precipitated by the pain of arthritis, the individual consumed a large number of pills in a deliberate manner in order to end her life. Therefore, this death would be ruled a suicide. Furthermore, if the intervals among the three levels are narrow, the determination between an accident and suicide is more difficult and resolving the manner of death depends on the information contained in the death investigation report or the results of a psychological autopsy (see Chapter 11).

The effect that a drug has upon an individual varies because of tolerance, accumulation, and general health. Tolerance is generated by repeated exposure to the drug. Drinking regularly will result in the body building up a tolerance for the effects of alcohol, thus requiring a greater amount of alcohol to achieve an effect similar to that of someone experiencing a beer for the first time. A heavy drinker can function relatively normally at a level of blood alcohol concentration (BAC) that would incapacitate a light drinker.

Over time, tolerance can be lost due to abstinence. This is typically seen among drug abusers released from prison who lost their tolerance of a drug while in prison. Upon release, they typically die from an overdose at a level that, prior to the incarceration, would have resulted only in a high. After a drug enters the body, it takes time for it to be eliminated. The time for the body to eliminate half of the substance taken in is called the "half-life" and each compound has a different half-life. Drugs such as ibuprofen have a short half-life; others like warfarin and digoxin have much longer half-lives. Half-life becomes important in cases where a substance has a long half-life and the individual consumes additional amounts; the result is a cumulative effect of the first and second doses. The health and age of the individual must also be considered. Individuals with disease of the liver and kidney might require altering the levels of medication more so than those with normally functioning organs.

The last pharmaceutical effect to consider is the synergistic or combined effect. The drug levels detected in the blood do not have to be in the lethal

Accidental Deaths

range to cause death. For example, if several different CNS depressant drugs, all within their individual therapeutic range, are consumed at the same time, the combined or synergistic effect would result in a massive suppression of the CNS, resulting in death.

Forensic Analysis of Drug Overdose
Body Fluids Collected
During all complete forensic autopsies the following body fluids are collected: blood, urine, bile, and vitreous fluid (eye fluid). In the case of a suspected drug overdose, the stomach contents are also carefully examined, collected, and sent for analysis. Blood specimens can be collected from the femoral and subclavian vessels in order to reduce the possibility of contamination and postmortem redistribution. However, in most complete autopsy cases the blood is collected directly from the chambers of the heart. In cases of an external-only examination, a long syringe is inserted into the left upper chest region, aiming for the heart, to recover blood. About 60 cc of blood is collected for analysis in both types of examinations.

The blood from individuals that die after receiving medical intervention (blood and plasma) or after several days of hospitalization may not show the presence of drugs or drugs may metabolize at the time of the autopsy. In most ER admissions, a blood sample is collected for typing and cross-matching. In these cases, blood drawn upon admission to the hospital would be of greater investigative value and should be obtained and analyzed. Among individuals that died at the scene or were discovered DOA, the body fluids collected during the autopsy are used for this analysis. The blood is the most important blood fluid used for toxicological analysis. The blood level of a compound has a direct effect on the individual at the time of death; drugs detected in the urine and bile, while having an effect on the individual, may not be present at the time of death.

Urine can be collected during an external examination and during a complete examination. The urine from inside the bladder is collected by inserting a syringe and recovering 60 cc of the fluid. Among hospitalized patients that are catheterized, if no urine is present in the bladder, urine contained within the catheterization bag can be used for analysis.

Located behind the liver is a small green sac, the gallbladder, which contains bile. This fluid can only be collected when a complete autopsy is conducted; about 30 cc are collected.

The vitreous fluid is collected by using a small syringe to collect about 5–10 cc of fluid from each eye; this is collected during both external and complete autopsies. The fluids collected from the two eyes are typically combined for analysis. After the biological samples have been collected, they are transferred from the autopsy suite to the toxicological section of the crime laboratory for analysis.

Toxicological Analyses

Forensic toxicology is the study and application of the science of toxicology for the purposes of the law. It has three main functions: (1) identification; (2) quantification of the drug, poison, or substance in the human tissue; and (3) interpretation of how these compounds affect the human body. Forensic toxicology laboratories are equipped with varying methods of analysis, including thin-layer chromatography, immunoassay, high-performance liquid chromatography (HPLC), and atomic absorption and emission spectroscopy.

The goal of the analysis concerning the compounds within body fluids is both qualitative and quantitative. The qualitative analysis provides the number of different drugs detected within the sample. If the blood sample contained acetaminophen, cocaine, and alcohol, the quantitative part of the analysis would report the levels or concentration of each compound—for example, acetaminophen: 0.017 mg%, cocaine: 76.91 mg%, and alcohol: 0.01 mg%. This means that the level of acetaminophen was within the therapeutic level, alcohol was below the toxic level, and cocaine was at the toxic level. The results of the toxicological analysis are presented in the toxicology report (see Figure 7.1).

The final determination to ascertain which drug played a role in the death is resolved by a meeting between the forensic toxicologists and the forensic pathologist. The forensic toxicologists present the results of the analysis and the drugs that they feel contributed to the death. The concentrations of drugs detected should not be interpreted in isolation. The forensic pathologist considers the toxicology report in conjunction with the medical history, death scene investigation, autopsy results, police investigation, and the circumstances leading to the death. The role of the forensic pathologist is to determine which compounds to list on the DC and then determine the manner of death. The forensic pathologist must consider whether the drugs were taken for medically designed pharmacological effects, for nonmedical pleasure-seeking effects, or as a means to end life. The final judgment as to the cause and manner of death is made by the forensic pathologist.

Forensic Epidemiological Investigation of Drug Overdose Deaths

The role of the forensic epidemiologist investigating deaths from a drug OD is, first, to describe the epidemiological characteristics of the individual, location, and types of drugs involved; second, to examine the types and concentration of drugs involved in the death; and, finally, to disseminate that information to the local police, emergency personnel, and national monitoring agencies.

Accidental Deaths

ALLEGHENY COUNTY CORONER'S OFFICE
DIVISION OF LABORATORIES

Autopsy # ▓ Deceased's Name ▓
Autopsy Prosector Dr. ▓   Blood Drawn by ▓   Date of Autopsy ▓
Specimen(s) Submitted by ▓   Specimen(s) Received by ▓
Date Submitted ▓   Time 1:00 pm   DoL Case # ▓

SPECIMEN(S) SUBMITTED:

Heart Blood	Bile	Urine	Eye Fluid	Grey Top
Chest Blood	Other Blood			
Brain	Liver	Kidney	Stomach Contents	
Drugs			Other	

CORE SPECIMENS:
Blood x
Bile   x
Urine x
Eye Fluid x

LABORATORY FINDINGS:

Core Blood:
Plasma Alcohol:
  Isopropanol 5 mg% or 0.005%
  Methanol and Ethanol – Not Detected
Elisa:
  Cocaine Metabolites – Not Detected
Carbon Monoxide – Not Detected
Cyanide – Not Detected
Benzodiazepines (GLC) – Not Detected
Phenytoin (TDX) – 1.09 ug/ml
Screen (GLC) – Not Detected

Core Urine:
Urine Alcohol – Not Detected
Acetone –15 mg % or 0.015%
Salicylate – Not Detected
Phenothiazine – Not Detected
Opiates TDX – Not Detected
Screen (GC/MS) – Lidocaine, Phenytoin, Fentanyl*

Core Bile:
Alcohol – Not Detected

Core Eye Fluid:
Alcohol – Not Detected
Glucose – 56 mg%

*Not Confirmed

Reported By ▓   Date ▓
, Director & Chief Toxicologist
Assistant Chief Toxicologist

Figure 7.1 Toxicology report.

The drug OD deaths can be investigated on four levels: basic descriptive, detailed drug analysis, local trends, and national comparisons.

The basic information that should be collected in a forensic epidemiological Investigation of drug OD deaths is listed in Table 7.6. These characteristics are important to show the profile of an individual that dies from an accidental drug OD.

The basic epidemiological data can be collected from the death investigation report and the DC. These data include the total number of deaths and the number by age, sex, and race. This information is important to identify

Table 7.6 Basic Information Collected in Drug OD Deaths

Characteristics	Variables
Basic epidemiological features	Age
	Sex
	Race
Incident: location	Residence
	Friend's residence
	Hotel
	Open area
	Other
Incident: time/date	Time
	Day of the week
	Month
Place of death	Scene
	Residence
	Hospital
Residence	Exact address
	Number of drugs detected
	Drug levels of each drug
Types of drugs	Legal:
	Medications: with/without prescription
	Nonprescribed medications
	Illegal:
	Combination of illegal/legal
Drug history	Yes/no
List of prescription medications	
Past medical history	

the population most at risk of dying from an OD and to understand the trend of OD deaths in a specific region. In addition, this information can provide baseline data that can be used to evaluate the level of effectiveness of changes in police tactics, sentencing, and drug prevention programs.

The forensic epidemiologist should display the data in a manner that is easy to understand and should start with the basic number per year and then the breakdown by sex and race. Figure 7.2 shows the number of OD deaths over a 9-year period. This type of presentation provides an easy means of comparing the total number of deaths over time in one location.

Figure 7.2 clearly indicates that the total number of OD deaths remained fairly stable, with around 100 deaths per year, until 2001, when the number nearly doubled; this was followed by a steady upward trend. This dramatic increase in the number of deaths has an impact on the staffing and workload of emergency medical response units, emergency rooms, poison control centers, police, the ME/C office, and forensic crime laboratories. The forensic epidemiologist must ascertain if the increase seen in the local data was

Accidental Deaths

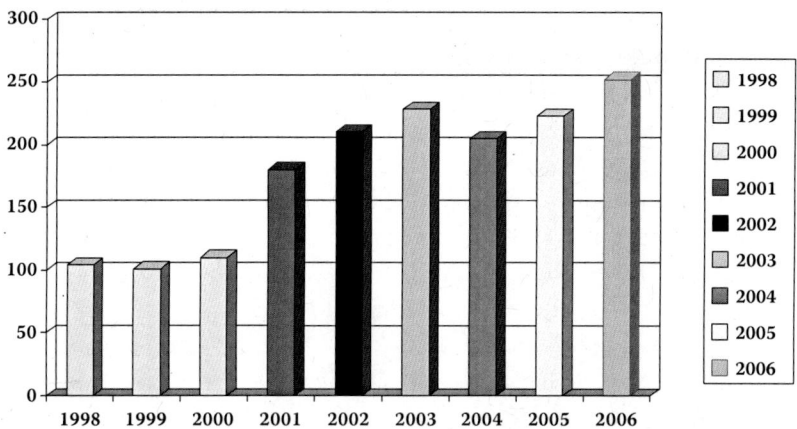

Figure 7.2 Total number of drug overdose deaths, 1998–2006, in Allegheny County.

also seen at the national level. If it only represents a local phenomenon, local police agencies must be notified of the dramatic increase and receive as much forensic epidemiological information as possible, such as the types of drugs involved, the locations of the drug deaths, and any other changes in the profiles of the victims.

The number of OD deaths can be examined by sex, race, and age of the victims. Table 7.7 shows the distribution of 223 OD deaths examined at the

Table 7.7 All Drug Overdose Deaths by Age, Sex, and Race, Allegheny County, 2005

Age	White male	White female	Black male	Black female	Total
20–24	12	4	—	—	16
25–29	13	8	1	—	22
30–34	7	3	2	—	12
35–39	19	8	3	1	31
40–44	29	10	3	2	44
45–49	26	10	6	4	46
50–54	18	8	5	2	33
55–59	5	1	4	1	11
60–64	—	2	1	—	3
65–70	—	—	1	—	1
≥70	1	—	1	—	2
Total (%)	130 (58.3)	54 (24.2)	27 (12.1)	10 (4.5)	223 (Includes one 23-year-old Asian male; one white male fetus)

Allegheny County, Pennsylvania, medical examiner's office in 2005 by sex and race and broken down by age. The data show that the vast majority of deaths occurred among individuals between the ages of 40 and 49 years old and predominantly among white males. The table also highlights the fact that no deaths occurred to persons under the age of 20. These types of data provide important information as to which part of the population is at risk and where to target intervention programs.

The data can also be displayed in several ways. As Figure 7.3 illustrates, among males, the distribution is bimodal with a peak at 21–25 years of age and then between 46 and 50 years of age. Females, on the other hand, have a bell-shaped distribution, with the maximum number of deaths at ages 41–45. Figure 7.4 shows the deaths by race and by age. Among whites, a steady upward pattern was seen with a peak at ages

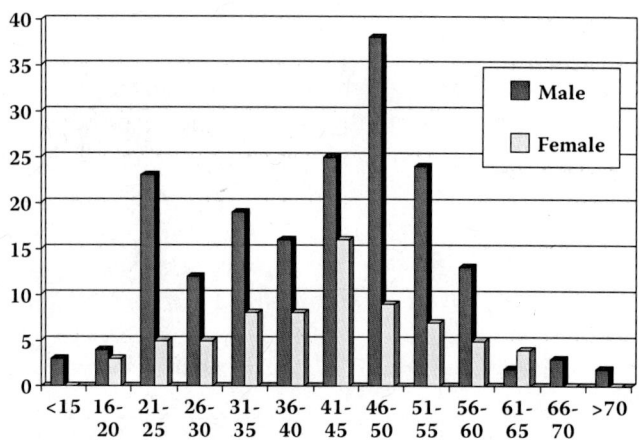

Figure 7.3 Total number of accidental overdose deaths by age and sex, 2005.

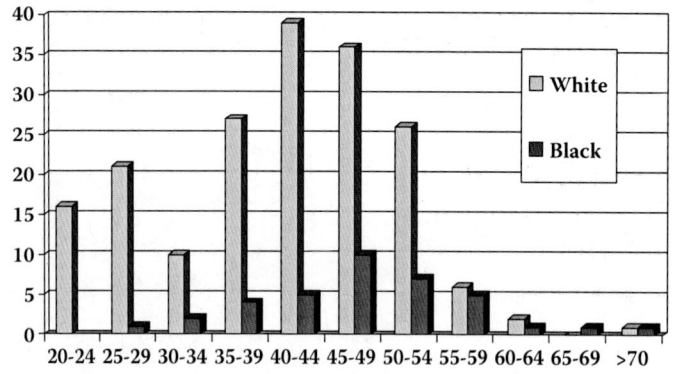

Figure 7.4 Total number of accidental overdoses by age and race, 2005.

Accidental Deaths

40–44, followed by a steady decline. Among blacks, the pattern resembles a bell-shaped curve, with the peak number of deaths among those ages 45–49 years old.

The location of death can be analyzed in three ways: exact address, municipality, and the physical location where the death occurred. The exact address where the body was discovered is information that can be obtained from the DC and can be used to plot the location on street maps and also to calculate the distance the victim traveled from his or her residence to the site of the fatal OD. The DC contains the residence address, and the death investigation report will list the location where the victim was discovered. Next, the region or area covered by the ME/C office is typically separated into legal borders, such as municipality, township, city, and counties, each with its own local police force. The collected data can be used to create area maps showing the number of ODs within each municipality, to highlight the types of drugs and the profiles of the victims, and as a means of presenting the data to show trends.

In order to accomplish this, at least 5 years' worth of data is required. A map should be made for each year and, when placed side by side, these can reveal the directional change profile of the victims or the change in types of drugs used. The goal of these maps it to illustrate the flow of drug deaths visually over time. This type of presentation would be invaluable to law enforcement agencies and public health researchers initiating prevention programs to target specific areas where increasing numbers of drug OD deaths are occurring. In Allegheny County, the deaths can be separated as in the city and in the county (nonurban area). Table 7.8 shows the number of OD deaths separated into those within the city limits and those outside. The table clearly indicates that the percentage of such deaths is increasing in nonurban areas and that the drug problem is moving from inner city to more affluent regions. An examination of the physical location where the events occurred can involve grouping the locations into residence, friend's residence, hotel, and public areas.

Table 7.8 Jurisdictions Where Drug Overdoses Occurred, 1999–2005

Year	Total OD deaths	Total deaths within city	Total deaths outside city
2005	223	98 (44%)	125 (56%)
2004	205	121 (59%)	84 (41%)
2003	228	116 (51%)	112 (49%)
2002	210	98 (47%)	112 (53%)
2001	180	87 (48%)	93 (52%)
2000	110	54 (49%)	56 (51%)
1999	101	53 (52%)	48 (48%)

The forensic epidemiological investigation can examine the number of drugs, types of drugs, and drug concentrations responsible for a death. In order to do this analysis, the forensic epidemiologist must examine both the DC and the toxicological report. The DC will list all of the drugs responsible for the death and the toxicological report will contain the levels detected for each drug. Remember that the toxicological report lists all the drugs tested for and the corresponding levels, rather than all the drugs with a positive level contributing to the death.

The drug OD deaths should first be grouped by the number of drugs contributing to the death. Table 7.9 shows the 223 drug OD deaths in a 1-year period grouped by the number contributing to the death. This type of information shows the types of drugs responsible for deaths in a particular area and what types of combinations result in death. A death by one drug indicates that the compound was at a lethal level to cause death; a death involving two or more compounds means that all the compounds were at a lethal level, all were within the therapeutic or toxic range, or some combination of both.

Once this grouping has been created, the individual levels of each drug should be added and analyzed. The forensic epidemiologist can then further reclassify each type of OD drug death as due to therapeutic, toxic, or lethal concentration or some combination of the three.

The drugs involved in a fatal OD are changing. In the past, the majority of drug deaths involved illegal or "street" drugs. Today, there is a shift away from these illegal drugs to the abuse of prescription and over-the-counter medications. The types of drugs responsible for the death should be reclassified as legal, illegal, or a combination of both. Legal drugs have been legally prescribed to the individual by a physician or, in the cases of alcohol and tobacco, used by an individual of legal age. An illegal-drug-related death includes a prescription medication obtained without a physician or without a medical or psychological condition requiring that medication; the use of alcohol or tobacco by an individual under the legal age requirements, or use of a drug that has no medical use. Figure 7.5 shows the drug OD deaths by legality of the drug involved in the death. During the 5-year period shown, the number of deaths involving only illegal drugs declined, the number of illegal in combination with legal drugs increased, and deaths from legal drugs alone also increased.

Advantages and Limitations of Forensic Epidemiological Investigation of Drug Overdose

Investigating drug OD deaths using ME/C office data has several advantages. First, the majority of ME/C offices conduct toxicological analysis of body fluid. Large ME/C offices are equipped with a toxicology lab in house; smaller offices typically use outside private chemical testing labs. Second, the analysis

Accidental Deaths

Table 7.9 Number of Drugs Identified in 223 Drug Deaths in 2005

Drug	No. deaths
One drug	
Heroin	25
Cocaine	28
Alcohol	13
Morphine	4
Fentanyl	3
Oxycodone	2
Methadone	4
Metroprolol	1
Phenobarbital	1
Paroxetine	1
Opiates	7
Salicylate	1
Total deaths	90
Two drugs	
Heroin + alcohol	8
Heroin + cocaine	28
Heroin + methadone	1
Heroin + hydrocdone	1
Heroin + fentanyl	1
Alcohol + zolpiden	1
Alcohol + opiates	2
Alcohol + methadone	2
Alcohol + oxycodone	4
Cocaine + methadone	4
Cocaine + morphine	3
Cocaine + opiate	7
Cocaine + alcohol	1
Cocaine + oxycodone	4
Cocaine + fentanyl	1
Morphine + olanzapine	1
Methadone + morphine	1
Methadone + fentanyl	1
Methadone + alprazolam	1
Methadone + nortriptyline	1
Oxycodone + hydrocodine	2
Opiate + benzodiazepines	1
Clozapine + clomipramine	1
Total deaths	77

Table 7.9 Number of Drugs Identified in 223 Drug Deaths in 2005 (continued)

Drug	No. deaths
Three drugs	
Heroin + cocaine + alcohol	4
Heroin + cocaine + methadone	1
Heroin + cocaine + diazepam	1
Heroin + cocaine + paroxetine	1
Heroin + alcohol + doxepine	1
Heroin + alcohol + benzodiazepine	1
Heroin + methadone + alprazolam	1
Heroin + propxyphene + tramadol	1
Methadone + benzodiazepine + amitriptyline	1
Methadone + alprazolam + oxycodone	1
Methadone + trazodone + nortriptiline	1
Methadone + diazepam + alprazolam	1
Methadone + alprazolam + sertraline	1
Alcohol + cocaine + hydrocodone	1
Alcohol + cocaine + amitriphyline	1
Alcohol + cocaine + amoxapine	1
Alcohol + cocaine + methanol	1
Alcohol + morphine + trazodone	1
Alcohol + methadone + alprazolam	1
Alcohol + codeine + phenobarbital	1
Alcohol + oxycodone + benzodiazepines	1
Oxycodone + alprazolam + methadone	1
Oxycodone + hydrocodone + alprazolam	1
Oxycodone + methadone + meprobmate	1
Cocaine + fentanyl + phenobarbital	1
Cocaine + fentanyl + diazepam	1
Cocaine + methadone + opiate	1
Cocaine + opiate + benzodiazepine	2
Cocaine + methadone + alprazolam	1
Cocaine + meprobamate + methadone	1
Cocaine + morphine + methadone	1
Cocaine + oxycodone + alprazolam	1
Fentanyl + tramadol + diazepam	1
Hydrocodone + alprazolam + cyclobenzopine	1
Total deaths	38
Four drugs	
Heroin + alcohol + trazodone + norpropoxyphene	1
Heroin + cocaine + alcohol + alprazolam	1
Cocaine + methadone + alcohol + propoxyphene	1

Accidental Deaths

Table 7.9 Number of Drugs Identified in 223 Drug Deaths in 2005 (continued)

Drug	No. deaths
Cocaine + methadone + amitriptyline + paroxetine	1
Cocaine + fentanyl + citalopram + alprazolam	1
Cocaine + alcohol + diazepam + methadone	1
Alcohol + benzodiazepine + darvon + citalopram	1
Alcohol + methadone + alprazolam + trazolone	1
Oxycodone + venlaforine + trazodone + alprazolam	1
Oxycodone + meperedine + hydroxyzine + amitriptyline	1
Citalopram + opiate + benzodiazepine + tramadol	1
Total deaths	11
Five drugs	
Cocaine + fentanyl + phenytoin + hydroxyzine + cyclobenzaprine	1
Cocaine + oxycodone + benzodiazepine + amitrptyline + citalopram	1
Cocaine + alcohol + trazodone + quetiapine + doxepin	1
Cocaine + methadone + paroxetine + benadryl + alprazolam	1
Citalopram + benzodiazepine + alcohol + quetiapam + phenytoin	1
Citalopram + methadone + metoprolol + topiramate + bupropion	1
Total deaths	6
Six drugs	
Methadone + quentiapine + nortriptyline + mirtazepine + metroprolol + benzodiazepine	1

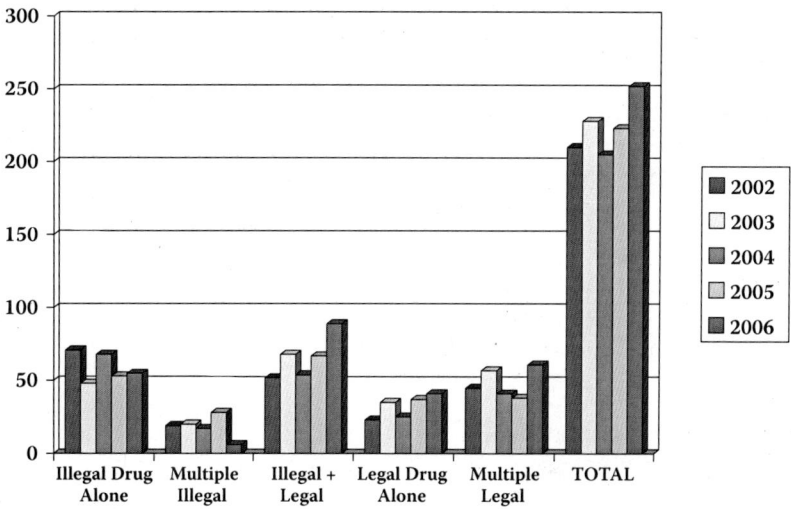

Figure 7.5 Drug overdose deaths by drug type, 2002–2006.

generates the number and concentration of the drug that caused the death. Finally, excellent geomapping data are provided.

The main limitation in this type of investigation involves delayed deaths. If the victim is hospitalized, the initial drug levels can be dilated or totally eliminated from the system at the time of postmortem analysis. Although the hospital tests for the presence of drugs, it may not calculate the concentration and the treatment modality is similar, regardless of the concentration.

Motor Vehicle Accident

Definition

A motor vehicle accident (MVA) is defined as a fatality occurring to an occupant of any vehicle with a motor used to transport individuals from one location to another that operates on the land, in water, or in air. Vehicles include cars, trucks, motorcycles, trains, airplanes, boats, lawn mowers, and electric wheelchairs.

Fatalities

In the United States, transportation accidents (ICD-10 codes: V01–V99, Y85) claimed a total of 48,441 lives in 2005. Among these deaths, motor vehicle accidents (ICD-10 codes: V02–V04, V09.0, V09.2, V12–V14, V19.0–V19.2, V19.4–V19.6, V20–V79, V80.3–V80.5, V81.0–V81.1, V82.0–V82.1, V83–V86, V87.0–V87.8, V88.0–V88.8, V89.0, and V89.2) accounted for 45,343 cases. Deaths from other land transport accidents (ICD-10 codes: V01, V05, V06, V09.1, V09.3–V09.9, V10, V11, V15–V18, V19.3, V19.8, V19.9, V80.0–V80.2, V80.6–V80.9, V81.2–V81.9, V82.2–V82.9, V88.9, V89.1, V89.3, and V89.9) accounted for 1,241 deaths. Death involving water, air, space, and other and unspecified transport accidents and their sequelae (ICD-10 codes: V90–V99, Y85) accounted for 1,857 deaths. Table 7.10 shows the breakdown of transportation accidents by total number, sex, and race for 2005 deaths.

Table 7.10 Transportation Accidents by Total Number, Sex, and Race for 2005 Deaths

Type	Total	Male	Female	White	Black
Motor vehicle accidents	45,343	31,631	13,712	38,041	5,491
Other land transport accidents	1,241	957	284	970	204
Water, air, space, and other and unspecified transport accidents and their sequelae	1,857	1,498	359	1,636	147

Fundamentals of MVA Accidents

In order for a forensic epidemiologist to study fatal MVAs, the basic factors that caused them to occur and the location of injuries resulting from them must be reviewed.

Causes of MVAs

The causes of MVAs in descending order of frequency (1) impairment to the driver, (2) human error, (3) environmental hazards, and (4) natural diseases. Impairment to the driver is typically caused by the influence of alcohol or other drugs; it has been estimated that between 65 and 75% of drivers killed in an MVA were under the influence of alcohol. While the impact of alcohol has received a great deal of attention, the role that prescription medication plays in fatal MVAs has only recently come to the foreground. In the United States, the population of individuals over the age of 65 has increased, resulting in an increase in the number of elderly drivers on the road. In turn, these drivers are typically prescribed numerous medications and the role of these medications, either singularly or in combination, on their driving ability has received limited study.

The second most common cause of an MVA is human error in the form of speeding, reckless driving, or falling asleep while operating a vehicle (typically seen with long-haul truckers). The third cause is environmental conditions at the time of the accident, including weather hazards such as ice, snow, rain, fog, or road hazards; poorly maintained roads; potholes; or animals such as deer or dogs on the roadway. The final causes are those resulting from a pre-existing medical condition or disease but these types of deaths are considered rare. These sudden deaths behind the wheel are commonly caused by a cardiac event such as ischemic heart disease or cerebrovascular disease. Studies of the phenomena conducted in the 1960s showed that between 15 and 19% of drivers involved in a fatal MVA died from natural causes. A detailed study of sober drivers that died from natural causes revealed that they posed a minimal risk to their passengers and other drivers on the road because of their ability to bring the vehicle to a stop. However, these studies are dated and the level of anatomical examination and scene recondition warrants a re-evaluation of the risk posed by elderly drivers with pre-existing medical conditions.

Types of MVA Impacts and Associated Injuries

MVA can be grouped into four types: front impact, side impact, rollover, and rear impact.

Front Impact

In a front impact crash there are actually three sequential impacts. The first is when the vehicle hits a fixed object such as a tree or other solid barrier. While the vehicle comes to a complete stop, the occupants are still moving due to forward acceleration. The second impact occurs when unrestrained occupants hit something in the interior of the vehicle (steering wheel, dashboard, or airbag) and restrained occupants hit the restraining system (belts or airbag). After the body stops, the internal organs are still in forward motion. Therefore, the third impact is the internal organs colliding with the skeletal structure.

Among unrestrained drivers, key injuries include the knees hitting the instrument panel, the chest hitting the steering wheel or airbag, and the head hitting the windshield or the airbag. Hitting the dashboard typically results in factures to the femur. The steering wheel hitting the chest causes external injuries such as imprinting, abrasions, and contusion, as well as internal injuries including fracture to the sternum and ribs, contusions of the lung and heart, transecting of the aorta, and lacerations to the liver and spleen. The most frequent thoracic injuries are transection of the aorta. The head hitting the windshield causes abrasions and superficial cuts to the forehead, nose, and face, but these are typically not serious due to the nature of the construction of the windshield. Beginning in 1966, automobiles were equipped with a laminated windshield consisting of two sections of glass sandwiched between a core of plastic. If the driver is restrained via a seatbelt, only the knees still hit; however, the head would flex forward with the chin hitting the sternum. Unrestrained front-seat passengers will display similar injuries except that their heads will hit the dashboard.

Side Impact

Side impact accidents normally occur at intersections when one vehicle is struck broadside by another vehicle. Seatbelts and frontal airbags offer little protection to the occupants in these types of accidents and "dicing" injuries are commonly encountered in a side impact. Dicing injuries are due to the breaking of the side windows, which are made of temperate glass that, when broken, breaks into small angular fragments that produce superficial cuts to the face. Drivers will receive these types of injuries to the left side of the face and front-seat passengers to the right side of the face.

Rollover

Rollover accidents are most lethal if the occupants are ejected from the vehicle; they account for ~18.8% of all fatal MVAs. Rollovers account for 15.1% of fatal MVAs among passenger cars, 36% for utility vehicles, 24.5% for pickups; 20.3% for vans, and 13.8% for large trucks. Most rollovers are caused when

Accidental Deaths

the vehicle runs off the road and the driver dramatically turns the wheel to overcorrect, causing the vehicle to skid sideways and begin to tip over. If there is sufficient lateral momentum, the tires will plow the surface and the vehicle will roll over. The point where the vehicle begins to roll is where the tire marks end. Factors that determine the likelihood that vehicles will roll over include (1) side momentum, (2) height of the vehicle, and (3) nature of the road surface.

Rear Impact

The least common type of fatal MVA is the rear impact type because occupants of the struck vehicle are protected by the structure of the trunk and the rear passenger compartment. The occupants of the impacting vehicle are protected by the engine compartment of their vehicle.

Forensic Investigation of MVA Deaths

Fatal MVAs are investigated by the local or state police and by the ME/C office. The level of police investigation is dictated by the type of accident. Single vehicle accidents (SVAs) with only a single occupant (driver) will receive a standard level of investigation by the law enforcement community, who will ascertain the speed of the vehicle, activity of the driver (speeding, driving recklessly), road conditions, and other road hazards that might have contributed to the accident. The role of the police is to protect the scene until the ME/C has arrived to process the scene and ensure that hazards such as broken glass and downed power lines have been addressed. Law enforcement takes a more active role if the accident involves multiple fatalities and survivors. The investigation focuses on whether the driver had a valid driver's license, was impaired by alcohol or drugs, or violated any traffic law (speeding, illegal turn, or failure to signal).

Death investigators at an accident scene collect data about the scene, vehicle, and occupants. Information collected about the scene includes the type of roadway, condition of the pavement, weather conditions, and any environmental hazards around the accident scene. All vehicles involved in the accident are photographed, measurements between the vehicles or impacted objects are noted, and detailed diagrams are created. If skid marks are present, their lengths are measured and distances from the vehicles are calculated. All vehicles involved in the accident are described in terms of their make, model, color, traveling direction, estimated speed, position in the road, airbag deployment, and final resting position. The VIN number is noted to determine the registration. The location and level of damage to the vehicles are described and multiple images of the scene are made.

The occupants within each vehicle are described in terms of position within the vehicle or, if ejected, distance from the vehicle; the use of safety systems (belted, unbelted, helmeted, not helmeted); and of the visible injuries. If the occupants were transported to the ER and died, after the scene investigation has been completed, the death investigation would transfer the bodies and the medical records from the hospital to the morgue. The death investigator prepares a death investigation report using information from the emergency medical services (EMS) reports, police and fire reports, and his or her own investigation to provide the forensic pathologist with an accurate description of the events leading up to the accident and possible causes.

The role of the ME/C, aside from determining the cause and manner of death, is to determine the position of all of the occupants within the vehicle at the time of the accident. This task is relatively easy among restrained occupants, but it becomes more difficult if they were unrestrained or ejected from the vehicle. The determination is made based on the injury patterns. A driver will have dicing injuries to the left side of the face due to the breaking of the driver's side window, while these injuries will be on the right side of the face for the front-seat passenger. Other types of external and internal injuries can also distinguish driver from passengers.

The function of the autopsy is to determine if the crash was caused by physical impairments, environmental factors, behavioral actions, or a pre-existing medical condition. Physical impairment includes testing positive for alcohol or other drugs that affect perception, reaction time, or judgment. Environmental factors include hazardous weather or road conditions, or wildlife on the road. Behavioral actions include speeding and other risky behavior such as trying to beat a train at a crossing. The most difficult determination is whether a pre-existing condition caused the accident. Did the driver have a heart attack before hitting the bus? The examination of the heart can show severe blockage of the coronary arteries—but did the heart attack occur, causing him to lose control of the vehicle? Forensic pathologists are most confident to conclude this sequence when witnesses state they saw the driver slumped over the wheel or appearing to be unconscious immediately prior to the crash.

The complete autopsy will list the location and severity of all external and internal injuries and the DC will list the injuries that directly contributed to the cause of death. The toxicological analysis will list the names and levels of the detected drugs. Upon completion of the forensic investigation, the ME/C office completes and submits a fatality analysis reporting system (FARS) report, which is then sent to the U.S. Department of Transportation.

Accidental Deaths

Table 7.11 Available Forensic Data by Source

Source	Available data
Death scene investigation report	Time and date of accident
	Detailed description of accident
	Basic epidemiological data
	Time/date of incident
	Type and number of vehicles
	Number and location of each occupant
	Use of restraints/helmet
	Airbag: deployed
	Skid marks/length
	Type of roadway
	Posted speed limit
	Weather/road conditions
Final autopsy report	Current health state of the occupant
	Internal organs: pathology/weight
	Type of autopsy conducted: complete/external only
Toxicological report	Number/type/level of drugs at time of accident
Police investigation reports	Detailed description of accident
	Determination of fault
	Diagram of the accident scene
EMS reports	Time of notification
	Response time
	Medical treatment
	Method of transport to hospital: ground/air
Accident reconstruction reports	Calculation of speeds of vehicles involved
FARS report	Brief description of accident
Death certificate	Immediate cause of death
	Contributory cause of death
	Time/date/place of death
	Basic epidemiological data

Forensic Epidemiological Investigation of MVAs

Forensic epidemiologists conducting research on fatal MVAs must first obtain copies of the following reports from the ME/C office: death scene investigation report, final autopsy report, toxicological report, police investigation reports, EMS reports, accident reconstruction reports, FARS report, and the DC. The specific data available from the various sources are listed in Table 7.11.

The basic data collected from deaths involving an MVA are shown in Table 7.12. The role of a forensic epidemiologist in investigating deaths resulting from an MVA is to (1) describe the epidemiological characteristics of the accident in terms of the fatalities, location, types of vehicles involved, and

Table 7.12 Basic Data Collected from Death Involving an MVA

Characteristics	Variables
Basic epidemiological features	Age
	Sex
	Race
Location of incident	Single-lane roadway
	Double-lane roadway
	Multiple-lane roadway
	Rural road
	Highway
	Parking lot
Type of vehicle	Passenger car
	Sport utility vehicle
	Van
	Jeep
	Light truck
	Heavy truck
	Delivery truck
	Emergency vehicle: ambulance, fire truck
	Tractor trailer
	Bus: school, public, commercial
	Motorcycle
Numbers and types of vehicles	
Incident: time, day of the week, month	
Time/date of death	
Place of death	Scene
	Residence
	Hospital
	Long-term care facility
Weather at scene	Clear
	Fog
	Rain: light, medium, heavy
	Snow: light, medium, heavy
	Hail
Road surface condition	Clear
	Wet: rain, snow, ice
Type of surface	Asphalt
	Concrete
	Loose gravel
	Dirt
Posted speed limit	
Control of roadway	Posted speed limit
	Stop sign
	Traffic light
	Two-way stop
	Three-way stop
	Four-way stop

Accidental Deaths

Table 7.12 Basic Data Collected from Death Involving an MVA (continued)

Characteristics	Variables
Fatality	Driver
	Front seat passenger
	Rear seat passenger: right, center, left position
	Blood alcohol concentration
Pre-existing medical condition	Cardiovascular
	Hepatic
	Vision
	CNS
	Neurological

environmental factors; and (2) identify risk factors that can be modified to reduce such deaths.

The forensic epidemiological investigation begins with describing the basic demographic characteristics (age, sex, and race) of the occupants. This information is available from multiple sources and can be presented in a number of ways by grouping the fatalities into: driver in SVA, drivers involved in two-vehicle accident, drivers involved in a three-vehicle accident, and passengers. Next, add the age, sex, and race of the victims. Table 7.13 shows the demographic characteristics of vehicular fatalities by occupant and number of vehicles involved in Allegheny County in 2005. The majority of the MVAs involved SVAs; the victim was a white male, mostly between the ages of 20 and 29.

These data can be further examined by separating the groups into the specific types of vehicles involved in the accident—for example: were the types of vehicles involved in the seven SVAs among those aged 20–24 different from those in other age groups? The fatalities among the passengers tended to be either very young or very elderly. Deaths of those less than 20 years old should be examined to determine whether proper restraint systems were used as well as their position within the vehicle. Deaths of those over 65 years old should be examined to determine whether these deaths were caused by the initial trauma or were delayed deaths.

Forensic epidemiologists will normally present the total number of deaths typically over a several-year period to allow comparisons over time. Table 7.14 shows the total number of deaths in fatal MVAs over a 7-year period. This table illustrates a common problem of many data sets where, over time, more detailed data are collected and presented. In this case, a more detailed breakdown of the driver's vehicle was provided for 2 of the 7 years. In order to make multiple-year comparisons, the forensic epidemiologist must obtain the older data and complete the table.

Table 7.13 Demographic Characteristics of Vehicular Fatalities by Occupant and Number of Vehicles Involved, Allegheny County, 2005

	Driver (single vehicle)	Driver (two vehicles)	Driver (three vehicles)	Passenger
Total cases	36	29	6	10
Age				
1–4	—	—	—	1
5–9	—	—	—	1
15–19	—	2	—	1
20–24	7	3	—	—
25–29	7	4	1	2
30–34	3	—	—	—
35–39	4	3	—	3
40–44	2	1	—	—
45–49	3	1	1	—
50–54	3	1	—	—
55–59	2	2	3	—
60–64	2	—	—	—
65–69	—	4	1	—
70–74	1	3	—	—
75–79	1	2	—	1
≥80	1	3	—	1
Race and sex				
White	29	26	5	7
Male	24	23	5	3
Female	5	3	—	4
Black	7	3	1	2
Male	7	1	1	1
Female	—	2	—	1
Other	—	—	—	1
Male				—
Female				1

The forensic epidemiological investigation of an MVA can examine the following: (1) types and numbers of vehicles involved in the accident, (2) environmental factors, and (3) behavioral factors of the driver.

The types of vehicles involved in the accident can be obtained from information contained in the death investigation report or the police report. The forensic epidemiologist should first use general terms to describe the vehicle, such as passenger car, SUV, van, truck (light truck, tractor trailer), motorcycle, bus, or bicycle. Table 7.15 lists the types of vehicles, the number of vehicles involved, and the role of the fatality (driver or passenger). This table also contains some methodological errors: Pepsi truck should be replaced with

Accidental Deaths

Table 7.14 Total Number of Fatal Motor Vehicle-Related Accidents by Role of the Victim, Allegheny County, 1999–2005

Decedent role	1999 Number (%)	2000 Number (%)	2001 Number (%)	2002 Number (%)	2003 Number (%)	2004 Number (%)	2005 Number (%)
Driver	46 (58.9)	45 (62.5)	68 (66.0)	58 (65.1)	52 (62.6)	52 (59.7)	71 (76)
Passenger Vehicle						41	56
Motorcycle						9	10
Bicycle						1	3
ATV						1	1
Scooter						—	1
Passenger	12 (15.4)	11 (15.3)	13 (12.6)	17 (19.1)	11 (10.8)	13 (14.9)	10 (11)
Pedestrian	20 (25.6)	16 (22.2)	22 (21.3)	14 (15.7)	22 (26.5)	22 (25.3)	11 (13)
Total	78	72	103	89	85	87	92

delivery truck and PAT bus should be replaced with public transportation bus. When listing multiple-vehicle accidents, the first vehicle listed denotes the one with the fatality. Detailed analysis of these data would include creating a profile of the driver by vehicle type, the estimated speed by vehicle type, and the location and level of damage to the vehicle by the impacting object (tree, other vehicle).

The second factor of the forensic epidemiological investigation is to examine environmental factors, which include the road surface, surface condition, and the type of weather at the time of the accident. The death investigation and the police report will both note the environmental conditions at the time of the accident. The road surface can be described as asphalt, concrete, loose gravel, or dirt. This information is important when considered in conjunction with the estimated speed the vehicle was traveling at the time of the accident. The condition of the road surface is noted immediately upon arrival at the scene as well as the time the observation was made. The description of the road surface will indicate that it was clear, wet, snow covered, or icy. The weather at the time of the accident includes terms such as clear; fog; light, medium, or heavy rain; light, medium, or heavy snow; or hail. Forensic epidemiological investigations can focus on the role that the road conditions and weather played in the accident; therefore, the accident should be separated by road and weather conditions. Questions to investigate include whether certain types of vehicles are more likely to become involved in accidents under certain weather conditions.

Table 7.15 Types and Numbers of Vehicles Involved in MVAs by Victim's Position in Vehicle, Allegheny County, 2005

Type of vehicle	Driver (single vehicle)	Driver (two vehicles)	Driver (more than two vehicles)	Passenger (one vehicle)	Passenger (more than two vehicles)
Car	12	—	—	2	—
Van/light truck	11	—	—	1	—
Jeep	1	—	—	—	—
Motorcycle	9	—	—	1	—
ATV	1	—	—	—	—
Bicycle	2	—	—	—	—
Car versus car	—	7	—	—	6
Car versus light truck	—	6	—	—	—
Car versus Pepsi truck	—	1	—	—	—
Car versus access bus	—	1	—	—	—
Car versus tractor trailer	—	1	—	—	—
Car versus van	—	1	—	—	—
Car versus Blazer	—	1	—	—	—
Car versus SUV	—	1	—	—	—
Blazer versus car	—	1	—	—	—
Motorcycle versus car	—	1	—	—	—
Blazer versus tractor trailer	—	1	—	—	—
Van versus car	—	1	—	—	—
Van versus tractor trailer	—	1	—	—	—
Truck versus car	—	1	—	—	—
Truck versus PAT bus	—	1	—	—	—
Truck versus tractor trailer	—	1	—	—	—
Scooter versus car	—	1	—	—	—
Bicycle versus car	—	1	—	—	—
Car versus car versus car	—	—	2	—	—
Car versus Blazer versus car	—	—	1	—	—
Car versus truck versus tractor trailer	—	—	1	—	—
Car versus tractor trailer versus truck	—	—	1	—	—
Blazer versus tractor trailer versus tractor trailer	—	—	1	—	—
Total	36	29	6	4	6

Table 7.16 Blood Alcohol Levels of Fatalities by Number of Vehicles Involved in Accident, Allegheny County, 2005

BAL (mg/%)	Single vehicle	Single motorcycle	Passenger	Two vehicles	Three or more vehicles	Total
None detected	16	5	9	21	4	55
≤50	1	1	—	—	—	2
050–099	—	—	—	—	—	—
100–149	2	—	1	—	—	3
150–199	—	1	—	5	1	7
≥200	8	2	—	3	1	14
Total	27	9	10	29	6	81

The third factor investigated by the forensic epidemiologist is behavioral factors of the driver. These include driving under the influence of alcohol and illegal and legal drugs, the use of safety devices, engaging in unsafe driving behavior, and the natural biological effects of ageing.

In almost every MVA, blood is collected and analyzed for blood alcohol content and a number of other compounds. The BAC level can be separated by levels that are above and below the legal definition of intoxication for that area or into various ranges, as shown in Table 7.16. The investigation should concentrate on individuals with a BAC level equal to and above 100 mg%. Although the association between alcohol and MVA has been well established, the role of prescription medications has not. The toxicological report also lists the types and levels of prescription medications. The forensic epidemiologist will examine the types of medications and, most importantly, their effects on the CNS and their synergistic effects.

Two separate profiles should be constructed, one for the driver involved in a single vehicle accident and the other for accidents involving more than one vehicle. Among accidents involving two or more vehicles, the role of the decedent should be determined. Although it is not the role of the ME/C to determine fault of an MVA, the detail of the information at the ME/C office will allow the forensic epidemiologist at least to list the actions of the driver under broad groupings, such as legally intoxicated, traveling at an unsafe speed for conditions, operating a vehicle recklessly, violation of a traffic law (turning against the light), or not at fault.

Another behavioral factor to consider in MVAs is the occupants' decision to use the safety systems. Part of the death scene investigation report is noting the use of safety devices: seatbelts in motor vehicle accidents and helmets in motorcycle accidents. Table 7.17 presents analysis of the use of a safety device by occupant type and number of vehicles involved in the accident. The table clearly shows that among those driving a car, truck, or van who are involved in an SVA, 70.8% were not using a seatbelt at the time of the

Table 7.17 Seatbelt/Helmet Status of Motor Vehicle Operators and Passengers by Type of MVA, Allegheny County, 2005

	Seatbelt used/ helmet worn	Seatbelt not used/helmet not worn	Unknown	Total
Driver—single vehicle				
Car/truck/van	2	17	5	24
Motorcycle	4	4	1	9
ATV	1	—	—	1
Bicycle	—	—	2	2
Total	7	21	8	36
Passenger—single vehicle				
Car/truck/van	2	1	—	3
Motorcycle	—	1	—	1
Total	2	2	0	4
Driver—two vehicles				
Car/truck/van	4	11	11	26
Scooter	—	1	—	1
Motorcycle	—	1	—	1
Bicycle	—	1	—	1
Total	4	14	11	29
Passenger—two vehicles				
Car	1	4	1	6
Total	1	4	1	6
Driver—three vehicles				
Car	4	1	1	6
Total	4	1	1	6
Grand totals	18	42	21	81

accident. Among motorcycle operators, only 44% were wearing a helmet at the time of their accident.

An area within the role of medications that requires further investigation is the role of pre-existing medical conditions and the normal effects of aging. Pre-existing medical conditions such as prior cardiovascular conditions, diabetes, or cerebral vascular accident (CVA) may place the driver and others on the road at risk. In addition, the normal physiological effects of the aging process itself should be examined. As people age, reaction time, vision, hearing, and speed of mental processing abilities decrease. The forensic epidemiologist should begin to collect data on the frequency and role of pre-existing medical conditions and the general health of the internal organs by age to start understanding the possible role of these factors in MVAs.

Figure 7.6 Fatality analysis reporting system (FARS) report.

Fatality Analysis Reporting System (FARS)

The FARS national reporting system became operational in 1975 with the objective of providing an overall measure of highway safety, to help suggest solutions, and to aid in providing an objective basis to evaluate the effectiveness of motor vehicle safety standards and highway safety programs. FARS contains data on a census of fatal traffic crashes within the 50 states, the District of Columbia, and Puerto Rico. To be included in the FARS, a crash must involve a motor vehicle traveling on a traffic way customarily open to the public, and it must result in the death of an occupant of a vehicle or a nonmotorist within 30 days of the crash. Upon completion of the final autopsy report and the DC, personnel from the ME/C complete the FARS report (see Figure 7.6). FARS data are collected from the following sources: coroner and medical examiner reports, police accident reports, state vehicle registration files, state driver licensing files, state highway department data, vital statistics, death certificates, hospital medical reports, emergency medical service reports, and other state records.

The National Highway Traffic Safety Administration (NHTSA) has a cooperative agreement with an agency in each state's government to provide information on all qualifying fatal crashes in the state. These agreements are managed by regional contracting officer's technical representatives located in the 10 NHTSA regional offices. Trained state employees, called "FARS analysts," are responsible for gathering, translating, and transmitting their state's data to the National Center for Statistics and Analysis (NCSA) in a standard format. The number of analysts varies by state, depending on the number of fatal crashes and the ease of obtaining data. FARS data are obtained solely from the state's existing documents.

From these documents, the analysts code more than 100 FARS data elements. Regarding MVA-related deaths, the FARS data system is categorized as accident variables, vehicle variables, and person variables. Table 7.18 shows some of these. Each analyst enters data into a local microcomputer data file, and daily updates are sent to NHTSA's central computer database. The data collected within FARS do not include any personal identifying information, such as name, address, or social security number. Thus, any data kept in FARS files and made available to the public fully conform to the Privacy Act. Each year the office creates an annual report.

The mission of NHTSA is to reduce the number of motor vehicle crashes and deaths on our nation's highways and, subsequently, reduce the associated economic loss to society resulting from those motor vehicle crashes and

Table 7.18 Partial List of FARS Variables

FARS variable	Accident variable	Vehicle variable	Person variable
Day of week	X		
Lighting condition	X		
Roadway surface type	X		
Speed limit	X		
Impact point		X	
Vehicle make		X	
VIN number		X	
Number of occupants		X	
Number of vehicles		X	
Age			X
Sex			X
Alcohol level			X
Seating position			X
Protective system used			X

Accidental Deaths

fatalities. FARS data are critical to understanding the characteristics of the environment, traffic way, vehicles, and persons involved in the crash.

Advantages and Limitations of Forensic Epidemiological Investigation of MVAs

The advantage of investigating fatal MVAs using ME/C data is that a large volume of data from multiple sources is generated. Reports are generated from the emergency responding units, the emergency room, the police, and the ME/C office. Each agency generates its own independent assessment of the accident and provides a slightly different perspective of the incident. These reports can be used to cross-reference data and, in the case of any discrepancy, to compare several sources to resolve the issue.

The limitation involved in MVA research is the level of investigation, which varies greatly among ME/C offices across the country. In some areas, the cause and manner of death are based solely on an external examination of the body and the collection of blood to determine the BAC. In addition, an SVA involving only a driver may receive a more limited police investigation, mainly because the case will not go to court as there is no one to charge with a violation. Other locations conduct a complete postmortem investigation, including toxicological analysis.

The number of completed autopsies among victims of MVA has been steadily declining over the past 5 years. The percentage of MVA victims that underwent a complete versus external-only autopsy in Allegheny County between 2000 and 2004 is shown in Table 7.19. This increase in the number of external examinations can lead to a greater possibility of missing pre-existing medical conditions that could have contributed to the accident. A complete autopsy will provide anatomical and physiological data and allow for a detailed examination of the possible role that a pre-existing medical condition and other acute conditions played at the time of the accident.

Table 7.19 Percentage of MVA Victims Who Underwent Complete versus External-Only Autopsies, Allegheny County, 2000–2004

Year	Complete	External only	Unknown	Total
2000	67 (81.7%)	14 (17.1%)	1	82
2001	72 (88.9%)	9 (11.1%)	0	81
2002	90 (83.3%)	17 (15.7%)	1	108
2003	77 (81.9%)	17 (18.1%)	0	94
2004	85 (77.3%)	25 (22.7%)	0	110

Falls

Definition

A fall is defined as blunt force trauma (BFT) inflicted when an individual tumbles from the same level or from one elevation to a lower one, causing immediate or delayed death facilitated by the injury. Falls from one level to a lower level include stepping off a curb, rolling out of a bed or chair, falling down a flight of steps, falling from a ladder, and falling out of a building (open window) or from another structure (down an open elevator shaft). Falls on the same level include slipping, tripping, and stubbing.

Fatalities

In 2005, there were over 19,656 deaths due to accidental falls (ICD-10 code: W00–W19) in the United States. Table 7.20 shows the total number of fatal falls by sex and race that year.

Fundamentals of Deaths by a Fall

The result of any fall is blunt force trauma. Injuries caused by BFT can be grouped into (1) abrasions, (2) contusions, (3) lacerations, and (4) bone fractures. An abrasion is an injury to the top layer of the skin caused by friction. There are three types of abrasion: (1) scrape or brush abrasions caused by a blunt object scraping off layers of skin (examples include falling off a bike or being dragged over a surface), (2) impact abrasions caused by a blunt force directly perpendicular to the skin crushing it, and (3) patterned abrasions caused by colliding with an object, such as a pipe, that gets imprinted onto the skin.

The most commonly encountered BFT injury is the contusion or bruise. The contusion is an area of hemorrhage due to a rupture of blood vessels caused by the trauma. The skin can present with a contusion, but so can the underlying internal organs, such as heart, lungs, and brain. The severity and extent of these BFT injuries depend on the following: (1) the amount of force delivered to the body, (2) the time over which the force was delivered, (3) the region of the body struck, (4) the extent of body surface over which the force was delivered, and (5) the structure of the object hitting the body.

Table 7.20 Accidental Deaths from Falls by Sex and Race, United States, 2005

Total	Male	Female	White	Black
19,656	10,154	9,502	18,113	1,027

Accidental Deaths

Other factors affecting the severity and development of fall-related injuries include the age of the individual, health status, and type of medications being taken. Older individuals can develop contusions through only a minimal amount of force. The health of the individual may affect the amount of time required for a contusion to heal. Certain medications, such as blood thinners, will cause simple lacerations to bleed more profusely. A laceration is a tearing of the tissue caused by a crushing force such as being hit by a baseball bat, a fall, or impact with a vehicle. The force results in irregular edges, abraded margins, and cross bridges, which are pieces of tissue that connect both sides of the margins. A laceration can be produced on the skin and in the internal organs. The last type of BFT is fractures of the bones.

The site of the BFT will dictate the underlying organs most likely to be affected. BFT to the chest can result in structural injures to the heart—specifically, lacerations to the pericardium or to one or more of the three major blood vessels of the heart. BFT to the chest region of a healthy young athlete has been shown to cause sudden death: The blunt impact to the chest causes a disruption of the normal electrical cardiac rhythm. Examination of the external chest region and the heart would display no visible trauma. This type of death is called a cardiac concussion. Trauma to the upper right region of the abdomen can cause a laceration of the liver and trauma to the left upper region of the abdomen can cause a spontaneous rupture of the spleen. The level of injuries to the extremities and brain is dictated by the height of the fall and the type of surface on which the victim lands.

Forensic Investigation of Death from a Fall

The forensic investigation of a death by a fall typically involves collection of data relating to activities prior to the fall, the cause of the fall, injuries received during the fall, prior medical history (especially prior history of falling), and a list of medications. Deaths of individuals that suffer blunt force trauma caused by a fall in a public place, nursing home, hospital, or residence are investigated by the ME/C office. Victims of a fall are transported to the local ER or pronounced dead at the scene. The location of the event dictates the type of information collected by death investigators.

The majority of falls occur in the home. They can be a same-level fall or a change in elevation. Same-level falls are caused when the individual slips on a loose rug or a wet floor, or trips over an electrical cord or a dog. The most common type of an elevation type of fall is falling down a flight of stairs. The death investigators first ascertain the location of the event, photograph that area, and then attempt to determine the physical structure that caused the fall. If it was a trip or slip type of fall, they identify the object that caused the fall and then describe the objects that would have been hit after the fall, such as a corner of a table, bookcase, or floor. The type of floor would be described as carpeted, wooden, or other. In the case of a fall involving steps, the following information is collected: the construction material of the steps (wood, carpeted), number of steps, surface of the landing (concrete, dirt, wood, carpet), the type of railing, lighting system, and the height from the top of the stairs to the bottom or the stair landing.

Falls occurring in a nursing home, in most states, require a forensic death investigation. The most common types of falls encountered there include falling out of a bed, chair, or wheelchair. Patients in nursing homes are by their nature suffering from a number of health conditions that make them more susceptible to life-threatening injuries from otherwise minor trauma. In a case where a patient fell out of bed, the investigation would measure the distance fallen, type of floor surface, whether the bed had rails, and, if so, in what position they were in. The investigation of falls from a chair or wheelchair would collect similar information.

The elderly not only bruise more easily than their younger counterparts but also require a longer period of time to heal, and they may be taking medication that retards the healing process. Therefore, caution must be exercised when a large number of bruises are discovered during examination of an elderly victim so as not immediately to suspect elderly abuse.

The investigation of a fall out of a structure from an open window would first focus on determining whether the victim was pushed (homicide), deliberately jumped (suicide), or accidentally fell. Young children may fall out open screened windows when they apply more pressure to the screen than it can support. Data regarding the distance of the fall, landing surface, and type of structure (apartment, warehouse, abandoned building) are all collected.

The forensic investigators next focus on the individual. The death investigation report will describe the activity in which the individual was engaged prior to the fall and his or her physical and psychological state. Behavior such as alcohol consumption and/or any drug (legal or illegal) use would be determined as well as past medical history, such as heart disease, low blood pressure, diabetes, neurological conditions (dementia, Alzheimer's), decreasing mental capacity, decreased vision, and a list of current medications. This information would be obtained from a review of the medical records and information provided by the next of kin. The fall history is obtained to list the number and dates of prior falls.

These investigations also attempt to ascertain what role alcohol and drugs played in the death. As the composition of the U.S. population over the age of 65 increases, age-related factors must be considered: the role that prescription medication and neurological conditions such as dementia and Alzheimer's play in contributing to the death. These areas require increased research.

Accidental Deaths

The results of a complete forensic autopsy will provide pathological information on the condition of the internal organs in addition to blood, urine, bile, and vitreous fluid for toxicological analysis.

Deaths involving a fall vary within the jurisdiction of ME/C offices due to the level of investigation in each case. In some cases, the ME/C will issue the DC based on the death investigation report and a review of the medical records. In other cases, the body will be brought into the morgue; although most will receive a complete forensic autopsy, a small number will undergo an external-only examination.

Forensic Epidemiological Investigation of a Fall

The basic data that should be collected by a forensic epidemiologist investigating death involving a fall are shown in Table 7.21. The forensic epidemiologist will first describe the epidemiological characteristics of the deceased, the location where the fall occurred and the cause, and then identify risk factors that can be modified to reduce such deaths. There are three ways of examining the causes of falls: (1) environmental, (2) biological, and (3) chemical. Environmental examples look for structural factors that increase the risk of a fall, such as slipping on uneven sidewalks, extension cords, or loose carpeting. Biological causes include neurological impairments such as CVA, dementia, or Alzheimer's. Chemical causes include the possible effects of prescription medicines, over-the-counter medications, alcohol, and illegal drugs.

The forensic epidemiological investigation of accidental falls can begin by presenting the basic epidemiological characteristics of the total number of deaths, as well as the total by age, sex, and race. This will provide a profile of the typical fall victim. Table 7.22 shows data for deaths from falls covering a 7-year period in Allegheny County. The total number of deaths varies from year to year. The age distribution of the county should be ascertained and compared to the 7-year period.

An examination of the age and sex distribution among victims of falls occurring in 2005 is shown in Table 7.23. This type of presentation would identify the population at greatest risk of dying after a fall. The total number of deaths from falls increases with age and a dramatic increase was noted after the age of 74. Forensic epidemiologists should create a profile of the cause of death within each age group because these types of data would be invaluable to injury prevention programs in identifying the age group to target.

The location where the fall occurred should be described next. Table 7.24 shows the location of falls over a 5-year period; the vast majority occurred in a residence, with nursing homes a distant second. Falls in residences should be further divided into falling down steps, slipping on loose carpeting, tripping over objects, and falling out of a bed or chair. The forensic epidemiological investigation of falls at home should concentrate on collecting information

Table 7.21 Basic Forensic Epidemiology Data in Investigation of Deaths Involving a Fall

Characteristics	Variables
Basic epidemiological features	Age Sex Race
Location of incident	Residence Nursing home Hospital Public location Open area
Type of structure	Residence: house Medical facility: nursing home, hospital Public building: mall, parking lot, bridge Public structure: curb, sidewalk, stairs Nonpublic building: abandoned building, warehouse, industrial buildings Open area: park, field, woods
Incident: time, day of week, month	
Time/date of death	
Place of death	Scene Residence Hospital Long-term care facility
Type of fall	From one elevation to a lower elevation: ladder/down steps/chair/bed Slipping Tripping Stumbling
Height of fall	Feet and inches
Landing surface	Wood, metal, carpet, concrete, dirt, water
Fall involved steps	Number of steps Types of steps: wood, metal, carpeted, concrete Surface of landing
Prescription drugs: type, concentration	
Pre-existing medical condition	Cardiovascular Hepatic Vision CNS Neurological

Table 7.22 Deaths from Accidental Falls, Allegheny County, 1998–2005

	1998	1999	2000	2001	2002	2003	2004	2005
Total number of cases	82	123	73	56	67	93	113	74

Table 7.23 Deaths from Accidental Falls by Age, Sex, and Race, Allegheny County, 2005

Age	White male	White female	Black male	Black female	Total
20–24	—	3	—	—	3
35–39	2	—	—	—	2
40–44	1	1	—	—	2
45–49	1	—	1	—	2
50–54	2	2	—	—	4
55–59	1	3	—	—	4
60–64	3	1	—	—	4
65–69	3	1	—	—	4
70–74	3	2	1	1	7
75–79	5	7	—	1	13
80–84	8	4	1	—	13
85–89	6	7	1	—	14
90–94	2	—	—	—	2
Total (%)	37 (50%)	31 (41.9%)	4 (5.4%)	2 (2.7%)	74

on the architectural layout of the residence; the consumption of drugs, alcohol, and prescription medications; and pre-existing medical conditions. This type of information would indicate that the injury prevention researcher should explore the home environment for modifiable risk factors.

The death investigation report will provide a general layout of the residence. This information is most important in deaths involving falls down steps, slipping, and tripping. If the fall was down a flight of steps, data on the types of steps, presence or absence of safety devices such as handrails, and level of illumination should be collected. If the injury was due to slipping or tripping, the type of object that caused the fall (a loose rug, an electrical cord, a toy, the dog) should be noted. If the fall occurred in a bathtub or shower, the presence or absence of safety devices such as hand rails and non-skid surface pads will be collected. Again, the main purpose of these data is to assist injury prevention specialists in recommending changes in the home to reduce the risk of injuries from falls.

The behavior of the victim must also be examined. The examination of the toxicological report will determine if alcohol or other drugs played a role in the death. An examination of postmortem blood alcohol level (BAL) or blood alcohol concentration (BAC) over an 8-year period is shown in Table 7.25 and reveals that only a small percentage of individuals who died from a fall were positive for alcohol. On the other hand, a small percentage of deaths have an extremity high BAL. These cases should be examined further to determine what role alcohol played in the death.

The forensic epidemiologist should explore the possible role of drugs, especially those that could impair balance, coordination, and judgment.

Table 7.24 Location of Falls, Allegheny County, 2001–2005

Location	2001 Number (%)	2002 Number (%)	2003 Number (%)	2004 Number (%)	2005 Number (%)
Residence	33 (58.9)	43 (64.2)	67 (72.0)	83 (73.4)	54 (72.9%)
Nursing home (hospice)	10 (17.8)	9 (13.4)	10 (10.7)	6 (5.3)	6 (8.1%)
Outside	7 (12.5)	8 (11.9)	8 (8.6)	10 (8.9)	6 (6.7%)
Work	4 (7.1)	2 (2.9)	—	2 (1.8)	—
Hospital	1 (1.8)	4 (5.9)	5 (5.3)	8 (7.0)	2 (2.7)
Church	—	—	1 (1.1)	—	—
Hotel/motel	—	—	—	1 (0.9)	—
Jail	—	—	—	—	1 (1.3)
Shopping center	—	—	—	2 (1.8)	4 (5.4)
Highway	—	—	—	1 (0.9)	—
Sidewalk	—	—	—	—	1 (1.3)
Bar/restaurant	1 (1.8)	1 (1.5)	2 (2.2)	—	—
Total	56	67	93	113	74

Table 7.25 Postmortem Blood Alcohol Levels in Accidental-Fall Fatalities, 1998–2005

BAL (mg/%)	1998	1999	2000	2001	2002	2003	2004	2005
All deaths	82	123	73	56	67	93	113	74
Not detected	82	121	55	47	62	76	93	65
≤50	—	—	3	3	3	5	4	4
51–99	—	—	—	1	—	2	—	2
≥100	—	2	5	5	2	6	9	3
Unknown	—	—	8	—	—	4	1	—

The elderly population—most at risk from a fall—is prescribed the greatest number of drugs. The toxicology report can also provide important information to determine whether the individual was taking prescription medication and, if so, at the correct dosage. An elderly individual who fails to take medication for low blood pressure might have fallen due to an unsafe drop in blood pressure. A vastly under-researched area is the synergistic effects of these multiple drugs and their role in deaths from falls among the elderly. In addition, the role of pre-existing medical conditions should be examined in terms of their severity and possible contribution to the fall.

The examination of the completed forensic autopsy report can provide the following information: specific site of the injury, organs affected and severity of injuries, and whether the death was immediate or due to secondary complications associated with the fall. This type of information would provide clues to the biomechanics involved in the fall. Research into types of injuries

Accidental Deaths

from different heights can be conducted and a comparison made between the types and severity of the injury received between those that fall out of bed onto a carpeted floor versus onto a hardwood floor. The death investigation report, autopsy report, and medical records can be used to understand the sequence of events after a fall. The deaths should be divided into immediate and delayed deaths. In an immediate death, the victim is pronounced dead at the scene. A delayed death implies that the victim died sometime after the event due to injuries received from the fall or from secondary complications precipitated by the injury received from the fall.

For example, an elderly woman trips over a dog and falls, causing her to fracture her right leg. Although the fracture is not life threatening, it does require bed rest. The prolonged bed rest causes a severe case of pneumonia, which causes death. The DC would read:

Immediate cause of death: pneumonia
Due to: fracture of right leg
Due to: fall

Advantages and Limitations of Forensic Epidemiological Investigation of Falls

The data collected by the ME/C offices regarding falls are unique compared to data for other types of deaths, such as MVAs, homicides, and ODs in that the ME/C office is the only agency collecting information regarding this type of death. For example, data regarding MVAs are independently collected by the ME/C office, police, EMS, and FARS. Homicide data are collected by the ME/C office, police, FBI, and victim advocate groups. Therefore, falls are typically only investigated by the ME/C office.

One of the major limitations of ME/C data regarding deaths from falls is that all DCs that list an injury caused by a fall in part I with the manner listed as accident must be filtered through the ME/C office and only a percentage of all falls received are fully investigated—that is, a death scene investigation, complete autopsy, and medical history review. A large percentage of DCs for falls are completed as OWI (see Chapter 4). In these cases, the ME/C office issues the DC based on information contained within the medical records and the body is not examined.

A more serious limitation is the under-reporting of deaths by fall, especially those due to secondary complications. This typically occurs in a hospital setting where the patient dies from pneumonia or other respiratory infection and the physician signs the DC out as a natural death. The physician fails to determine the sequence of events that led up to that infection. Forensic epidemiologists can determine the number of under-reported cases by ascertaining the number of admissions to a hospital with the chief complication of trauma due to a fall and then compare the final discharge summary and the DC to see whether they were listed as natural or accident.

Researchers examining deaths for falls based solely on the DC have one major limitation. A review of the classification of the circumstances surrounding the fall occurring within the residence based on information cited on the DC between 1992 and 1998 revealed that 63% did not record the cause of the fall. Therefore, the specific mechanism leading to the injury could not be determined.

Fire

Definition

Fire is defined as a rapid oxidation process with the evolution of heat and light.

Fatalities

In 2005, there were 3,197 accidental exposures to smoke, fire, and flames (ICD-10 code: X00–X09) in the United States. Table 7.26 shows a breakdown of these deaths by sex and race that year.

Fundamentals of Deaths by Fire

Four components are required for a fire: fuel, oxygen, heat, and an uninhibited chemical reaction.

- Fuel can be any substance that will burn or support combustion and can take the shape of a solid, such as wood; a liquid, such as gasoline; or a gaseous vapor, such as natural gas. Note that the fuel can only be volatilized in the vapor state; therefore, when wood burns, the burning takes place at the surface of the wood where the vapors are created by heat and ignited.
- Oxygen acts as the oxidizing agent required to support combustion.
- Heat is required to increase the temperature of the fuel in the presence of oxygen to cause ignition. Heat is the energy possessed by

Table 7.26 Fire Deaths by Total Number, Sex, and Race, United States, 2005

Total	Male	Female	White	Black
3,197	1,886	1,311	2,351	746

Accidental Deaths

a material due to its molecular activity. The five types of heat production are chemical, mechanical, electrical, compressed gas, and nuclear.
- The last condition for a fire is a chemical reaction that must be continuously and precisely reproduced to maintain combustion. This reaction must contain the oxidation reaction producing sufficient heat to maintain continuous oxidation, the fuel mass must be broken down and liberated (vaporized) from the mass itself, and the vapors must combine with the oxygen.

The causes of deaths associated with a fire are smoke inhalation and burns. The manner of death can be accidental, suicide (self-immolation), or homicide (arson). The most common causes of accidental fire death are associated with smoking, cooking, candles, and electrical malfunctions. The role of the death investigator in fire-related deaths is to work closely with the fire marshal and police arson teams to ascertain whether the origin of the fire was accidental or deliberate (suicide or homicide). The forensic autopsy is conducted in the same manner regardless of preliminary opinions as to the cause of the fire, and all fires are treated as suspicious. The external examination of the body would note the types of burns (first, second, and third degree), the location of the burns, and the percentage of the body burned based on the rules of nines (explained later). Body fluid would also be collected in the standard manner.

A critical medicolegal question involved in fire deaths is whether the victim was alive or dead when the fire started. To make this determination, the airway of the victim is carefully examined. If the victim was alive when the fire started and failed to exit the structure because he or she was overcome by smoke or suffered a cardiac event, the victim would have inhaled the smoke and other gases in the atmosphere. An examination of the airway would reveal soot deposited in the nostrils, mouth, larynx, trachea, and bronchi. Caution should be taken because an absence of this feature is not a proof-positive indication that the victim was dead at the start of the fire; a toxicological analysis of the blood should be conducted. Analysis of the blood would be positive for carbon monoxide and possibly other airborne compounds such as cyanide, commonly given off by burning furniture and some flooring materials. If, on the other hand, the victim was already dead when the fire started and the fire was used to conceal a homicide, an examination of the airway would show no soot and analysis of the blood would be negative for carbon monoxide.

Mechanisms

The two main mechanisms of death associated with a fire are burns and smoke inhalation. A less common mechanism is blunt force trauma (BFT) caused by falling debris.

Burns are caused by the body coming into contact with a hot surface over 70°C and may be classified into first, second, and third degree. The determination is based on the depth of the burns in the skin. First-degree burns are superficial burns similar to sunburn. Second-degree burns are deeper (partial thickness) and are characterized by the formation of blisters. Third-degree burns are deep (full thickness) with destruction of the epidermis and dermis. The extent of burns to the body is determined by using the "rules of nines." This rule states that the head is 9%, the upper extremities are 9% each, the front of the torso is 18%, the back is 18%, each lower extremity is 18%, and the perineum is 1%. The calculation of the total body burned is by adding up all the surfaces with burn injuries.

Individuals that die in a fire may not display visible external injuries; in these cases the cause of death is by smoke inhalation. During a fire, the atmosphere contains carbon monoxide (CO), cyanide, and other toxic gases. The classic signs of CO poisoning are a cherry-red coloration of the muscles, internal organs, and blood. Carbon monoxide is a colorless, odorless, tasteless toxic gas produced as a by-product of combustion. The sources of this gas include fires, fireplaces, gas stoves, and automobile exhaust. The medical effects of CO inhibit the hemoglobin of the red blood cell from binding with oxygen. The symptoms of concentrations of CO are shown in Table 7.27.

Death from fire can be immediate or delayed. Immediate deaths are caused by direct thermal injury caused by burns to the body or from smoke inhalation. Deaths that occur days after the fire (delayed deaths) are the result of shock, fluid loss, or acute respiratory failure caused by inhalation of gases that injured the respiratory system. Deaths occurring several weeks after the event are caused by sepsis or chronic respiratory insufficiency.

Table 7.27 Carbon Monoxide Concentration and Its Effects on the Body

Concentration	Symptoms and medical effects
10%	None (heavy smokers can have a CO concentration ~ 9%)
15%	Mild headache
25%	Nausea, severe headache
30%	Symptoms intensify
45%	Unconsciousness
50%+	Death

Accidental Deaths

Table 7.28 Basic Forensic Epidemiological Data Used in Investigation of Death Involving Fire

Characteristic	Variables
Basic epidemiological features	Age
	Sex
	Race
Location of incident	Residence:
	Occupied
	Vacant
	Business
	Vehicle
Time/date of incident	
Place of death	Scene
	Residence
	Hospital
Smoke detectors	Installed and operating
	Installed but not operating
	None
Origin	Location of start of fire
Cause	Electrical
	Cooking
	Smoking
	Matches
Total amount of body burned	%
Survival time	

Table 7.29 Accidental Deaths from Fire, Allegheny County, 1998–2005

	1998	1999	2000	2001	2002	2003	2004	2005
Number of cases	21	17	10	17	14	12	17	15

Forensic Epidemiological Investigation of Fires

Forensic epidemiologists investigating fire deaths should begin by collecting the data listed in Table 7.28. The investigation of fire deaths can be conducted on four levels: basic epidemiological characteristics, cause of the fire, cause of death, and the roles of drugs or pre-existing medical conditions in the deaths. In addition, data collected on fire fatalities can also highlight risk factors that could prevent future deaths.

The annual number of fire-related fatalities and a profile of these victims by age, sex, and race are essential to illustrate the population most likely to die in an accidental fire. Table 7.29 shows the total number of fire fatalities

Table 7.30 Accidental Deaths from Fire by Age, Sex, and Race, Allegheny County, 2005

Age	White male	White female	Black male	Black female	Total
15–19	1	—	—	—	1
35–39	1	—	—	—	1
40–44	2	—	—	—	2
45–49	3	1	—	—	4
55–59	1	—	—	—	1
60–65	—	—	2	—	2
75–79	1	1	—	—	2
80–84	—	—	1	—	1
85–89	—	—	—	1	1
Total	9	2	3	1	15

Table 7.31 Number of Deaths from Fire during Different Time Periods, Allegheny County, 2001–2005

Time	2001	2002	2003	2004	2005
0000–0600	5	5	2	5	7
0601–0900	—	1	—	3	3
0901–1200	5	4	—	1	2
1201–1600	6	1	4	1	1
1601–2000	—	2	1	4	2
2001–2400	1	1	5	3	—
Total	17	14	12	17	15

covering an 8-year period. To place this number into perspective, the number of fire deaths in other locations of similar demographics would be required.

The profile of the fire victims in 2005 is shown in Table 7.30. The victims ranged in age from 15 to 89 and the majority was white males. Because of the small number of cases, several years of data should be used to gain a better representation of the fatalities. Once this larger population has been obtained, the cause of the fire can be described within each age grouping. Questions to ask include whether the causes of fires are a function of age.

The forensic epidemiologist can also examine the time and month of the fires. The time that the fire started is an important piece of information because it can be used to explain, for example, why individuals may have failed to escape. A 5-year analysis of the time a fire started (Table 7.31) clearly shows that the majority of fires occurred between midnight and 6:00 am. Typically, during these times, individuals are sleeping and may be disorientated upon waking due to the smoke, pass out from the carbon monoxide levels, or suffer a cardiac event in an attempt to flee the house. The month that

Accidental Deaths

Table 7.32 Number of Deaths Occurring Each Month, Allegheny County, 2001–2005

Month	2001	2002	2003	2004	2005
January	—	1	1	6	3
February	—	5	1	1	3
March	3	1	—	4	1
April	1	1	1	2	—
May	4	—	2	—	4
June	—	—	4	—	—
July	2	—	—	2	2
August	2	1	1	—	—
September	2	2	1	—	—
October	—	—	—	—	—
November	—	1	—	1	—
December	3	2	1	1	2
Total	17	14	12	17	15

Table 7.33 Source of Fire, Allegheny County, 2001–2005

Activity	2001	2002	2003	2004	2005
Cooking	5	2	2	2	3
Smoking	4	4	2	2	5
Electrical malfunction	2	1	3	3	1
Driving	1	—	1	1	—
Oxygen tank	—	—	—	—	2
Heater	—	—	—	—	1
Fire for warmth	—	1	—	—	2
Candle	—	—	2	1	—
Unknown	5	6	2	8	1
Total	17	14	12	17	15

the fire occurred can be an indication of the cause of the fire. Fires in the cold winter months can be related to the use of a fireplace, candles, or electrical overload. This is supported by data shown in Table 7.32, which indicate that the majority of fires occurred in the colder months. Important comparisons could include the time, cause versus month, and cause of the fire.

The role of the ME/C office is to determine the cause and manner of death; the office often relies on the skills of outside agencies to assist them in this duty. In most fires, the fire marshal's office will conduct an independent investigation of the fire to determine its cause and its point of origination, and will rule as to the type of fire. The reports also note the number, location, and level of operation of smoke detectors within the residence. The fire marshal's office can rule the fire as accident, arson, or cause unknown. Table 7.33 shows the causes of fires in Allegheny County between 2001 and 2005. The two most common causes were associated with smoking and cooking.

Forensic epidemiological research can classify house fires into preventable and nonpreventable. Preventable fires are those associated with behaviors or activities that increase the risk for a fire, such as smoking, unsupervised cooking, using candles, and unsafe use of heaters and fireplaces. Nonpreventable fires are typically associated with unseen risks such as poor wiring and malfunctioning electrical equipment. Based on the information from the fire marshal's report, residential fires can be separated by the operating level of the smoke detectors into (1) none, (2) present but nonoperational, or (3) present and operational.

Advantages and Limitations of Forensic Epidemiological Investigation of Fires

The main advantage of forensic epidemiological investigation of deaths involving fire is that these types of deaths undergo several types of independent investigation, including the ME/C office, the fire marshal's office, and the police. The forensic investigation of the body provides information on the effects of fire and smoke inhalation upon the body and the toxicological analysis provides the chemicals released into the atmosphere and inhaled by the victims. The limitation of investigating fires is minimal; the main limitation is that, in a number of fires, the cause of the fire remains undetermined.

Industrial Deaths

Definition

An occupational or industrial death is a fatality that occurs during or as a result of employment (that is, working for pay, compensation, or profit) when one is engaged in a legal activity or present at the site of the incident as a requirement of one's job. The injury causing death must result from an intentional (homicide or suicide) or unintentional (accident) trauma or damage to the body. The acute exposure, trauma, or other specific event should occur within a single workday or shift.

Fatalities

The calculation of the number of fatalities that occur on the job is more difficult than for the other categories of accidental deaths because the cases can be scattered over a number of different causes and manners of death.

Accidental Deaths

For example, if a roofer falls off the roof and dies from BFT to the chest, that death would be listed under the ICD-10 code "fall" and the manner would be "accident." However, if a shop owner is killed during a robbery, that death would be listed under the ICD-10 code "assault by discharge of a firearm" and the manner would be "homicide." In order to determine the number of occupational deaths at a national level, the following sections of the DC must be electronically compiled: (1) cases with Part 30C checked as "yes," (2) a place of injury listed in Part 30, and (3) part 1a describing the type of occupation.

Fundamentals of Industrial Deaths

The first role of the death investigation is to ascertain whether the death occurred while the victim was working or "on the clock" at the time of the incident. A construction site is defined as one where active construction is in progress. In off-site industrial deaths, the victim was off the construction site but transporting or picking up supplies from one location to deliver to another job-related site.

An industrial death is a joint investigation involving the ME/C and the Occupational Safety and Health Administration (OSHA). The role of the ME/C office is the same as for any death: to determine the cause and manner or death. In addition to completing the DC, the ME/C office completes an industrial reports form (Figure 7.7) that is sent to OSHA. The role of the OSHA investigation is to detect unsafe working environments and recommend changes to decrease work-related injuries and deaths.

Forensic Epidemiological Investigation of Industrial Deaths

Basic epidemiological characteristics collected on all industrial deaths are shown in Table 7.34. The basic epidemiological characteristics of individuals that die in an industrial-related death should be presented by the number of deaths annually and then further broken down by age, sex, and race. Table 7.35 shows industrial deaths over an 8-year period; the majority of deaths occurred among white males, with the mean age around 50–54 years.

Forensic epidemiologists investigating industrial deaths should classify the site of the event as one of the following: construction, manufacturing, transportation, public utilities, agriculture, forestry, fishing, mining, wholesale or retail trade, finance, service industry, or business office. This would allow determination of the most dangerous occupations in that area. Next, the type of activity in which the victim was engaged should be described within each of the preceding job classifications at the time of the event. These pieces of data can be obtained from the death investigation report.

Allegheny County Coroner's Office
PITTSBURGH, PENNSYLVANIA
INDUSTRIAL ACCIDENT REPORT

| M.E. CASE NO |
| POLICE FILE NO. |
| DATE REPORTED |

NAME OF DECEASED (Last, First Middle)

AGE   RACE   SEX   MARTIAL STATUS

DATE OF DEATH   CODED OCCUPATION

ADDRESS OF EMPLOYMENT   WORK PHONE

SUPERVISOR'S NAME

LOCATION OF INCIDENT

LYING FACE-UP IN BED.
SITE OF DEATH

SUMMARY REPORT OF DEATH IN DETAIL

DEPUTY COMPLETING REPORT   DATE

TO BE COMPLETED BY SECRETARY FROM DEATH CERTIFICATE
CAUSE OF DEATH

MANNER OF ACCIDENT

DATE SENT TO OSHA   DATE SENT TO NIOSH

COMPLETED AND SENT BY   DATE

Figure 7.7 Industrial reports form.

The mechanism that caused death can be divided into trauma, exposure, asphyxiation, gunshot wound, or natural conditions (see Table 7.36). The deaths caused by trauma can be further divided into the region of the body. Deaths from exposure can be grouped into chemical, electrical, radiation, or thermal exposure. Industrial deaths can be divided into those that were natural and those caused by accident, homicide, or suicide. Deaths from natural conditions can be grouped by the affected organ.

Advantages and Limitations of Forensic Epidemiological Investigation of Industrial Deaths

The main advantage to the investigation of industrial deaths is that all nonnatural deaths occurring during working hours are, by law, required to be investigated by a forensic investigator from the ME/C office and by OSHA. This

Accidental Deaths

Table 7.34 Basic Epidemiological Characteristics Collected on All Industrial Deaths

Characteristic	Variables
Basic epidemiological features	Age
	Sex
	Race
Location of incident	Work site
	Office
	Construction site
	Off-site
	Vehicle
	Time/date of incident
Place of death	Work site
	Hospital
Type of industry	Agriculture, forestry, fishing, mining
	Construction
	Manufacturing
	Transportation and public utilities
	Wholesale and retail trade, finance, insurance, real estate services
Job title	
Cause of death	
Manner of death	
Number of drugs	One, two, three, etc.
Types of drugs	
Drug levels	
Pre-existing medical conditions	

ensures complete ascertainment of these types of work-related deaths. The limitation comes in the form of when the cause of death is natural in nature. Take, for example, a 55-year-old accountant working at his desk who suffers a massive myocardial infarction and dies. Does the forensic pathologist call this death a natural or an industrial death? Some will call it natural because if that same death had occurred a few hours later, it would have been called natural. Others would argue that the stress of the job contributed to the cardiac event and that stress is reduced at home. The forensic epidemiologist must inquire of the ME/C regarding the protocol for assigning the death as industrial-related fatality.

Medical Misadventure Deaths

Definition

Medical errors can occur from a health care provider choosing an inappropriate method of care or choosing the right method of care but carrying it out

Table 7.35 Demographic Characteristics of Industrial Accidental Deaths, Allegheny County, 1998–2005

Age	1998	1999	2000	2001	2002	2003	2004	2005
15–19	—	—	—	—	—	—	—	1
20–24	3	—	1	—	—	—	—	2
25–29	1	—	1	—	—	1	—	—
30–34	—	—	1	1	—	—	—	1
35–39	—	3	—	3	1	2	2	—
40–44	1	3	3	3	1	—	—	2
45–49	2	1	2	3	1	3	2	2
50–54	—	—	1	5	1	—	4	1
55–59	—	1	1	7	1	2	4	1
60–64	—	—	—	1	—	—	1	—
65–69	—	—	—	1	—	—	—	1
≥70	—	—	1	—	—	—	1	1
Total	7	8	11	24	5	8	14	12
Race and sex								
White male	7	7	10	20	5	6	13	12
White female	—	—	—	2	—	—	—	—
Black male	—	1	—	1	—	2	1	—
Black female	—	—	—	1	—	—	—	—
Asian male	—	—	1	—	—	—	—	—
Total	7	8	11	24	5	8	14	12

incorrectly. Errors can also occur by giving the wrong dose, wrong medication, or medications that are contraindicated for a patient. Errors can also occur before, during, or after a medical or surgical procedure.

Fatalities

In 2005, there were 2,653 deaths due to complications of medical and surgical care (ICD-10 codes: Y40–Y84, Y88) in the United States. Table 7.37 shows U.S. medical misadventure deaths by total number, sex, and race that year.

Fundamentals of Medical Misadventure Deaths

Of the 33.6 million people admitted to hospitals each year in the United States, 2.9–3.7% of them will suffer an adverse event and between 8.8 and 13.6% will suffer a fatal event. The number of medical misadventures (medical errors) resulting in death has been estimated to be between 44,000 and 98,000 people a year in U.S. hospitals, according to the National Institute of Medicine. Put another way; 1 out of every 500 individuals admitted to a U.S. hospital is killed by a mistake. The report estimated that medical errors may be the fifth leading

Accidental Deaths

Table 7.36 Mechanisms of Death for Industrial Cases, Allegheny County, 1998–2005

Mechanism	1998	1999	2000	2001	2002	2003	2004	2005
Industrial vehicle (collision)	1	—	2	—	—	—	—	—
Crushed by an object	3	4	1	—	2	—	2	—
Fire related	—	1	—	—	—	—	—	—
Smoke inhalation	—	—	—	2	—	—	—	—
BFT head	—	—	—	7	—	4	—	3
BFT trunk	—	—	—	2	—	1	1	1
Extensive BFT	—	—	—	—	1	—	—	—
High voltage	3	1	2	—	—	1	—	1
Asphyxiation	—	—	—	—	—	—	2	—
Falls	—	2	1	—	—	—	—	1
Compression of torso	—	—	—	—	—	1	—	3
Anaphylactic shock	—	—	1	—	—	—	—	—
GSW	—	—	2	—	—	—	—	—
Excited delirium	—	—	—	—	—	—	—	1
ASCVD	—	—	2	10	2	1	4	2
Hypertrophic cardiomyopathy	—	—	—	2	—	—	1	—
Cardiac tamponade	—	—	—	1	—	—	—	—
Lung disease	—	—	—	—	—	—	2	—
Exposure	—	—	—	—	—	—	1	—
CVD	—	—	—	—	—	—	1	—
Total	7	8	11	24	5	8	14	12

Table 7.37 Medical Misadventure Deaths by Total Number, Sex, and Race, United States, 2005

Total	Male	Female	White	Black
2,653	1,220	1,433	2,170	434

cause of death. It must be kept in mind that these figures do not represent fatal mistakes that occur in other health care facilities such as ambulatory care settings, surgical centers, office practices, home health care, and nursing homes. Medical errors are not reserved to errors made only by physicians; they include those made by pharmacists, nurses, and other health care professionals.

The miscalculation can cause immediate or delayed death from error-related complications. Examples of complications include pneumothorax or hemothorax related to central catheter placement, infections related to central and peripheral catheters, superficial wound infections when the skin is closed, postoperative surgical hemorrhage, wrong surgical site, and unscheduled return to surgery. These deaths can be classified as either avoidable or unavoidable. The most frequent cause of avoidable complications is technical error. Medical errors include such items as medication errors, failure of medical devices, errors in blood transfusions, surgery on the wrong body part or wrong patient, improper insertion of catheters or feeding tubes, and a variety of medical misadventures that cause serious injury or death.

To improve medical safety, more information needs to be collected about errors and how they occur. All practice settings need to implement a reporting system to capture information about medical errors that will allow for learning about errors and improvement in health care quality. Unless information about errors and medical near-misses is available to the states, the federal government, practitioners, and consumers, it will not be possible to learn from these occurrences.

Forensic Epidemiological Investigation of Medical Misadventures

Forensic epidemiological methods of investigating medical misadventure can be classified in terms of a time line, the site (organ), or by the procedure. Medical errors can be divided into three time frames: before the operation or procedure (preoperative), during the operation or procedure (operative), or sometime after the operation or procedure (perioperative). Table 7.38 shows these stages and some associated events that result in death.

These errors can be ascertained by examining the affected organ or extremities. The last method of grouping these deaths is by the procedure. The forensic epidemiologist should gain some basic understanding of the medical procedures encountered.

Advantages and Limitations of Forensic Epidemiological Investigation of Medical Misadventure

The main advantage in the investigation of deaths by medical misadventure is that cases investigated by an ME/C office have complete access to all the medical information concerning the period leading up to, during, and after the procedure. However, the ascertainment of all deaths associated with a medical practice is in question. Unlike deaths from a homicide, a death from a medical error may not be reported to the ME/C office. A large number of these deaths are not reported due to the assumption that death is just one of the possible outcomes of the procedure. The risk of this assumption is that without a thorough postmortem examination, the true cause of the death may never be known. However, the possibility that some of these deaths are deliberately obscured must also be considered. The forensic epidemiologist investigating these types of deaths might start by examining the types and numbers of medical procedures conducted by each hospital and the number of deaths investigated by the ME/C office.

Table 7.38 Medical Errors by Time of Error

Time line	Event
Prior to	
Surgical or medical procedures	Failure to follow sterile procedures
	Anesthetic management
	Radiology and radiotherapy (reaction to dyes)
Medical devices associated with adverse incidence in diagnostic and therapeutic use	Anesthesiology devices associated with adverse incidence
	Radiological devices associated with adverse incidence
During	
Surgical or medical procedures	Abnormal reaction
	Accidental cuts, punctures, perforations
	Unexpected or unexplained hemorrhage
	Foreign object left in body
	Mechanical failure of instruments
	Heart catheterization
	Surgical operation
	Dialysis
	Failure of dosage
Drugs, medicinal, and biological substances in therapeutic use	Prophylactic reactions
	Allergic (hypersensitivity reaction)
	Wrong drugs
	Wrong dosage
	Incorrect dilution
After	
Surgical and medical procedures (abnormal reaction of patients or later complication, without mention of misadventure at time of procedure)	Displacement or malfunction of prosthetic devise
	Hepatorenal failure
	Malfunction of stoma
	Postoperative intestinal obstruction
	Rejection of transplanted organ
	Infection

Drowning

Definition

Drowning is a form of asphyxia in which the lungs are prevented from obtaining oxygen due to submersion of the face in water or some other fluid, filling the lungs.

Table 7.39 Drowning Deaths by Total Number, Sex, and Race, United States, 2005

Total	Male	Female	White	Black
3,582	2,818	764	2,819	556

Fatalities

In 2005, there were 3,582 deaths due to accidental drowning and submersions (ICD-10 codes: W65–W74) in the United States. Table 7.39 shows the total number of drowning deaths by sex and race in the United States that year.

Fundamentals of Drowning Deaths

Drowning can be classified as typical drowning (also called wet drowning) or atypical drowning (such as dry drowning, immersion syndrome, and submersion while unconscious). Drowning can take place in freshwater or saltwater. A wet drowning is the inhalation of water into the lungs and stomach. The first type of an atypical drowning is a dry drowning, when a small amount of water enters the nasopharynx or larynx; it triggers an intense laryngeal spasm mediated as a vagal reflex. This spasm prevents water from entering the respiratory tract but also prevents oxygen exchange and death is due to asphyxia. The second type is immersion syndrome, which is a sudden exposure to very cold water that causes a vagal inhibition, which triggers a cardiac arrest. The last type is submersion while unconscious. This type of drowning occurs in individuals with a medical history of epilepsy, seizures, or severe coronary artery disease. The individual will first suffer a cardiac event, become unconscious, and then submerge underwater.

The forensic examination of a drowning death should concentrate on basic changes in the (1) respiratory tract, (2) biochemistry of the blood, (3) presence and features of water in the stomach and intestines, and (4) presence and types of diatoms. In a drowning, the respiratory tract, especially the mouth and nose, would be filled with a fine froth, a classic sign of edematous lungs. The lungs will be heavy, waterlogged; when they are cut, a bloodstained, frothy fluid flows out. The respiratory tract may contain foreign matter, such as algae, weeds, mud, and sand.

The biochemistry of the blood should be tested for hemodilution and lowered viscosity in freshwater drowning, and hemoconcentration and increased viscosity in saltwater drowning. The stomach and intestines must be examined for the presence of algae, weeds, and other foreign material. The inhaled or swallowed water may contain diatoms, which are microscopic, unicellular algae made of siliceous cell walls that resist acid digestion and putrefaction; diatoms are found in all types of water. If the blood is circulating, the diatoms will distribute into all the organs, including the bones.

Accidental Deaths

The process of isolating diatoms from the organs involves dissolving them in strong mineral acid, thus allowing for microscopic examination that will determine the presence, types, and numbers of diatoms.

Mechanism of Drowning

The cause of death in a drowning is asphyxia due to irreversible cerebral anoxia. The mechanism varies by the type of water. The mechanism of a freshwater drowning is that large amounts of water enter the lungs; the water crosses the alveolar members and enters into the circulating blood stream, which results in the following conditions: marked hypovolemia, rupture of the red blood cells (RBCs), and a significant release of potassium. The result is that the heart becomes anoxic; the large amount of potassium causes the heart to go into ventricular fibrillation and death occurs within 4 or 5 minutes.

The mechanism in a saltwater drowning is characterized by marked hypertonicity, an influx of fluid from the circulation into the lungs, pulmonary edema, and progressive hypovolemia. These conditions cause shock and lead to cardiac asystole; death follows in 8–12 minutes.

Drowning requires only a few inches of water—just enough to cover the mouth and nose. Reports have cited small children drowning after falling into a 5-gallon bucket holding only a few inches of water and intoxicated individuals drowning after falling face first into puddles of water only inches deep.

Forensic Epidemiological Investigation of Drowning

Basic epidemiological characteristics should be collected on all drowning deaths (see Table 7.40). Forensic epidemiological methods of investigation of drowning include the profiles of the victims, activity engaged in at the time of the drowning, location of the event, features of the fluid, medical history that increased the risk of drowning, and the role of alcohol.

The basic profile collected on drowning victims includes the age, sex, and race of victims. The age distribution is important to establish the population at greatest risk of death. When these deaths are grouped by age, the standard 5-year interval should be modified among those under the age of 10 years to a 1-year interval; those under 1 year old should be grouped into month intervals. This would provide a more accurate picture of those at risk.

The type of activity engaged in prior to death can be obtained from the death investigation report. Categories include recreational actives such as swimming, fishing, boating, water sports (rafting, cannoning, row boating, kayaking), or in close proximity to water while hiking. The activity may provide clues to the sequence of events that led to the death. Among those that died while swimming or in close proximity to water, their swimming

Table 7.40 Basic Epidemiological Characteristics Collected on All Drowning Deaths

Characteristic	Variables
Basic epidemiological features	Age
	Sex
	Race
Location of incident	Bathtub
	Hot tub
	Public pool (identify)
	River (identify)
	Stream (identify)
	Lake (identify)
	Ocean (identify)
	Exact location (GPS)
	Time/date of incident
Activity	Swimming
	Boating
	Fishing
	Bathing
	Near water
Place of death	Scene
	Hospital
Type of fluid	Freshwater
	Saltwater
	Other
Characteristics of fluid	Temperature
	Flow rate
	Depth
	Type of bottom
Diatoms	Species
	Density
	Distribution
Type, number, level of drugs	
Pre-existing medical conditions	

proficiency should be ascertained through information within the death investigation report or by conducting interviews with the next of kin, family, and friends. In cases involving a watercraft, the rate of capsizing the craft, the type of safety equipment worn (life preserver, helmet), and the level of experience of the operator should be colleted. The behavior of the victim prior to the event should also be examined, including drinking and using drugs. An individual partying in a boat might fall into the water and, due to intoxication, drown.

Deaths occurring in a public pool or water park should be investigated in terms of the size of the pool, the average demographics (age, sex, race, swimming experence), and the number and level of training of the lifeguards on duty at the time of the accident.

The water type can be grouped into freshwater and saltwater and these groups further subdivided into specific categories. Freshwater can be divided into bathtubs, private and public pools, ponds, lakes, streams, and minor and major rivers; saltwater can be divided into brackish waters and oceans. Regardless of the water type, the following information needs to be collected: water temperature; average flow rate; average depth, including the depth at the site of the drowning; and composition of the bottom.

The U.S. Coast Guard is responsible for all major U.S. waterways; this includes oceans, major lakes, and inland waterways such the Mississippi, Ohio, Allegheny, and Monongahela Rivers. It is also charged with collecting the temperature, flow rates, depth charts, contour of the bottom, and location of water hazards such as sunken ships, old bridge structures, and other structures. Determining the exact location by use of global positioning system (GPS) would be beneficial, especially in river drownings where there are no identifiable landmarks. The forensic epidemiologist should work with the Coast Guard to overlay the location of victims with its data regarding current, depth, and bottom type to identify areas that should be put off-limits to swimmers and boaters due to a high number of deaths or dangerous features of the water such as a strong undertow.

The investigation must also examine the death in terms of the role that a pre-existing medical condition may have played. The forensic epidemiologist must review the medical records for evidence of a pre-existing medical condition such as a severe cardiac condition, seizure, epilepsy, or any other medical condition that may increase the risk of becoming unconscious and falling into the water. This should be compared to the results of the forensic autopsy. In cases where an individual was diagnosed and prescribed medicines for seizures, a determination should be made whether the postmortem level was detected to be within the effective therapeutic range.

As in all deaths, the toxicological report should examine the levels of alcohol or other drugs to determine if they had a role in the death. Remember that a BAL equal to or above 0.8 is considered legally intoxicated on land or when operating a watercraft.

The forensic epidemiologist can examine the distribution of diatoms in varying water types. The species, frequency, and a description complete with an image of each diatom by the water type in that region would be a great database to access in future cases.

Advantages and Limitations of Forensic Epidemiological Investigation of Drowning

The main advantage of forensic investigation of deaths by drowning is that the cause of the death is rarely an issue. The determination of manner of death is the main limitation of this type of investigation. Even with a psychological autopsy, the true intent of the victim many not be ascertained.

Death by Suicide 8

Introduction

The act of taking one's own life is a personal decision made for many reasons. The precipitating trigger for a successful suicide can range from relationship problems to economic difficulties to health-related issues. The method chosen is dictated as much by the means available as by the level of confidence that an individual has in a particular method. A hunter with a high level of familiarity with guns may choose to use a firearm, whereas an elderly women living in a nursing home may choose a plastic bag over her head.

This chapter will define suicide and discuss the number of suicide fatalities, the forensic investigation of deaths by suicide, various methods of committing suicide, and the application of forensic epidemiological investigation to suicides.

Definition

The classification of a death as suicide implies that the death occurred as a result of intentional self-inflicted injuries or acts with a singular motive of killing oneself. A suicide is the deliberate termination of one's own life.

Fatalities

In the United States in 2005, there were 32,637 deaths due to intentional self-harm (suicide) (U03, X60–X84, Y87.0) with 17,002 due to a firearm (X72–X74). Death by suicide is the 11th leading cause of death in the United States. Table 8.1 shows the total number of U.S. deaths by suicide by sex and race in 2005. Table 8.2 shows a breakdown of the 32,637 deaths by mechanism of death by sex and race.

Table 8.1   2005 Suicide Deaths by Sex and Race

Total number	Male	Female	White	Black
32,637	25,907	6,730	29,527	1,992

Table 8.2   2005 Suicide Deaths by Cause of Death, Sex, and Race

Cause of death	Total	Male	Female	White	Black
Intentional self-harm by discharge of firearm	17,002	14,916	2,086	15,681	1,009
Intentional self-harm by other and unspecified means and their sequelae	15,635	10,991	4,644	13,846	983

Fundamentals of Deaths by Suicide

The reason someone chooses to end his or her life is a personal decision and varies from one individual to another. However, some general patterns have emerged based on the age of the victim. Suicide committed among the younger population commonly revolves around a failed relationship. Typically, an adolescent male will commit suicide after his girlfriend ends the relationship. In many instances, the male will communicate a threat to commit suicide in the hope that the girl will reconsider the relationship, but does not attempt to end his life. In a smaller number of cases, the male successfully commits the act. In these cases, the boy usually leaves a long suicide note explaining how he cannot live without his girlfriend or that she was the only girl for him. Suicides in the middle-aged population are often precipitated by economic problems and loss of a job. Relationship problems affect this age group also and frequently revolve around a pending divorce proceeding. During the senior years, primary factors include declining health, chronic pain from disease such as arthritis or osteoporosis, and loneliness or depression after losing a lifelong partner.

The suicide act can be a well thought-out, detailed plan or an almost impulsive act. The well planned suicide involves obtaining the mechanism of death, securing a location, and finally ensuring that no rescue is possible. If the mechanism is a firearm, the individual obtains the gun and ammunition, understands the workings, and is comfortable handling the firearm. If the mechanism is by hanging, the individual typically locates a ligature from items within the house such as rope, extension cord, or even the electrical cord from a vacuum cleaner. The location is any place where one end of the ligature can be tied to a support beam, rafters, or tree limb; the victim places the noose around his or her neck and then stands on a chair, ladder, or other platform from which he or she can step or jump.

The location chosen to commit suicide is critically important because the individual does not want to be discovered during the act and possibly saved; therefore, this part of the preplanning involves making certain that the location, typically a residence, is empty. The individual will inquire how long the family members are going to be shopping or the length of the movie to ensure that he or she will not be interrupted. Although the individual does not want to be saved, he or she wants to be discovered after the act but before decomposition begins. The main reason is a desire for an open casket; other reasons may include preventing damage to the residence or questions of identity. In some cases, suicide is committed in the bathroom. With its ceramic tile and uncarpeted floors, this room provides for easier cleanup than if the suicide were committed in the living room. To ensure discovery, just prior to committing suicide the individual may call a family member or friend to reveal what he or she is going to do—knowing that the friend or the police will be unable to arrive in time to prevent the death. Other means of ensuring a delayed detection include sending a letter or e-mail message.

The most common method chosen to commit suicide is by firearms—mainly because of the ease of obtaining and availability of firearms and the high level of lethality. Although firearms are fairly accessible to most people, not everyone is comfortable handling one. A failed suicide with a firearm is caused by placing the barrel at the wrong angle or position, resulting in a nonfatal, painful, and often disfiguring injury. An individual may have physical limitations, such as severe arthritis of the hands, that makes it difficult to pull the trigger.

The ligature is primarily used because it can be fashioned from materials easily found in a home, such as ropes, electrical cords, wires, cables, and belts. Step-by-step instructions of how to create the classic hangman's noose can be found on the World Wide Web. Among the prison population, ligatures, belts, and shoelaces are removed in order to prevent suicide; however, inmates typically use strips made out of bed sheets, attaching one end to the bars of the cell and dying from asphyxiation.

Another method of committing suicide is by a fatal overdose of pills. The individual simply exceeds the medically prescribed dosage. Individuals may horde prescription pills until they have stockpiled a large quantity and then ingest them all.

Suicide using carbon monoxide typically occurs in a garage and requires planning and some mechanical ability. For this, the location must be available without disturbance during the construction of the apparatus. The hose used must first be connected and secured to the exhaust pipe and the other end placed inside the vehicle. The vehicle should be sealed to present the CO from escaping and fresh air from entering the interior. The level of risk in this type of suicide is high because a neighbor or passersby might hear the running vehicle inside the garage and discover the victim before he or she is beyond life-saving medical treatment.

The presence of a suicide note is a strong indication that the death might be a suicide; however, the lack of a note does not mean that it is not a suicide. The role of a suicide note can provide an explanation to the next of kin of why the deceased felt committing suicide was the only answer or a final good-bye message to family and friends. It can be an angry and vicious letter venting toward an individual from someone who felt hurt or wronged or, in some cases, a collection of rambling sentences, statements, and figures whose meaning in only known to the author. These notes can be handwritten, typed, located in an unprinted computer file, or posted on Web sites such as Facebook or MySpace. These notes vary from a few words to over 50 pages. In general, only between 10 and 37% of suicide victims leave a note.

Investigation of Suicide Deaths

The first action in any death investigation is to photograph the scene, paying particular attention to the location and position of the victim, the suicide mechanism, the relationship between the two, and the general condition of the surrounding scene. The role of the death investigation of a possible suicide is to remain neutral and consider all possible explanations for the death, including an intentional suicide, a homicide masquerading as a suicide, or an unintentional death (accidental). The identification of the mechanism that caused the death, in most cases, is fairly clear, such as a gunshot wound to the head, hanging from a tree, or a hose running from the tail pipe to inside the vehicle. A scene should be searched in an attempt to determine whether a suicide note was left. The victim's computer hard drive should undergo a forensic audit in order to determine whether the Web was searched for sites on suicide or methods to commit suicide and for the presence of a suicide note.

The key components of the investigation are the statements provided by the next of kin, family, and co-workers to the death investigators. The immediate cause of death is known; however, the manner is in question. Statements such as that the victim was acting depressed, seemed distant, stopped engaging in activities that were previously enjoyed, or any communications centering on suicide ideation or statements reflecting a will to end life would be important. The next of kin should be questioned about whether the individual started giving away any personal possessions or talked about his/her funeral, the clothing they wish to be buried in, or the disposition of their remains.

The investigation also attempts to determine any personal event that may have led to the suicide. The investigation should inquire into key areas such as the victim's current relationship status, financial situation, legal problems, and health status. Relationship issues can include a recent separation, divorce proceedings, or the death of a spouse. Often an upcoming divorce can be a trigger for a suicide and a number of suicides have occurred on the day the final divorce papers were received. Financial problems such as a losing a business or a job, mounting medical bills, or a gambling problem can be detected by an examination of banking records.

Individuals accused of a crime may commit suicide to save the public disclosure of the alleged crime. Someone may commit suicide when accused of sexually molesting a daughter in order to protect the family from a public trial. Individuals who know that they will be found guilty and cannot handle a life of incarceration often commit suicide prior to the trial. Declining health or an impending medical condition or diagnosis of diseases such as cancer or Alzheimer's can also trigger a suicide. For example, an elderly person that lived through the hardship of watching a spouse suffer and die from Alzheimer's, upon learning of the same diagnosis for himself or herself, may commit suicide to ensure that family does not go through the pain again.

Mechanisms of Suicides

The list of methods that individuals have invented to commit suicide is endless. The mechanisms chosen can vary, but the end results are always the same. The biomechanics that cause death for various methods of suicide are listed in Table 8.3. The simplest methods require no equipment—such as jumping from a height or consuming a great number of pills—while other methods require more thought and planning, such as pulling a trigger, constructing

Table 8.3 Biomechanics That Cause Death for Various Methods of Suicide

Method	Biomechanics
Firearm	Damages vital organs (brain or heart)
Asphyxia	Failure of cells to receive oxygen
Ligature strangulation (hanging)	Blocks blood supply to the brain
Gas (carbon monoxide)	Prevents oxygen from binding to RBC
Pills	Depresses the CNS
Jumping from height	BFT injuries to the brain or heart
Drowning	Asphyxiation
Hit by train	Massive blunt force trauma
Exsanguination	Blood loss
Driving car into a tree	Blunt force trauma

a noose, connecting a hose from the exhaust pipe causing the redirection of the exhaust into the vehicle, or driving a vehicle into a tree.

Suicide by Firearm

The most common method used to commit suicide is by a firearm due to easy availability and the high level of lethality. In these types of cases, the investigation focuses on the features of the wounds to the body and the firearm. Any firearms discovered at a scene are first unloaded and then transported in a safe manner to the firearm (ballistics) division of the crime laboratory.

The forensic examination of the body focuses on determining the entrance and exit wounds. The entrance wound can offer evidence that can assist in estimating the firing distance and the hand can provide evidence of gunshot residue (GSR).

The external examination begins by collecting evidence from the hands that later will be tested for the presence of GSR using an atomic absorption kit. A detailed macroexamination of all the wounds of the body will then be conducted to ascertain entrance and exit wounds. The tell-tale signs of an entrance wound include imprints from each end of the barrel, soot, and gun powder around or within the wound; exit wounds do not contain these features. Full-body x-rays are then taken to determine whether the bullet passed through the body or if it is still lodged within the body cavity. As they pass through the body, certain projectiles (bullets) deposit small metal fragments along their path.

The body may undergo an external-only examination if the x-ray indicates that the bullet passed through the body; the scene investigation and, at times, a police investigation also support that conclusion; and the death appears to be a suicide. However, if the bullet did not exit the body, a complete autopsy will be conducted. The forensic pathologist will determine the point of entrance, the path within the body, and the point of exit of each bullet. The distance of the firearm from the body is also estimated based on the distribution pattern of soot and gunpowder around the point of entrance. See Chapter 9 for a detailed description of the properties of firearm by types and injury patterns.

The role of the Firearm Division is to (1) determine that the recovered firearm is operational, (2) classify the firearm as a handgun (revolver or automatic), shotgun, or rifle, and (3) determine if GSR was detected on the hands of the victim. In a case of suicide, one would expect that the hands would be positive for GSR. One big question asked by the death investigator concerns handedness; if the victim was right handed, then one would expect him or her to use the right hand to hold and fire the handgun.

Suicide by Asphyxiation

A death by asphyxiation means that some mechanism is preventing or interfering with oxygen reaching the cells of the tissues. Deaths by asphyxiation can be classified into suffocation, strangulation, and chemical asphyxia.

A death by suffocation is caused by a failure of oxygen to reach the blood. Causes of this include (1) inadequate supply of oxygen in the environment, (2) mechanical obstruction of the external airway, (3) obstruction within the airway, (4) external pressure on the body preventing respiration, or (5) displacement of oxygen with another gas incapable of carrying oxygen to the tissues.

Strangulation is a type of asphyxiation caused by closure of the blood vessels and the air passages of the neck as a result of external pressure. There are three types of strangulation: (1) hanging, (2) ligature strangulation, and (3) manual strangulation. The majority of deaths involving hanging are suicides; the other two types of strangulation are homicides. In all three types, the cause of death is cerebral hypoxia secondary to compression resulting in the occlusion of the internal carotid arteries, vertebral arteries, and the small spinal arteries.

Hanging is the second most common method of suicide, primarily because the necessary materials are easily available to the average person, compared with firearms or lethal poison. In hanging, asphyxia is caused by the compression of the blood vessels of the neck caused by a noose that is tightened by the weight of the body. Death is caused by an insufficient amount of oxygenated blood reaching the brain. Compression of the trachea can cause obstruction of the airway.

The victim of a hanging can be in one of two positions: fully suspended or only partially suspended; both will result in death by asphyxiation. The typical image of a victim totally suspended from a crossbeam or a tree limb is an example of a full suspension hanging. An individual does not have to be fully suspended to die from a hanging death. In a partial (incomplete) suspension, the area below the neck can be resting on the ground with only the head suspended by the ligature. In order to comprehend how death can occur in this position, two facts need to be understood: the pressure required to occlude the varying vessels of the neck and the weight of the human head. The amount of pressure required to compress the jugular vein is 4.4 pounds; the carotid artery, 11 pounds; vertebral artery, 66 pounds; and trachea 33 pounds. The weight of the average head, 11 pounds, is sufficient to restrict the arterial blood flow of the carotid artery. This type of suicide is typically seen among the prison population.

In most suicidal hangings, the noose is placed under the chin with the location of the knot to the side or the back. Over time, the noose will cause a furrow around the neck that runs around the front of the neck, slants upward past the ears toward the back, and then fades at the point of suspension. The pattern of the noose will, over time, be transferred to the skin of the neck to the point where, if a highly decorative belt is used, the pattern will become clearly visible on the neck.

The most frequent type of asphyxiation death among young and middle-aged individuals is by hanging; among the elderly, suicide is committed by smothering. Asphyxiation by smothering is caused by the mechanical obstruction of the external airway (mouth and nose). The most common form is by placing a plastic bag over the head, particularly the thin, filmy plastic bags associated with dry cleaners.

The death scene investigator would pay particular attention to how the victim was positioned at the time of discovery and who found the victim and at what time. In many cases, the next of kin instinctively cut the rope and lower the victim to the ground and often remove the noose from the neck of the victim. Therefore, the investigation relies on witnesses' statements as to the exact position of the victim upon discovery. The time last seen alive and the time discovered can be useful to help establish a time of death while also using core body temperature and other signs of decomposition. In a vast majority of deaths by asphyxiation, the victim is beyond medical treatment. The type and height of the structure used to support the body are noted, as well as the possible item the victim stood on. The scene is searched for a suicide note. The next of kin and other family members are asked about any events in the individual's life that may have caused him or her to commit suicide.

At the forensic autopsy, the body is examined. The postmortem changes are compared to the statements made at the scene as to the last time the victim was seen alive and the time of discovery. The stated position upon discovery is compared to dependent lividity patterns. The injuries to the neck are examined and the following are noted: the pattern imprinted onto the neck from the noose and the angle of the furrow produced by the noose. The noose is examined and the type, length, and location of the knot are described.

Suicide by Carbon Monoxide

Carbon monoxide (CO) is a colorless, odorless, nonirritating gas; car exhaust is one of the most common sources. The mechanism of CO poisoning is the completion between the oxygen molecule and CO molecule to binding with the hemoglobin molecule on the red blood cell (RBC). Carbon monoxide has an affinity 250–300 times greater than oxygen to bind with the hemoglobin molecular. This results in the displacement of oxygen with CO and results in an insufficient amount of oxygen being delivered to the tissues of the body, thus resulting in death from hypoxia of the brain.

Death by Suicide

The carbon monoxide level in the blood is measured by the percentage of hemoglobin combined with carbon monoxide to form carboxyhemoglobin. The characteristic cherry-colored appearance of the skin is caused by the carboxyhemoglobin. In the case of a suspected CO-induced death, the rapid analysis of the blood for the level of carboxyhemoglobin is critical. There are two methods of measuring it in the blood: by spectrophotometer and by chromatography. The level of carbon monoxide in the blood is expressed as a percentage of saturation. This represents the extent to which the available hemoglobin has been converted to carboxyhemoglobin. Table 8.4 shows the effects of different concentrations of carbon monoxide.

Suicide by Overdose

Drug overdose is defined as the consumption of a lethal level of drugs for the intention of ending one's life. The death scene typically offers limited clues to the cause and manner of death. No visible external trauma to the victim, no viable means of death, and often no suicide note will be found. If the forensic autopsy does not reveal an internal cause of death such as an obstructed airway or a natural cause (cirrhosis, cardiovascular event), the role of the forensic tox-

Table 8.4 Effects of Different Concentrations of Carbon Monoxide on the Body

Level of carboxyhemoglobin in the blood (%)	Effects on the body
0.0	Normal level
0–10	Headache
30–39	Throbbing headache
30–40	Throbbing headache Nausea Vomiting Faintness Drowsiness even at rest
40	Slightest exertion causes drowsiness Pulse and respiration rapid Falling blood pressure
40–60	Mental confusion Weakness Loss of coordination
≥60	Loss of consciousness Cheyne–Stokes respiration Convulsion Depressed heart action Respiratory failure Death

icologist becomes critical to ascertaining the cause of death. (See Chapter 7 for a detailed explanation of therapeutic, toxic, and lethal levels of compounds.)

The forensic pathologist uses several factors to determine the manner of death. He or she first reviews the findings of the autopsy, considering useful information provided by the next of kin, such as presence of lung cancer, to the autopsy results. Second, the forensic pathologist examines the levels of the substances detected within the blood. Third, any statements made by family and friends regarding any stressors in the form of personal, economic, legal, or health problems that could have precipitated a suicide are considered. Finally, other factors are considered, including past attempts, the content of the suicide note, and general location, time, and compounds used to commit suicide.

Suicide by Vehicle

A fraction of single motor vehicle accidents (MVAs) are, in reality, suicides. The driver will deliberately steer the vehicle into a fixed object, such as a tree. At first glance, the scene looks very similar to the scene of a single-vehicle accident. However, upon closer examination, the following key points will emerge: (1) lack of skid marks, (2) sufficient time to avoid impact, and (3) pedal pattern on the sole of the shoes indicating that the foot was on the accelerator at the time of the impact, rather than on the brake pedal. Interviews with the next of kin typically reveal prior suicide attempts or a verbalized threat by the victim to commit suicide. The results of the toxicological analysis are important, especially the alcohol level.

Suicide by Train

Committing suicide by walking or lying on railroad tracks is rare. The cause of death in most cases is from extensive blunt force trauma or by decapitation for those that lie on the tracks. The investigation must determine whether the death was an accident or suicide. Signs that would indicate a suicide include walking on the tracks, a failure to respond to the horn of the train, being alone, and previous suicide attempts.

Suicide by Exsanguination

Exsanguination is death by blood loss due to cutting of a major blood vessel. The wounds typically seen are located on the wrist or forearm; those seen in the wrist region typically consist of several horizontal cuts. Although these wounds appear to be deep, they rarely extend beyond the fat layer and do not involve any of the major blood vessels. They are commonly called "hesitation marks" and are not fatal. However, the cutting of the neck region, which

Death by Suicide

has a large number of vessels close to the surface, is fatal. Deaths by exsanguination are rare.

Forensic Epidemiological Investigation of Suicides

The forensic epidemiological investigation of deaths by suicide includes the description of the basic epidemiological characteristics of the victim, location of the act, specific method used, role of the suicide note, anatomical location of the fatal injury, and identification of the precipitating event leading to the suicide. In addition, the role of the forensic autopsy is to confirm any medical illness, disease or other diagnosis, and role toxicological analysis in determining the effects of alcohol and other drugs in contributing to the death. The basic information to collect on deaths by suicide is shown in Table 8.5.

The forensic epidemiological examination of deaths by suicide begins with an examination of the basic epidemiological characteristics, which include the annual number of cases, followed by a breakdown by age, sex, race, marital status, living arrangement, and month and day of the week on which death occurred. The basic information can be obtained from the DC; data regarding the living arrangement need to be obtained from the death investigation report. The most basic epidemiological data for deaths by suicide over an 8-year period is shown in Table 8.6. The annual number of deaths appears to be fairly stable during this period, with an average of 146 deaths per year.

The table also presents deaths by sex and race. An examination of suicide by sex and race shows that the greatest risk of committing suicide is among white males. However, this must be put into perspective by determining the population breakdown and presenting this as rates within each of the four categories. The most traditional method of presenting these types of data is illustrated by Table 8.6. It provides the actual number of deaths by sex and race over a time period. However, the same data can also be presented as in Figure 8.1. The advantage of this type of figure is that trends over time can be shown. The figure clearly shows that over the 8-year period, the total number of suicides among whites increased, while the number among black males decreased. The next question to ask is whether the population of blacks and whites shifted during these 8 years.

The total number of deaths by age, sex, and race is required to understand the trend of a region and develop baseline data. It can be used to evaluate the level of effectiveness of any suicide prevention program.

The next basic epidemiological characteristics to examine are the ages of the victims. This information is important because it identifies the population most at risk within a specific region. Overall, there were three peaks within the age distribution: between 20 and 24, 45 and 49, and 65 and 69

Table 8.5 Basic Information Collected on Suicide Deaths

Characteristics	Variables
Basic epidemiological features	Age
	Sex
	Race
	Living arrangement
Marital status	Single
	Married
	Divorced
	Windowed
Location of incident	Resident
	Workplace
	Public area
	Woods
	Time/date of incident
Place of death	Scene
	Residence
	Hospital
Method	Firearm
	Asphyxiation:
	Hanging
	Carbon monoxide
	Plastic bag
	Overdose
	Jumping from height
	Blunt force trauma
	By vehicle
	Sharp object
Methods of previous suicide attempts	Date and method
Suicide note	Yes/no
Specific location of injury	Head
	Neck
	Chest
	Abdomen
	Extremities
Toxicological results	Number of drugs
	Concentration of drugs
Precipitating event	Relationship
	Legal
	Economic
	Health
List of prescription medications	
Past medical history	

Table 8.6 Demographic Characteristics of Suicide Deaths, 1998–2005, Allegheny County

Race/sex	1998	1999	2000	2001	2002	2003	2004	2005
Total	150	136	138	135	133	150	163	154
White male	110	99	100	103	90	112	111	112
White female	23	23	17	21	28	25	33	29
Black male	15	10	17	8	11	10	14	9
Black female	2	2	3	3	2	1	1	2
Other	—	2	1	—	2	2	4	2

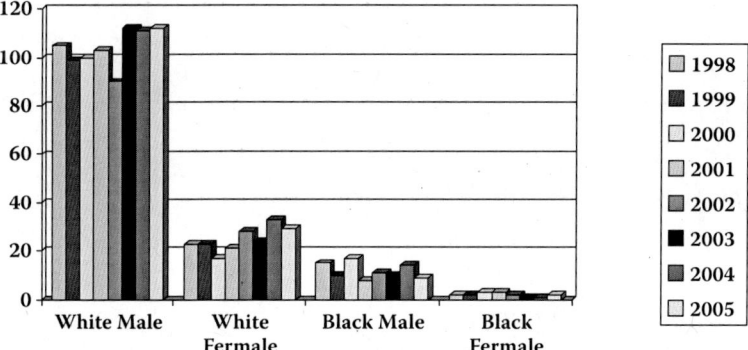

Figure 8.1 Demographic characteristics of suicide deaths by sex and race, 1998–2005.

(Table 8.7). The age distribution should also be examined by sex and race. The victims can be regrouped into three general categories: young, middle age, and elderly. Future examination can explore the associations of marital status/living arrangement, the precipitating event, method of suicide, and the level of planning to the age and sex of the victim.

The marital status is listed on the DC and the living arrangements are described within the death investigation report. These factors may provide some insight into or sign of a possible clue to the suicide. It has often been cited that those who live alone are more prone to commit suicide. Table 8.8 shows the living arrangements of victims at the time of the suicide. The data show that those living alone had an overall lower risk of committing suicide when compared to those living in a family unit. To understand the role of living arrangements better, those classified as living with a family should be regrouped into living with parents, significant other, spouse, or roommate. Those listed as living alone should be regrouped as recently moved out of parent's house, attending college/university, recently divorced, or recently widowed.

Table 8.7 Suicide Broken Down by Age, Race, and Sex, 2005, Allegheny County

Age	White male	White female	Black male	Black female	Total[a]
10–14	1	—	—	—	1
15–19	6	1	—	1	8
20–24	7	4	—	—	11
25–29	6	1	—	—	7
30–34	8	1	1	—	10
35–39	8	3	1	—	12
40–44	11	1	1	—	13
45–49	12	7	4	1	24
50–54	17	2	1	—	20
55–59	5	1	1	—	7
60–64	4	2	—	—	6
65–69	9	3	—	—	12
70–74	3	1	—	—	4
75–79	4	—	—	—	4
80–84	5	1	—	—	6
85+	6	1	—	—	7
Total (%)	112 (71.8%)	29 (18.6%)	9 (5.8%)	2 (1.3%)	154[a]

[a] Two others (non-white; non-black).

Information concerning the circumstances surrounding the suicide includes time, location, method, and level of planning.

Part 32d of the DC lists the time that the suicide was committed. The actual time in most circumstances is an estimate, at best. In rare instances, a spouse or relative may hear the sound of a firearm discharging and then discover the victim dead. The timing of the suicide is not random; a suicide typically illustrates deliberate forethought in the planning. Table 8.9 shows the time at which suicides were committed. The greatest number of suicides occurs during hours when family members are at work or possibly out running errands.

The location where the suicide was committed is listed in part 32g on the DC. The location data provide the most likely place where a suicide event would occur. Table 8.10 shows the location where individuals have committed suicide. The vast majority of the deaths occurred within the residence. This is expected because the materials to commit suicide are within easy access and the traffic of individuals within the residence is well known.

The location an individual chooses to commit suicide can be described in terms of being discovered and in terms of making a final statement. For example, suicides in open areas and public places such as parking lots ensure rapid discovery. On the other hand, death in a hotel room or residence where the schedules of people are known to the victim ensures that discovery will

Table 8.8 Living Arrangements at Time of Suicide 1998–2004, Allegheny County

Where victim lived	1998 Number (%)	1999 Number (%)	2000 Number (%)	2001 Number (%)	2002 Number (%)	2003 Number (%)	2004 Number (%)
Alone	37 (24.6)	22 (16.2)	36 (26.0)	60 (44.4)	51 (38.3)	44 (29.3)	50 (30.7)
With family	64 (42.6)	75 (55.1)	68 (49.3)	64 (47.4)	64 (48.1)	75 (50.0)	60 (36.8)
With boyfriend/girlfriend	15 (10.0)	13 (9.6)	10 (7.2)	6 (4.4)	13 (9.7)	9 (6.0)	13 (7.9)
With relative	—	1 (0.7)	—	—	—	2 (1.3)	9 (5.5)
With friend	5 (3.3)	2 (1.5)	4 (2.9)	3 (2.2)	1 (0.7)	6 (4.0)	5 (3.1)
In an institution	1 (0.7)	3 (2.2)	6 (4.4)	2 (2.2)	4 (3.0)	1 (0.6)	2 (1.2)
In a retirement home	—	2 (1.5)	—	—	—	—	1 (0.6)
In a mental institute	—	—	—	—	—	1 (0.6)	1 (0.6)
Unknown	28 (18.7)	18 (13.2)	14 (10.1)	—	—	12 (8.0)	22 (14)
Total	150	136	138	135	133	150	163

be delayed. The site of the suicide can also act as a final statement by the individual. Examples include an ex-boyfriend committing suicide by hanging himself in front of his ex-girlfriend or a son committing suicide in his father's place of business.

The investigation of the place of death has implications in preventing future suicides. Because a high percentage of suicides occurs in the home, possible methods for committing suicide should be removed from residences of individuals at increased risk for that behavior. If an individual is at risk for suicide, all firearms, nonvital medications, and other methods of self-destruction should be removed from the home, at least temporarily.

The method of death can be obtained be examining the "immediate cause of death" (part 27) of the DC. An analysis of the methods used to commit suicide over a 7-year period revealed that, overall, the most frequent method involved a firearm, followed by hanging and then deaths by overdose (Table 8.11). Each method can be examined and broken down in more detail. The deaths involving a firearm can be examined by the type of firearm (handgun, rifle, or shotgun), the number of shots fired, and to whom

Table 8.9 When Suicides Occurred, 1998–2004, Allegheny County

Time	1998	1999	2000	2001	2002	2003	2004
12:01 a.m.–04:00 a.m.	7	10	15	8	19	10	8
04:01 a.m.–08:00 a.m.	15	14	20	10	14	15	20
08:01 a.m.–12:00 p.m.	34	31	32	28	18	26	33
12:01 p.m.–04:00 p.m.	36	27	18	38	33	46	39
04:01 p.m.–8:00 p.m.	40	30	33	40	30	40	44
08:01 p.m.–12:00 a.m.	18	24	20	11	19	13	19
Total	150	136	138	135	133	150	163

the firearm was registered. In a number of suicides involving a firearm, the individual will first fire the weapon, typically hitting a wall. This is done to be sure that it works and to gain an understanding of how it feels at the moment of discharge. The report generated from the firearm examiner will contain the classification of the firearm, caliber of the bullets, number of live and spent shells recovered at the scene, and a trace of the registration number of the firearm.

Forensic epidemiological research on suicide by firearm can compare the frequency of this method between two diverse locations with similar population demographics but with different gun-control regulations. This could determine whether a stronger gun regulation had any impact on the number of deaths by firearm (a decrease) and, if it did, whether deaths by other methods increased. The gunshot wound can be analyzed by location, type of firearm, sex of the victim, and the reason for the suicide.

The level of planning can be extracted by reviewing the information cited in the death investigation and police reports. The possible classifications include impulsive, low, medium, high, and complicated. An example of an impulsive suicide is when, during a domestic argument, a man takes a gun and shoots himself in the head. Low-level suicides are those that require little or no equipment and minimal planning—for example, jumping off a bridge. A medium-level suicide requires some equipment and a small amount of planning—such as hanging, which requires locating suitable material that can be made into a functioning noose, having the knowledge to create a noose, and having a sufficient structure (crossbeam or tree) accessible from which to hang the noose to commit the suicide.

Items to look for include the time required to set up the mechanism, the time available to commit the suicide, the location, and the chance of being discovered. High-level suicides are those that require the method to be constructed and a large amount of planning. The best example is suicide by carbon monoxide poisoning, which requires the following: time to construct the apparatus, a secure location to commit the act, and knowledge of the movement of the family members to prevent discovery. Complicated suicides

Table 8.10 Locations of Suicides, 1998–2004, Allegheny County

Place of death	1998 Number (%)	1999 Number (%)	2000 Number (%)	2001 Number (%)	2002 Number (%)	2003 Number (%)	2004 Number (%)
Abandoned house/alley	—	2 (1.5)	1 (<1)	—	—	—	—
Street/pavement	4 (2.7)	4 (2.9)	—	—	—	—	5 (3.1)
Height (bridge, balcony, porch)	—	—	6 (4)	3 (2.2)	5 (3.7)	7 (4.6)	5 (3.1)
In car	11 (7.1)	2 (1.5)	10 (8)	1 (0.7)	2 (1.5)	7 (4.6)	10 (6.1)
Cemetery/church	—	2 (1.5)	—	—	—	1 (0.6)	—
Forest, field, backyard	11 (7.3)	2 (1.5)	2 (1)	2 (1.5)	1 (0.7)	—	3 (1.8)
Friend's/relative's residence	1 (0.7)	2 (1.5)	3 (2)	7 (5.2)	2 (1.5)	4 (2.6)	9 (5.5)
Garage	6 (4.0)	2 (1.5)	—	1 (0.7)	12 (9.0)	1 (0.6)	5 (3.1)
Hospital	2 (1.3)	1 (0.7)	2 (1)	3 (2.2)	2 (1.5)	1 (0.6)	2 (1.2)
Motel/hotel	2 (1.3)	3 (2.2)	—	1 (0.7)	1 (0.7)	3 (2.0)	5 (3.1)
Park (woods)	4 (2.7)	1 (0.7)	3 (2)	6 (4.4)	4 (3.0)	1 (0.6)	4 (2.4)
Parking lot	3 (2.0)	4 (2.9)	1 (<1)	—	3 (2.2)	3 (2.0)	1 (0.6)
Penal institution	1 (0.7)	3 (2.2)	4 (3)	2 (1.5)	4 (3.0)	4 (2.6)	3 (1.8)
Residence	96 (64)	102 (75)	97 (70)	100 (74)	92 (69.2)	108 (72.0)	105 (64)
River, stream, canal, lake	3 (2.0)	2 (1.5)	6 (4)	3 (2.2)	—	4 (2.6)	5 (3.1)
Street/highway	1 (0.7)	—	—	3 (2.2)	—	—	1 (0.6)
Store/warehouse	1 (0.7)	2 (1.5)	—	1 (0.7)	—	1 (0.6)	—
Train tracks	1 (0.7)	2 (1.5)	2 (1)	1 (0.7)	2 (1.5)	3 (2.0)	—
Place of work	3 (2)	—	1 (<1)	—	—	—	—
Total	150	136	138	135	133	150	163

are rarely encountered; they consist of engaging in several methods of suicide simultaneously—for example, a man stands on a chair, places a noose around his neck, and then shoots himself in the head. The theory is that if the gunshot wound is not fatal, the force of the shot will cause him to fall off the chair and die from asphyxiation.

Table 8.11 Methods of Suicide, 1998–2004, Allegheny County

Method	1998	1999	2000	2001	2002	2003	2004
Carbon monoxide poisoning	15	8	8	7	11	6	8
Drowning	4	2	6	6	—	4	5
Drug overdose	16	16	12	6	10	5	25
Firearm	73	72	66	59	62	85	80
Hanging	28	23	35	47	41	34	35
Jumping/falling	6	6	5	5	5	9	8
Asphyxiation	2	—	—	1	—	—	1
Struck by train	—	1	2	—	2	3	—
Asphyxiation by plastic bag	—	3	—	—	1	2	3
Cutting (exsanguination)	5	3	2	2	1	2	5
Poisoning	—	—	2	2	—	—	1
Explosives (fireworks)	—	—	—	—	—	—	1
Burns	—	—	—	—	—	—	2
Total	150	136	138	135	133	150	163

The object of a forensic death investigation is to determine the cause and manner of death, but the investigation does not have to determine the reason for the event. An 18-year-old boy is found hanging in his bedroom. The cause of death is asphyxiation and the manner is suicide. Knowing that he was bullied in school does not change the DC, but information such as this could prevent other deaths. Understanding the reason or precipitating event that resulted in the death is significant and can be investigated in the suicide note and by examining the victim's social, mental, economic, legal, and health states at the time of the suicide.

Death investigators are trained to search the scene of a possible suicide case for a suicide note and, if one is discovered, to bring it back to the ME/C office, where a copy is placed in the permanent case file. Deaths by suicide should be first separated into those that leave a note and those that do not. A profile should be created of those that leave a note by age, sex, race, and method of suicide. Questions that should be examined include whether the age, sex, or race plays a role in whether or not a note is left. The note can be examined in terms of its format, length, tone, and purpose. The format can be handwritten, typed, or contained within a computer file. The length can be grouped by the number of pages or number of words. The possible grouping of the tone can include: angry, apologetic, rationalizing, or consisting of rambling thoughts. An informational note is one that simply provides the type of funeral, the clothing to be laid out in, the checking and saving account numbers, other financial information, and where the will is located. Note that the DC does not indicate where a note was discovered at the scene.

The understanding and identification of the precipitating event for the suicide are important for two reasons: to assist the forensic pathologist in assigning the correct manner to the death and to help prevent future suicides by identifying markers or behaviors that can be intervened in before the attempt. Reviewing the death investigation and police reports may provide clues to the factors that contributed to the suicide.

Information from the forensic autopsy and toxicological analysis can provide a state of health and level of control for physical and mental diseases at the time of the event. The investigation of anatomical information, including the progression of lung cancer, joint disease, or the confirmation of Alzheimer's disease, depends on the type of examination conducted. Investigators must first ascertain the percentage of complete autopsies conducted on victims of suicide within the ME/C office. In cases of a complete autopsy, the premortem (before death) diagnosis can be compared to postmortem (after death) findings in terms of accuracy, level of involvement, and missed diagnosis. Studies can explore the relationship of different types of terminal conditions and the interval between diagnosis and suicide.

Regardless of the type of autopsy, blood and urine are collected for toxicological analysis. The number and concentration of alcohol and other drugs at the time of death can be investigated to show whether they are related to the method employed. In addition, the postmortem level of prescription medications can be compared to the level at which they were prescribed. A question that can be investigated would be whether the individual was below his or her medication levels at the time of the suicide. This would be especially important information about individuals with psychological conditions.

The epidemiology, anatomy, psychology, and methods of suicide can be investigated in terms of multiple comparisons. The investigator can explore how different variables interrelate. The forensic epidemiologist can choose two variables within the same group or choose one variable from two different groups (Table 8.12). Possible comparisons include age versus the method of suicide, race versus the method of suicide, marital status versus method, role of drugs and method of suicide, triggering event and age, and anatomi-

Table 8.12 Factors Associated with Suicide

Group 1	Group 2	Group 3
Age	Method of suicide	Trigger for suicide
Sex	Anatomical location of trauma	Past attempts
Race	Organ affected	Suicide note
Marital status	Toxicology results	Search for supplementary information
Time of suicide	Pre-existing medical conditions	
Day of the week		
Place		

cal location and sex—to name just a few. The investigation can compare the method used to the type of information obtained via books or from the Web.

One example of a multiple comparison is to examine the age of the victim and the methods used. Table 8.13 shows victims' ages grouped into 10-year intervals and the methods used to commit suicide collected over a 10-year period. The analysis of the data shows that the use of firearms occurred among individuals under the age of 51, while deaths by smothering are more frequent over the age of 60. Future analysis would separate this table by sex and race.

Forensic epidemiological investigators also are interested in the characteristics of the victim and methodology of suicide over time; this is trend analysis. If the characteristics of the population change, new legislation is enacted, or other external factors are introduced to a specific location, do they have any positive or negative effect on the individual or methods used to commit suicide?

Advantages and Limitations of the Forensic Epidemiological Investigation of Suicides

The major advantage in researching deaths by suicide is that most ME/C offices conduct a forensic investigation into the death and collect a large amount of data; in most jurisdictions, the police also carry out an investigation. The available information from the ME/C records can provide researchers with basic epidemiological data, a narrative of the circumstances surrounding the death, toxicological analysis, and detailed information about the mechanism of death.

The main limitation is that a significant number of individuals that commit suicide undergo an external-only forensic examination, which does not provide anatomical, gross, or microscopic examination of the internal organs. Table 8.14 shows the ratio of complete to external-only examination based on mechanism of death. Among individuals that die from hanging, the ratio is 1:2.4—for every victim that undergoes a complete autopsy, 2.4 victims will receive an external-only examination.

Table 8.13 Mechanisms of Suicide by Age of Suicide Victim

Mechanism	Age range									Total number (%)
	11–20	21–30	31–40	41–50	51–60	61–70	71–80	81–90	91–100	
Firearm injuries	46	128	145	117	69	67	88	34	2	696 (48)
Stabbing/ incised wounds	0	4	5	4	4	6	7	1	0	31 (2)
Hanging	19	60	76	43	23	18	10	8	3	260 (18)
Smothering	0	1	5	3	2	5	6	3	5	30 (2)
Carbon monoxide poisoning/ smoke inhalation	1	22	45	26	17	16	11	4	0	142 (10)
Drug overdose	5	23	44	43	20	14	10	4	0	163 (11)
Jump from a height	4	25	11	10	4	8	4	1	0	67 (5)
Drowning	3	5	13	8	8	5	2	0	1	45 (3)
Motor vehicle	0	0	4	0	0	0	0	0	0	4 (0.3)
Train	0	1	6	0	1	0	0	0	0	8 (0.6)
Total (%)	78 (5.4)	269 (18.6)	354 (24.5)	254 (17.5)	148 (10.2)	139 (9.6)	138 (9.5)	55 (3.8)	11 (0.8)	1,446 (100%)

Table 8.14   Ratio of Complete Autopsy to External-Only Examination Based on Suicide Method

Method	Ratio of complete autopsy to external-only examination
Firearm injuries	1:1.8
Stabbing/incised wounds	1:1.4
Hanging	1:2.4
Smothering	1:1.7
Carbon monoxide poisoning/smoke inhalation	1:3.3
Drug overdose	7.2:1
Jump from a height	2.4:1
Drowning	10.3:1
Train	7:1

Death by Homicide 9

Introduction

Among the many different manners of deaths investigated by the ME/C office, homicide cases are one type that typically go beyond the walls of the ME/C office and enters the legal and judicial systems. The information collected at the crime scene, the results of the autopsy, and the analysis of the forensic evidence must all have been identified, documented, and collected in a manner that conforms to established scientific principles and practices and also be admissible in a court of law. Every member of the ME/C staff involved in an investigation must understand and be trained in the proper procedures of collecting, processing, and analyzing the evidence as well as the principles of the chain of custody.

In this chapter we will define various types of homicide, number of fatalities, fundamentals of the ME/C investigation of a homicide, various mechanisms of homicide, and the methods used by a forensic epidemiologist to investigate and interpret homicide data. In addition, the features of the FBI's Uniform Crime Report (UCR), Supplementary Homicide Report (SHR), and the National Incident-Based Reporting System (NIBRS) will be delineated.

Definition

Homicide is defined as the killing of one human being by the act, procurement, or omission of another and the term applies to all such killings, whether criminal or not. Homicide is considered noncriminal in a number of situations, including deaths as the result of war and putting someone to death by the valid sentence of a court. Killing may also be legally justified or excused, as it is in cases of self-defense or when someone is killed by another person who is attempting to prevent a violent felony. Criminal homicide occurs when a person purposely, knowingly, recklessly, or negligently causes the death of another. Murder and manslaughter are both examples of criminal homicide.

Types of Homicide

Homicide is a neutral term. It merely describes the act and does not pronounce a judgment as to its moral or legal quality. There are instances when homicide may be committed without any criminal intent and without criminal consequences. Execution is homicide, but it is carried out as a lawful judicial sentence. Other noncriminal or justifiable homicides may include a homicide committed in self-defense or a police officer causing a homicide as the only possible means of arresting an escaping felon. Homicide is ordinarily classified in one of three ways: justifiable, excusable, or felonious.

Justifiable homicide is committed intentionally, but without any evil design or motive. It is also committed under such circumstances of necessity or duty as to render the act proper and relieve the party from any blame whatsoever. Justifiable homicides include self-defense, a killing to prevent the commission of a felony, or an execution carried out by the state.

Excusable homicide is the killing of another by misadventure or by self-defense. There may be an element of fault, error, or omission, but that element is so trivial that it is excused from the guilt of a felony. Excusable homicide is best defined as the unfortunate killing of another during the commission of a lawful act without any intention to hurt.

Felonious homicide is criminal homicide. It is the wrongful killing of a human being without justification or excuse. There are two degrees of criminal homicide: murder and manslaughter. Murder is further subdivided into first, second, and third degrees. There are two degrees of manslaughter: voluntary and involuntary.

First-degree murder is the intentional killing of a human being. It is characterized by a plan or lying in wait. First-degree murder lacks spontaneity.

Second-degree murder is committed when the slayer is the principal or an accomplice in the perpetration of a felony. It is more commonly known as "felony murder." There exists an intention to carry out the felony, but not the intention to commit the murder. Examples may include the killing of another human being during a bank robbery or the death of a person as the result of arson.

Third-degree murder is simply all other kinds of homicides that cannot be categorized as intentional or as having been committed during the commission of a felony.

Voluntary manslaughter is the killing of a person without lawful justification while acting under sudden and intense passion resulting from a serious provocation by the individual killed. A person may also be guilty of voluntary manslaughter if another is killed with the unreasonable belief that the killing is justified. For example, a person may kill another while under the mistaken and unreasonable belief that self-defense is necessary to protect himself or herself.

Involuntary manslaughter is the death of another as the direct result of an unlawful act carried out in a reckless and grossly negligent manner. Additionally, a lawful act conducted in a reckless or grossly negligent manner that results in the death of another may give rise to the determination of involuntary manslaughter.

Fatalities

The homicide rate in the United States has fluctuated over the years from an annual low during the 1950s and 1960s of around 5/100,000 to a peak in the 1980s of 10.2/100,000. This was followed by a fall in the early 1980s, which was followed by another rise in the 1990s and then a steady decline between 1992 and 2000. The most recent data show that the rate is slowly increasing. Homicide (U01, U02, X85–Y09, Y87.1) is the 15th leading cause of death within the United States, with a total of 18,124 deaths in 2005. A breakdown by sex and race showed that 14,376 males, 3,748 females, 8,770 whites, 8,669 blacks, and 9,354 other races were the victims of homicide. Homicide involving the use of a firearm comprised 12,352 of the total deaths. Table 9.1 shows homicide broken down using the ICD-10 codes and by sex and race.

Fundamentals of Homicide Death Investigation

Any crime scene is a site of interest but a homicide scene brings a massive response, first by emergency medical services (EMS) and fire personnel, and then law enforcement, the always present news media, and lastly by the ME/C

Table 9.1 Homicides Broken Down Using the ICD-10 Codes and by Sex and Race

Cause of death	Total	Male	Female	White	Black	Other
Homicide by discharge of a firearm (U01.4, X93–X95)	12,352	10,561	1,791	5,266	6,703	383
Homicide by other and unspecified means and their sequelae (U01.0–U01.3, U01.5–U01.9, U02, X85–X92)	5,772	3,815	1,957	3,504	1,966	302

office. The moment the individual is pronounced dead, either at the scene or the hospital, the location where the criminal act occurred becomes a forensic crime scene and comes under the jurisdiction of the ME/C office. Nothing within that scene can be touched, moved, or manipulated in any way without first obtaining permission of the ranking ME/C personnel at the scene.

A typical scenario: the 911 dispatcher receives a call of a man lying unresponsive on the street. The first to arrive at the scene, the first responder, is usually a patrol officer, emergency medical technician (EMT), or paramedic, who determines whether the victim is alive or dead on arrival (DOA). If the victim is beyond medical treatment emergency medical services will pronounce the victim and his or her role, aside from completing a trip sheet, is complete.

At this point, the role of the police officer is to radio in a request for the ME/C office and a supervisor, typically a homicide detective, to respond to the scene. The news media regularly monitor the police, fire, and emergency channels so they also dispatch a news crew to the scene. The role of the police officer is to ensure that a large enough area around the crime scene has been roped off and to prevent unauthorized personnel from entering the now controlled crime scene. The determination of the size of the crime scene is critical; if the area is too small, vital evidence may be lost or contaminated. Upon arrival, the ME/C personnel interview the officer as to what he or she saw and what actions he or she took after arriving at the scene. The police officer is allowed to leave the scene when relieved by superior officers or by homicide detectives.

The investigation of a homicide is conducted by both law enforcement and the ME/C office. The homicide investigators are responsible for collecting information by interviewing the victim's family, friends, and co-workers; additionally, they may canvass the neighborhood for additional leads. They will compare the characteristics of this crime to others on file, searching for any similarities; identify possible suspects; conduct interviews; and make arrests. The role of the death investigator is to identify, document, and collect forensic evidence at the scene; to ensure that the evidence does not degrade or become contaminated; and to maintain a chain of custody from the crime scene to submission to the crime laboratory.

Upon arriving at the scene, the death investigator will first take a quick survey in order to determine the level of investigation and equipment required to process the scene. If necessary, a mobile crime unit will be called to the scene. This van contains basic equipment such as gloves, booties, masks, biohazard suits, and floodlights—as well as a wide range of equipment to collect blood, body fluids, hair, fibers, fingerprints, impressions; document blood splatter; and determine bullet trajectories.

The first step of the death scene investigator is to document the scene. Before anything at the scene is altered or touched, it must be photodocumented by a crime scene forensic photographer. The photographer follows a specific protocol at the scene, first starting from a distance to provide perspective and then in a calculated and determined fashion drawing closer to the victim. For example, if a homicide occurred in the upstairs bedroom of a free-standing, two-story house, the photographing would start at the street level. Pictures would be taken up and down the street and from across the street; the house would be photographed from all four sides. Next, pictures would be taken of the house entryway and the stairs leading up to the bedroom, from the doorway leading to the bedroom, and then the bedroom from all four corners of the room. Multiple images of the victim would be taken to provide the forensic pathologist, homicide detective, and, later, the lawyers and jury with an accurate presentation of the crime scene. In addition to the photographs, measurements are taken between various objects, such as the distance between a victim and a possible weapon and the distance between victims and other objects at the scene.

Once the scene forensic photographer has completed the documentation, the death investigator can process the scene, beginning by surveying the scene for possible evidence such as fingerprints, impressions, body fluids, and other trace evidence that requires collection. The examination then switches to the body. The position of the body, the position and condition of the clothing, areas of trauma, the state of decomposition, and any smells are noted and any insects on or around the body are collected. The body is also examined for the presence of any trace evidence, which is collected at the scene to prevent loss during the body's transportation to the morgue. When a firearm is used, the victim's hands are placed in paper bags and secured to preserve any gunshot residue (GSR) evidence. Paper is used to prevent sweating (due to the fact that the body is still releasing heat) and to collect other trace evidence that may come loose from underneath the fingernails during transport. All physical and biological evidence collected at the crime scene by the forensic death investigators is submitted directly to the crime laboratory.

An internal core body temperature is taken at the scene by inserting a long thermometer through the skin at the lower right region of the abdomen into the liver. The same thermometer is also used to ascertain the ambient air temperature and then these two readings are used to make an estimation of the time of death. The normal body temperature is 98.6°F. Upon death, the body's internal temperature begins to decrease at a rate of 1.5°F per hour during the first 12 hours and then slows to a rate of 1°F per hour during the next 12–18 hours. At some point after death, the body's core temperature will equilibrate with the surrounding air temperature. However, many factors affect this process, including the layers and types of clothing, type of surface on which the victim is lying, immersion in water, sizes and types of injuries, and the health status of the individual. Core temperature is only one method to estimate time of death; the others include algor mortis and rigor mortis. The estimation of the postmortem interval can be significant in a trial. Once the body has been processed, it is then transferred onto a white sheet and placed into a body bag and transported to the morgue.

After arriving at the morgue, the body is placed on the stainless steel examination table where the victim is first photographed by an autopsy forensic photographer in the condition in which it arrived at the morgue. The body is photographed from head to toe, front to back, with multiple pictures of areas displaying injuries or trauma. The clothing is removed layer by layer by an autopsy technician and each piece is examined for evidence, described, and carefully documented. The clothing is then packaged up and delivered to the crime lab, where it will be examined for trace evidence and body fluids. Once all clothing has been removed, the body will be washed in cool water and the entire body is photographed again. Very often, homicide detectives are present during the autopsy. Evidence recovered during the forensic examination can include trace evidence (hair, fibers), ballistics (bullets and bullet fragments), and serological evidence such as saliva, semen, and blood—all of which are turned over to the crime lab for analysis.

The role of the forensic autopsy is to examine the body to determine the cause of death and the manner of death, supplemented by the information contained in the death investigation report, medical records, and police investigation reports. Forensic pathologists are frequently called upon to testify in a court of law as to how the cause of death was determined; the type of trauma and wounds observed; in the case of a shooting, the path of the bullets; what organs were affected; and, in cases of multiple injuries, which injury was the fatal one.

The identification, collection, and processing of evidence are important in all deaths; however, those related to a homicide have the added dimension that some or all of the evidence will be presented in a court of law. Photographic evidence is the most basic and most often used evidence collected relating to a homicide. With the ease of use and affordability of digital cameras, a large number of ME/C offices have switched from the traditional 35 mm camera to an all-digital format. In many offices, even the death investigators are equipped with a digital camera; thus, they can take photos at the scene and then return to the office and download the images immediately. This allows the forensic pathologist to view the scene and the position of the body prior to beginning of the autopsy.

Mechanism of Homicide

The type of evidence collected from the homicide scene varies and is dictated by the mechanism of the homicide. The methods used to carry out a homicide are endless; however, they can be divided into broad categories, such as distance killings via firearms or arson versus direct contact with the victim via stabbing, strangulation, and blunt force trauma. The biomechanics that

Table 9.2 Methods of Homicide and the Corresponding Mechanism That Causes Death

Method	Mechanism of death
Firearm	Damages vital organs (brain or heart)
Stabbing	Blood loss
Manual strangulation	Asphyxiation
Ligature strangulation	Asphyxiation
Drowning	Asphyxiation
Fire (arson)	Smoke inhalation/burns
Blunt force trauma	Damage to internal organs
Poisons	Organ failure

cause death vary by each method. Table 9.2 provides a number of methods of homicide and the mechanisms that cause such deaths.

Forensic Analysis by Method of Homicide

Homicide by Firearm

Among the numerous methods of committing homicides, the most frequently used weapon in the United States is a firearm. The forensic epidemiologist investigating deaths due to a firearm will have at least a basic understanding of the fundamental workings of a firearm, different types of firearms, features of the fired projectiles, characteristics of different firing distances, and the nature of the injury.

It is important to understand the basic sequence involved when a firearm is fired. First, the trigger is pulled, which causes the hammer to strike the back of the primer (a small cylinder containing lead styphnate, barium nitrates, and antimony sulfide). The impact of the hammer causes a small explosion; this in turn ignites the propellant, which expands and forces the bullet down and out of the barrel. In addition, to the bullet exiting the end of the barrel, small amounts of burned and partially burned propellants and components of the primer are also ejected. These particles are called gun shot residue (GSR) and they are useful in investigating deaths involving a firearm. Firearms can be divided into handguns, such as revolvers and pistols (automatics), and long rifles, which include shotguns, rifles, and assault weapons (AK-47, machine guns). The four types of firearms and some basic features are shown in Table 9.3.

A firearm discovered at a scene is unloaded and transported to the crime lab, where it is first sent to the latent fingerprint division to be dusted for fingerprints. The firearm is then submitted to the firearm or ballistics division

Table 9.3 Types of Firearms and Some Basic Features

	Revolver	Pistol (automatic)	Shotgun	Rifle	Assault rifle
Example	Smith & Wesson .45	Lugar 9mm	12 Gauge	30-30	AK-47
Capacity (rounds)	6	10-20	5	5-10	>30
Sequence to fire	Cock hammer → Pull trigger between each shot	Manually move the slide to the rear → automatically moves forward → ready to fire Pull trigger to fire each bullet	Level action: Drop level → raise level between each shot Bolt action: Draw bolt to the rear and then forward; then turn downward between each shot Pump action: Slide moved to the rear and then forward between each shot	Level action: Drop level → raise level between each shot Bolt action: Draw bolt to the rear and then forward; then turn downward between each shot Pump action: Slide moved to the rear and then forward between each shot	Semiautomatic Pull trigger between each shot Automatic: Continues to fire while the trigger is pulled
Anatomy of the bullet	Primer Propellant Bullet	Primer Propellant Bullet	Primer Propellant Wad Pellets/slug	Primer Propellant Bullet	Primer Propellant Bullet
Barrel	Land and grooves	Land and grooves	Smooth	Land and grooves	Land and grooves

of the crime laboratory. The firearm examiner is charged with examining the recovered firearm to determine whether it is operational and then the type, manufacturer, and serial number; determining the shooting distance between the victim and the actor; and analyzing the evidence colleted from the hands during the autopsy using an atomic absorption gunshot residue evidence collection kit. Bullets or bullet fragments recovered during the autopsy will be researched for the caliber of the bullets and the data regarding the bullet and cartridge casing data will be entered into the national forensic ballistics database known as the National Integrated Ballistics Information Network (NIBIN). This system allows for the matching of bullets or casings discovered at one crime scene to other crime scenes across all 50 states.

During the forensic autopsy, the role of the forensic pathologist is to determine the location of the entrance wound(s), path of each bullet, location of the exit wound(s), and the level of damage to the internal organs caused by each projectile. This information would be noted in great detail in the final pathological diagnosis report. During the autopsy, the body is x-rayed to help identify the location of bullets and fragments. In addition, the hands are checked for the presence of any GSR. The analysis of the firearm examination and the results of the GSR analysis are contained within the firearm examiner's report.

Special attention is paid to the entrance wound because of its forensic importance. Features around the entrance wound can be used to determine the distance of the end of the barrel from the victim and the positions of the actor and the victim at the time of the shooting. The size and shape of the entrance wound cannot be used to determine the caliber of the firearm.

Distance from the Victim

When an individual is shot, the determination of the distance between the shooter and the victim is critical. Statements made by the suspect are compared to scientific evidence presented by the firearm examiner. The ballistics examiner uses tell-tale physical markers at the entrance site to determine whether the shooter was (1) in direct contact, (2) in close proximity, or (3) a significant distance from the victim. The physical characteristics of these three types of shots are described in Table 9.4. Soot due to fine carbon particles around the entrance wound can easily be wiped off the skin. Tattooing is due to coarse particles of unburnt and partially burned powder being driven into the skin; it cannot be wiped off.

Homicide by Suffocation

Death by suffocation is caused by preventing oxygen from entering the lungs and methods include smothering, strangulation, and the use of a gag. Smothering is blocking the external airway, which includes the mouth and

Table 9.4 Physical Characteristics of Three Different Types of Gunshot Wounds

Wound type	Distance of barrel from skin	Muzzle impression on skin	Particles of the primer	Soot	Tattooing	Power residue
Contact	Against the skin	Yes	Located inside the body	Located inside the body	Located inside the body	Located inside the body
Close	≤18 inches from the skin	No	Disposed around the entrance wound	Disposed around the entrance wound	Disposed around the entrance wound	Disposed around the entrance wound
Distant	≥18 inches from the skin	No	No	No	No	No

nose; it is typically seen in deaths of infants and is accomplished by placing a pillow over the mouth and nose and pressing down. There is very little in the way of physical forensic evidence in these types of deaths. Smothering of adults may involve placing a plastic bag over the face.

Strangulation can be manual or by using some form of a ligature. Manual strangulation is when the victim's air supply is interrupted by an actor constricting the victim's neck with his or her hands. In the case of manual strangulation, the forensic pathologist examines the victim's neck region for signs of fingernail marks, areas of contusions, or bruises. In a ligature strangulation, the method involves encircling the neck with a cord, belt, or rope to interrupt the air exchange. In this case, the forensic examination looks for patterns left on the neck that can later be matched to the ligature used. A gag is any object, such as a rag, forced down the victim's throat or into the mouth that would block the internal airway.

Homicide by Fire

The causes of death associated with homicide using fire include suffocation by smoke inhalation, carbon monoxide poisoning, or from blunt force trauma injuries caused by falling debris. A fire can also serve as a cover to conceal a homicide that occurred elsewhere. The forensic pathologist plays a central role in determining whether the victim discovered in the ruins of a burned structure was alive or dead at the start of the fire. This involves a detailed examination of the airway, especially the mouth, throat, trachea, and lungs; toxicological evidence of soot will be found in the upper airway and the blood CO level will be elevated. If, on the other hand, the victim was dead at the start of the fire, the airways will be clear of soot and the level of CO in the blood will be zero.

Homicide by BFT

An injury that causes a disruption to the normal anatomical structure of any of the tissues of the body caused by the application of physical force to the body is known as blunt force trauma (BFT). BFT is caused by inflicting a significant amount of force by a hand, foot, or any object that results in significant injury to the body that immediately or subsequently causes death. BFT can be classified into (1) abrasions, (2) bruises or contusions, and (3) lacerations.

An abrasion is a superficial injury to the top few layers of the skin caused by friction or pressure between the skin and some rough object. Abrasions can be further classified into: (1) scratches, (2) grazes, and (3) imprints. A scratch is a linear injury produced by a sharp object, such as a fingernail running across the skin. A graze is an injury caused when a large area of skin slides or scrapes against a rough surface. An imprint or pressure abrasion is an injury produced as a result of direct impact with or pressure from an object that results in a reproduction of its shape and surface characteristics upon the skin.

A bruise is defined as an infiltration of blood into the tissues from the ruptured blood vessels as a result of the application of BFT. The hemorrhage into the skin may not be visible, especially among battered babies. In these cases, an incision must be made into the suspicious area to reveal the hemorrhage. As a general rule, infants, old people, women, and obese or alcoholic individuals with blood disorders bruise more easily than healthy individuals. Also, as greater force is used, bruising will be more extensive. Bruises are often associated with lacerations.

A laceration is BFT that causes the skin and underlying tissues to tear. The common characteristics of a laceration include ragged and irregular edges, bruising, abraded margins, cross-bridging, crushing of the underlying blood vessels, and deposit of foreign material in the wound. Lacerations can be classified into (1) split laceration (due to blunt perpendicular impacts), (2) stretch laceration (tangential impact), (3) avulsion (horizontal crushing impact), and (4) tears (irregularly directed impact).

Abrasions and bruises on the body can provide information of the site of impact, identification of the object inflicting the injury, the degree of the violence, cause and direction of the injury, and, to a limited degree, the age of the injury.

Homicide by Fear

Not all homicides produce a wound or a bruise or any type of visible trauma. Fear can be a method of killing. The act of deliberately pointing a shotgun at the face of an elderly homeowner at 3 a.m. during a robbery can induce a cardiac event resulting in death. The role of the forensic pathologist is to determine, to a degree of medical certainty, that the increased stress of that specific situation resulted in the cardiac event that caused the death.

Homicide by OD

Killing an individual by injecting him or her with a lethal level of a compound is investigated similarly to investigation of an accidental drug overdose. Body fluids are collected during the autopsy and, if the deceased received medical treatment, the hospital will send any fluids collected. (See Chapter 7 for a detailed review of the methods used to determine whether drugs contributed to a death.) The role of the ME/C is to determine that the cause of death was a lethal level of a drug. Once that has been established, the role of the law enforcement agencies is to prove that drugs were injected into the victim by someone other than the victim; even if the individual asked to be injected, the cause of death is homicide.

Homicide by Vehicle

Any object can be used to kill; one special category is homicide by vehicle, or vehicular homicide. The only difference between a vehicular homicide and other homicides is the use of a motorized vehicle as a weapon, as opposed to a gun or knife. This does not change in any way the elements required to be proved for murder. As long as the elements for murder can be proved, a vehicular homicide defendant can be tried for murder just as someone who uses a gun would be.

Vehicular homicide can be defined as the killing of a human being by the operation of an automobile, airplane, motorboat, or other motor vehicle in a manner that creates an unreasonable risk of injury to the person and constitutes a material deviation from the standard of care that a reasonable person would observe under the same circumstances. An individual commits vehicular homicide by (1) unintentionally causing death of another, or (2) operating a motor vehicle while intoxicated. All 50 states, except Arizona, Montana, Oregon, and Alaska, have vehicle-specific homicide statutes.

For example, in Georgia, homicide by vehicle is defined as the unlawful killing of another person using a vehicle. It does not require an intent to kill or malice aforethought or premeditation. This state has two degrees of vehicle homicide:

First-degree homicide by vehicle is a felony that, upon conviction, will result in a sentence of between 3 and 15 years of imprisonment with no parole for the first year. A first-degree homicide by vehicle includes a driver who unlawfully met or overtook a school bus, unlawfully failed to stop after a collision, was driving recklessly, was driving while under the influence of alcohol or drugs, failed to stop for or otherwise was attempting to flee from a law enforcement officer, or had previously been declared a habitual violator.

Second-degree homicide by vehicle is a misdemeanor that, upon conviction, will result in a sentence of up to 1 year or a fine of up to $1,000 (or both). A second-degree homicide by vehicle encompasses all other homicides by vehicle, involving any other violation of the law governing motor vehicles not classified as first-degree homicide.

Homicide by the State

The state has the ability to execute individuals after a jury of their peers has found them guilty of a capital crime punishable by death. The methods of state-sponsored execution have varied from burning at the stake during the eighteenth century to the civilized methods used today, which include lethal injection, electrocution, the gas chamber, hanging, and firing squad. After an execution, a physician must pronounce the individual dead, and then the body must undergo a forensic autopsy. The DC will list the manner of death as homicide. The following is a brief explanation of the current methods used to execute criminals in the United States.

Lethal Injection

The method most frequently used in the execution of inmates is lethal injection, which was first used in 1977. The inmate is injected with sodium thiopental, which puts him or her to sleep; this is followed by injection of Pavulon or pancuronium bromide, which stops respiration, and then potassium, which causes the heart to stop.

Electric Chair

The first electric chair was built in 1888. Once strapped to the chair, the inmate receives between 500 and 2,000 V over a 30-second period. At postmortem, the body is hot enough to blister someone who touches it, and the autopsy is delayed while the internal organs cool. There are third-degree burns with blackening where the electrodes met the skin of the scalp and legs, and the brain appears cooked in most cases.

Gas Chamber

In 1924, the use of the gas chamber was introduced as a more humane method of execution. The warden provides a signal to the executioner, who flicks a lever that releases crystals of sodium cyanide into a pail. This causes a chemical reaction that releases hydrogen cyanide gas. The inmate dies from hypoxia—the cutoff of oxygen to the brain. Prior to the postmortem, an exhaust fan sucks the poison air from the chamber, and the corpse is sprayed with ammonia to neutralize any remaining traces of cyanide. About half an hour after the execution, orderlies wearing gas masks and rubber gloves remove the victim. Their training manual advises them to ruffle the victim's hair to release any trapped cyanide gas before removal.

Firing Squad

The method of execution by firing squad was last used in 1996. In this method of execution, the inmate is typically bound to a chair with leather straps across the waist and head, in front of an oval-shaped canvas wall. A black hood is pulled over the head; a doctor locates the inmate's heart and pins a circular white cloth target over it. Five shooters, each armed with .30 caliber rifles loaded with single rounds, stand 20 ft from the inmate. One of the shooters is given a blank round. The prisoner dies as a result of blood loss caused by rupture of the heart or a large blood vessel, or tearing of the lungs. The person shot loses consciousness when shock causes a fall in the supply of blood to the brain.

Hanging

Hanging is still used in a number of states. The day before the execution, the inmate is weighed to determine the proper length of "drop" necessary to ensure a quick death. If the rope is too long, the inmate could be decapitated, and if it is too short, the strangulation could take as long as 45 minutes. The rope should be ¾ to 1¼ inches in diameter, and it must be boiled and stretched to eliminate springing or coiling and the knot lubricated with wax or soap "to ensure a smooth sliding action," according to the 1969 U.S. Army manual. Immediately before the execution, the prisoner's hands and legs are secured, the prisoner is blindfolded, and the noose is placed around the neck, with the knot behind the left ear. The execution takes place when a trapdoor is opened and the prisoner falls through. The prisoner's weight should cause a rapid fracture dislocation of the neck.

Delayed Homicide

The investigation into any death must determine the sequence of events that resulted in that death; in a number of rare cases, the initiating event occurred many years earlier. For example, a 35-year-old man dies from sepsis after 15 years of living in a long-term nursing home because he was a quadriplegic. The death investigator reviews the medical records from the nursing home in order to determine what caused the quadriplegia. Possible explanations for the conditions include a hunting accident or being shot during a burglary. If the records indicate that the condition was a result of a shooting that occurred 15 years ago, police records from that event will be obtained and reviewed. If the gunshot wounds occurred during the commission of a crime, the death will be investigated and ruled as a homicide and the key forensic evidence will focus on recovering the bullet.

The role of the forensic pathologist is to show, through the information contained within the medical records and the results of the autopsy, that the exact sequence of events from the time of the shooting is linked to the immediate cause of death. In this case, the man would not have developed a septic infection if he were not bedridden, he would not have been bedridden had he not been a quadriplegic, and he would not have become a quadriplegic had he not been shot in the back at the third cervical column of the spinal cord during a burglary.

Forensic Epidemiological Investigation of Homicide

The forensic epidemiological investigation of homicides can be explored in terms of *person, place, time,* and the *mechanism of death*. The homicide characteristics can be further examined by the relationship between the actor and the victim, illustrate hot spots, show the changing patterns of homicide, assist in the planning of resources, and assess the effectiveness of crime prevention programs. The basic epidemiological characteristics that will be collected in any forensic epidemiological investigation of homicides are shown in Table 9.5.

The basic epidemiological demographic personal characteristics that provide a profile of individuals that died from homicide include age, sex, race, marital status, and activity engaged in at the time of the homicide. These data are located in the DC or within the death investigation report. The yearly total of homicides that occurred in Allegheny County, Pennsylvania, between the years 1998 and 2005 is shown in Table 9.6 by sex and race. This type of information is commonly presented in this form because it is clear, concise, and easy to understand, and it can be used for multiple year comparisons. The data show that the total number of homicides for a county with a total population of 1.23 million remained fairly stable, with an average of 90 homicides per year.

The sudden increase that occurred in 2003 warrants further investigation. A detailed examination by sex and race showed the following: 73.6%

Table 9.5 Basic Data Collected on Homicide Deaths

Characteristic	Variables
Basic epidemiological features of the victim	Age
	Sex
	Race
	Marital status
	Occupant
Exact location of incident	Site address
Incident: location	Residence
	Street
	Vehicle
	Business
	School
	Open area
Incident: date, month, day of week	
Time/date of death	
Place of death	Scene
	Residence
	Hospital
Activity in which engaged	Working
	Leisure activity
	Illegal activity
Distance between actor and victim	By home residence
Relationship of actor to victim	Married
	Intimate partners
	Friends
	Co-workers
	Acquaintances
	Strangers
Mechanism of death	Firearm
	Penetration by a sharp object
	BFT
	Asphyxia
	Drugs
Core body temperature	
Number of victims	1, 2, 3, etc.
Victim 1: age, sex, race	
Victim 2: age, sex, race	
Basic epidemiological features of the actor	Age
	Sex
	Race

Table 9.6 Total Number of Homicides and Demographic Characteristics, Allegheny County, 1998–2005

	1998 Total (%)	1999 Total (%)	2000 Total (%)	2001 Total (%)	2002 Total (%)	2003 Total (%)	2004 Total (%)	2005 Total (%)	Grand total (%)
White male	20 (25.3)	17 (20.2)	20 (25.9)	15 (16.5)	17 (19.1)	14 (11.2)	9 (10.8)	8 (8.7)	120 (16.7)
White female	10 (12.7)	10 (11.9)	11 (14.3)	10 (11)	7 (7.9)	18 (14.4)	11 (13.2)	4 (4.3)	81 (11.2)
Black male	43 (54.4)	44 (52.4)	31 (40.3)	55 (60)	53 (59.5)	79 (63.2)	51 (61.1)	75 (81.5)	431 (59.9)
Black female	6 (7.6)	11 (13.1)	12 (15.6)	11 (12)	12 (13.5)	13 (10.4)	12 (14.5)	3 (3.3)	80 (11.1)
Other	—	2 (2.4)	3 (3.9)	—	—	1 (0.8)	—	2 (2.2)	8 (1.1)
Total	79	84	77	91	89	125	83	92	720
Total, white	30	27	31	25	24	32	20	12	201 (27.1%)
Total, black	49	55	43	66	65	92	63	78	511 (70.9%)
Total, male	63	61	51	70	70	93	60	83	551 (76.5%)
Total, female	16	21	23	21	19	31	23	7	161 (22.3%)

were black, 25.6% white, 74.4% male, and 24.8% female. The overall male-to-female ratio was 3.4:1.0 and the white-to-black ratio was 1:2.4. These basic demographic data can also be presented in different ways: in table forms, such as Table 9.6, or by using a graphic, such as Figure 9.1. Graphics have the advantage in that it is easier to present multiple years of data and to visualize trends using them. Figure 9.1 clearly shows that, during this time period, the number of homicides among white males steadily declined, slightly declined among white females, was in a steady state among black females, and increased strongly among black males.

Homicide victims can be described by age, and the age can be divided into age bracketing, typically using 5- or 10-year intervals. The CDC used the following parameters: <1 year, 1–4, 5–14, 15–24, 25–34, 35–44, 45–54, 55–64, 65–74, 75–85, and ≥85 years. Table 9.7 shows the breakdown of 2005 homicide victims by age, sex, and race. Note that the age grouping used in Table 9.7 was a finer separation of the ages than that used by the CDC. This type of breakdown allows finer pinpointing of the age range of individuals most at risk that are the target of intervention programs. The table shows that the majority of victims were between 15 and 29 years old.

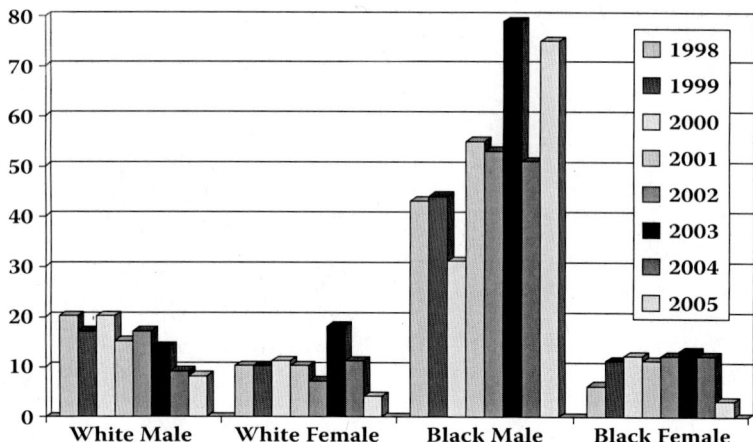

Figure 9.1 Total number of homicides by sex and race, Allegheny County, 1998–2005.

Table 9.7 All Homicides by Age, Sex, and Race, 2005

Age	White male	White female	Black male	Black female	Total
15–19	—	—	17	—	17
20–24	3	1	20	—	24
25–29	—	—	16	—	16
30–34	1	1	7	—	9
35–39	—	—	5	1	6
40–44	1	—	4	1	6
45–49	2	—	3	—	5
50–54	—	—	2	—	2
55–59	1	1	—	—	2
60–64	—	1	1	1	3
Total	8	4	75	3	92*

* Two other: 18-year old mulatto female; 23-year old Asian male.

Marital status is another personal feature that can be examined. It may be obtained from the DC or the death investigation report and divided into single, living with significant other, married, divorced, or widowed. The marital status can be examined by age, sex, and race. Questions that should be explored include whether marital status has any impact on being a victim of homicide or whether a relationship increases or decreases the likelihood of being a murdered.

Another feature of the individual's characteristics examined is the activity in which the victim was engaged at the time of the event. The class of activities includes working, leisure time activity, or illegal activity. The accuracy of this determination is in some degree subjective. For example, a group of teens is hanging out at a corner at 4:00 a.m. on a Wednesday; a car drives by and two of the teens are shot dead. The death can be ruled as a drug-related death, gang-related death, or simply a drive-by shooting. To determine the most likely cause for the death, the forensic epidemiologist will explore several sources of information that can include the death investigation report, police arrest report, and court transcripts, if available. Table 9.8 presents the activity that most likely was occurring just prior to the homicide. Presented with these types of data, a forensic epidemiologist should first attempt to ascertain whether any of the older cases (1997–2002) listed as under investigation have resulted in arrest. Also, attempts should be made to collect more information about those cases listed as "found on street."

The activity of the victim can also be examined by occupation. Not all homicide victims get killed during their off hours while engaged in criminal or marginally criminal activity. If an individual is killed while working, the death is classified not only as a homicide but also as an industrial death. The determination of whether a homicide occurred during work can be ascertained by examining part 30c of the DC, which will also provide the type of work in which the individual was employed (part 11a of the DC). Occupations can be divided into general types and then further into the exact job title. They may be classified as unskilled labor, skilled labor, service industry, management/administration, technical, professional, and executive. The exact job title and a description of the work can be obtained by reviewing the death investigation report or the police report. Questions that could be investigated include what the most dangerous occupation is, what places them at this increased risk, or what kinds of changes could be put in place to reduce the risk. Cases that should also be examined in greater detail include homicides that involved law enforcement personnel, domestic-related homicides, and those related to drug and gang activity.

Homicides can be explored in terms of location, which can be expanded in five ways: (1) the exact street address; (2) the township, borough, or municipality; (3) a physical description of the location; (4) the exact location within a structure; and (5) the distance between the victim's residence and the location of the homicide. The exact location (street address) where the homicide occurred can be found on the DC, in the ME/C report, and in the police reports. Some ME/C offices are now using GPS units to mark the exact location of victims. This method is very beneficial in pinpointing the locations of victims when no permanent landmarks are in close proximity to the body—especially in a wooded area or open highway or when bones are discovered scattered over a large area or open field.

This exact street location can be used to determine the specific municipality or township in which the homicide occurred, to plot the number of homicides within each given municipality, to show plot trend, and to differentiate the profile of homicide by method, age, sex, and race of the victims in

Table 9.8 Activity prior to Homicide, Allegheny County, 1997–2005

Activity	1997	1998	1999	2000	2001	2002	2003	2004	2005
Drug related	6	15	15	30	10	11	13	24	9
Gang related	6	1	10	—	4	6	3	—	1
Bar fight	—	—	—	1	—	6	—	—	—
At a party	—	—	—	1	—	1	1	—	1
Robbery	13	8	3	4	4	5	4	9	4
Carjacking	—	—	1	—	—	—	—	—	—
Over money	—	—	—	—	1	3	3	—	3
Drive-by shooting	8	8	2	1	4	1	4	3	3
Found on street	—	—	—	—	—	—	—	—	19
Found in car	—	—	—	—	—	—	—	—	9
Neighbor dispute	1	1	—	—	1	—	—	—	—
Law enforcement	1	4	2	2	2	1	1	—	5
Assailant (stranger)	—	20	11	2	—	17	5	14	12
Sexual assault	1	—	1	1	—	—	1	1	—
Arson	1	—	1	5	5	—	2	—	—
Racial killing	—	—	—	7	—	—	—	—	—
Sex related	—	—	—	—	2	—	—	—	—
Argument with friend	—	3	7	—	—	1	6	—	6
Altercation	—	—	—	7	7	—	2	—	—
Shaken baby syndrome	—	—	—	1	—	—	—	—	—
Overdose	—	—	—	—	2	—	1	—	—
Domestic dispute	15	16	16	12	18	18	26	17	6
Witness to homicide	1	—	—	—	—	1	—	—	—
Over clothing	1	—	—	—	—	1	—	—	—
Birth by midwife	—	—	—	—	—	1	—	—	—
Babysitter	1	—	—	—	—	1	—	—	—
Structure collapse	1	—	—	—	—	1	—	—	—
Playing w/gun	2	—	—	—	—	2	1	1	—
Under investigation	20	3	15	3	31	12	16	14	14
Total	78	79	84	77	91	89	125	83	92

each municipality. A map similar to the one shown in Figure 9.2 can be used to display the total number of homicides in each municipality by the actual number of cases or by different colors. To show trend data, at least 5 years' worth of data is required. A separate map is required for each year. On each map, the locations and the number of homicides should be plotted; then, the locations over the time period should be compared. Police agencies would find this type of information very useful.

The location of the homicide site should be described first in general terms, such as primary residence, friend's residence, business, warehouse, parked car, open field, or street corner. Using this information, data tables

Death by Homicide

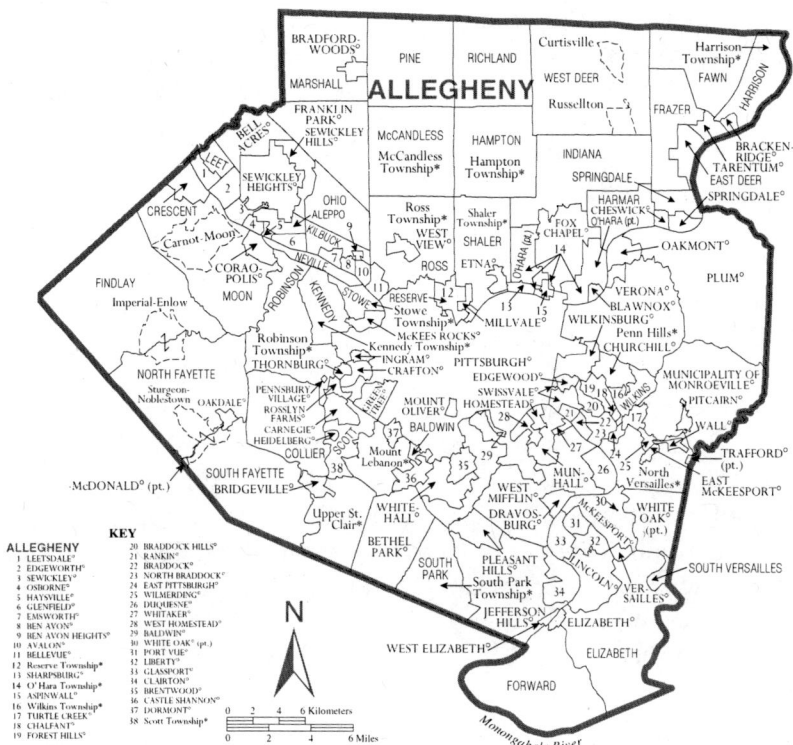

Figure 9.2 Map of Allegheny County.

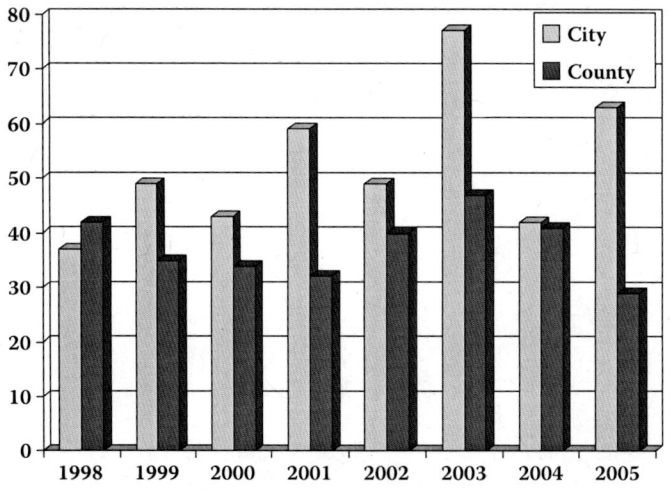

Figure 9.3 Total number of homicides by jurisdiction, 1998–2005.

will be created highlighting the most likely location for a murder to occur. Then, researchers can go from a general to a more specific description of the location, such as floor in bedroom of victim's residence, basement, vice president's office, third floor of abandoned warehouse, backseat of SUV, or at the corner of 5th Avenue and Brown Street.

Homicides can be explored in terms of time, which can be expanded to an examination of the number each month by the day of the week and the time the homicide occurred. Homicides can be displayed in terms of the numbers that occurred each month. The goal is to determine whether any yearly pattern emerges. The presentation shown in Table 9.9 allows easy yearly comparisons. The number of homicides per month over this 9-year period in Allegheny County appears to vary from year to year, illustrating the difficulty in predicting homicides (Table 9.9). Questions to be investigated include whether homicides increase around certain holidays or whether an association exists between homicide rates and colder months. More elaborate analysis can compare the types of homicides committed during each month.

The number of homicides can be examined by the day of the week the homicide was committed. Table 9.10 shows this for Allegheny County from 1997 to 2005. One would believe that a higher percentage of homicides occurred over the weekend period than during the week; however, the data shown in Table 9.10 do not appear to support that hypothesis strongly.

Homicides can also be examined concerning the time the event occurred. The data displayed in Table 9.11 show that a high percentage occurred during the early morning hours. Examination of this phenomenon can consist of comparing the type of homicide by time of the day, the

Table 9.9 Homicides by Month of Occurrence, Allegheny County, 1997–2005

Month	1997	1998	1999	2000	2001	2002	2003	2004	2005
January	11	7	8	6	9	6	10	13	6
February	4	7	4	7	9	7	5	5	7
March	6	8	5	7	4	5	14	5	6
April	8	5	11	9	8	5	4	6	5
May	5	10	11	1	11	11	9	7	7
June	4	9	6	7	9	8	16	5	9
July	6	2	3	11	8	5	3	8	10
August	3	7	1	5	12	4	21	5	9
September	10	5	7	7	8	11	13	3	9
October	6	6	7	4	4	6	14	13	8
November	6	4	10	7	5	14	7	5	5
December	9	9	11	6	4	7	9	8	11
Total	78	79	84	77	91	89	125	83	92

Table 9.10 Day of the Week on Which Homicide Occurred, Allegheny County, 1997–2005

Day	1997	1998	1999	2000	2001	2002	2003	2004	2005
Monday	5	11	11	13	11	10	18	12	11
Tuesday	13	10	14	7	8	7	23	13	13
Wednesday	10	10	9	7	14	12	15	14	12
Thursday	10	12	15	9	16	13	16	8	15
Friday	9	11	9	20	14	18	18	7	13
Saturday	16	11	15	14	14	20	14	18	8
Sunday	15	14	11	7	14	9	21	11	20
Total	78	79	84	77	91	89	125	83	92

Table 9.11 Time of Day When Homicide Was Committed, Allegheny County, 1998–2005

Time	1998	1999	2000	2001	2002	2003	2004	2005
12:01 a.m.–04:00 a.m	26	19	17	33	23	38	16	28
04:01 a.m.–08:00 a.m	8	14	9	10	7	12	8	6
08:01 a.m.–12:00 p.m	5	6	10	8	12	14	4	10
12:01 p.m.–04:00 p.m	12	10	11	8	9	13	19	12
04:01 p.m.–08:00 p.m	12	16	11	10	15	19	14	18
08:01 p.m.–12:00 a.m	16	19	19	22	23	29	22	18
Total	79	84	77	91	89	125	83	92

relationship between the victim and actor by time, and the location by time. Questions include: Do domestic-related homicides occur more frequently during the early morning hours? What role does alcohol play in the time of the homicide?

One note of caution when examining the time of the homicide is to ensure that the time of the homicide rather than the time of death is obtained. Although the vast majority of deaths occur at the scene, some individuals survive for hours, days, or even years after the event.

Homicides can be examined by the relationship between the personal characteristics of the victim and the actor; Table 9.12 displays this comparison. The sex of the victim can be obtained from the DC or the death investigation report and that of the actor can be obtained from police arrest reports. Among the cases where the sexes of the victim and actor are known, the majority were both male. When no arrests have been made, the sex of the actor is unknown and the forensic epidemiologist must expect a delay in the identification of the actor. In addition, older cases must be reviewed again to ascertain whether an arrest was made.

The relationship between the race of the victim and the attacker is shown in Table 9.13; the majority of homicides occurs among individuals of similar

Table 9.12 Sex of Actor Compared to That of Homicide Victim, Allegheny County, 1998–2004

Victim's sex	Actor's sex	1998 Number	1999 Number	2000 Number	2001 Number	2002 Number	2003 Number	2004 Number
Male	Male	23	12	30	34	29	37	16
Female	Male	9	10	17	11	15	18	16
Male	Female	1	2	2	2	2	5	—
Female	Female	2	1	1	2	—	1	—
Male	Unknown	37	48	19	28	26	50	36
Female	Unknown	4	10	3	6	3	9	3
Unknown	Unknown	—	1	—	—	—	—	—
Unknown	Male	—	—	—	—	—	1	—
Female	Multiple	1	—	1	2	2	3	4
Male	Multiple	2	—	4	6	12	1	8
Total		79	84	77	91	89	125	83

Table 9.13 Race of Actor Compared to That of Homicide Victim, Allegheny County, 1998–2004

Victim's race	Actor's race	1998 Number	1999 Number	2000 Number	2001 Number	2002 Number	2003 Number	2004 Number
White	Asian	—	—	1	—	—	—	1
Black	Black	14	9	28	32	37	36	27
White	Black	6	1	6	5	3	5	4
Hispanic	Hispanic	—	1	—	—	—	—	—
Hispanic	Black	—	—	—	—	—	1	—
White	Hispanic	—	1	—	1	—	—	1
Black	White	2	1	1	1	1	4	—
White	White	13	8	17	16	17	18	9
Asian	White	—	—	3	—	—	—	—
Black	Unknown	33	45	16	33	27	51	36
Unknown	Unknown	—	1	—	—	—	—	—
White	Unknown	11	17	5	3	4	8	4
Black	White/black	—	—	—	—	—	1	—
White	White/black	—	—	—	—	—	1	1
Total		79	84	77	91	89	125	83

race. These figures reflect that, most of the time, the race of the actor is unknown because no arrest has been made.

The next relationship that can be examined is the status of the relationship between the victim and the actor. This may be broken down into married, dating, boy-/girlfriend, family, friend, co-worker, acquaintance, or stranger.

The mechanism used to kill an individual can be obtained directly from the DC and the technique of presenting the data is by method of homicide or by the mechanism. Table 9.14 shows the data for homicide cases in Allegheny County over a 6-year period. The presentation has some errors in it that mixes method and mechanism in reporting the data. For example, arson is a method, but smoke inhalation is a mechanism, and BFT and strike/hit with an object both describe a similar mechanism.

Forensic epidemiologists must be aware of the different types of forensic evidence associated with different mechanisms of homicide. Table 9.15 illustrates some of the types of forensic evidence collected by mechanism of death.

Table 9.14 Methods Used to Commit Homicide, Allegheny County, 2000–2005

Method	2000 Total (%)	2001 Total (%)	2001 Total (%)	2003 City/county	2004 Total	2005 City/county
Asphyxia by plastic bag	—	1 (1.1)	—	—/1	—	—
Asphyxiation	—	—	3 (3.4)	2/1	—	—
Compression of neck	—	—	—	—/2	—	—
BFT	—	—	—	10/6	4	—
Beating by hands	6 (7.8)	9 (9.9)	8 (8.9)	—	—	—
Struck/hit w/object	—	1 (1.1)	4 (4.5)	—	—	—
Strangulation	2 (2.6)	1 (1.1)	1 (1.1)	1/1	1	—
OD	1 (1.3)	2 (2.2)	—	—/1	—	—
Gunshot	52 (70.9)	66 (72.5)	63 (70.8)	49/29	68	56/23
Carbon monoxide poisoning	—	—	—	2/—	—	—
Stabbing	8 (10.4)	6 (6.6)	9 (10.1)	10/3	9	8/5
Smoke inhalation	—	5 (5.5)	—	2/1	—	—
Maternal assault	—	—	—	—	—	—
Exsanguination	—	—	1 (1.1)	—	—	—
Arson	5 (6.5)	—	—	—	—	—
Thermal burns	1 (1.3)	—	—	—	—	—
Shaken baby syndrome	1 (1.3)	—	—	—	—	—
Starvation	—	—	—	—/1	—	—
Therapeutic termination of pregnancy	—	—	—	—/1	—	—
Physical sexual abuse	—	—	—	—	1	—
ASCVD	1 (1.3)	—	—	1/1	—	—
Total	77	91	89	77/48	83	64/28

Table 9.15 Forensic Evidence Collected by Mechanism of Death

Mechanism	Forensic evidence
Firearm	Firearm: type, caliber, manufacturer
	Bullets: types, number shot
	Casing: types, number discovered
	Features of the entrance wound
	Path
	Exit
	Organs affected
	GSR
Stabbing	Knife: number, type, dimensions
	Trace evidence: blood
	Blood splatter
	Number of stab wounds
	Organs affected
Asphyxiation	Ligature
BFT	Contusions
	Fractures
	Object causing trauma
Drowning	Diatoms
Arson	CO level
	Accelerants
	Soot in airway
Assault	DNA
	Trace evidence

National Violence Data Reporting System

National Databases

Typically, forensic epidemiologists working at an ME/C or a health department examine homicide data at a local level. However, they are often asked to compare their local homicide characteristics with those of other counties, states, or the nation as a whole. Several national data reporting systems collect and analyze homicides in the United States. These include the FBI's Uniform Crime Report (UCR), the Supplementary Homicide Report (SHR), the National Incident-Based Reporting System (NIBRS), and the National Violence Data Reporting System. The forensic epidemiologist must be aware of the limitations of each type of database.

FBI Uniform Crime Report (UCR)

The FBI has been operating the UCR program since the 1930s. The initial primary objective of the program was to generate information for use in law enforcement administration, operation, and management; however, over the

Death by Homicide

years, these data have become a source for criminologists, sociologists, legislators, and other researchers. Law enforcement agencies collect and submit information to the FBI monthly. The UCR gathers offense data on violent and property crimes but does not contain all crimes reported to the police. Rather, it only contains information on those crimes listed in part I and part II of the UCR. Part I offenses are only counted if the offense is reported to the police and police record (see Table 9.16). Offenses listed in part II are only counted if a person has been arrested and charged with a listed crime (Table 9.17).

The UCR is a summary-based measure of crime; this means that it presents the homicide as a summary or total crime count reports for individuals in a city, state, or county. The FBI is using the collected data from the UCR to publish an annual report titled "Crime in the United States."

The UCR has five main weaknesses that must be understood:

1. It does not count all crimes but only those listed in parts I and II.
2. Each state has different operational definitions of a crime.
3. The UCR data reported to the FBI come from information submitted by local law enforcement agencies, resulting in a great level of inconsistency between reporting agencies with the possibility of missing data.
4. There are technical insufficiencies of the reporting agencies in the form of staffing shortages to collect and enter the data and aging computer systems incapable of submitting the information.
5. The most serious weakness is the hierarchy rule to classify crimes. If there are two or more crimes committed by the same individual, only the most serious crime is counted. Hierarchy rule governs multiple-offense reporting. If more than one crime was committed by the same person or group of persons and the time and space intervals separating the crimes were insignificant, then the crime highest in the hierarchy is the only offense reported. For example, a person commits burglary + rape + grand theft auto; in this case, only the rape charge is counted in the UCR report. During the trial, all the charges will be adjudicated.

Supplementary Homicide Report (SHR)

The SHR began in 1961 as a supplement to the UCR. Local law enforcement agencies provided detailed information on homicide cases only. The supplemental data about homicide incidents are submitted monthly with details on location, victim, and offender characteristics. These reports include information on the month and year of an offense; on the reporting agency and its residential population, county and metropolitan statistical area (MSA)

Table 9.16 List of Part I Offenses of the UCR

Part I offenses of the UCR

Criminal homicide

a.) Murder and non-negligent manslaughter: the willful (non-negligent) killing of one human being by another. Deaths caused by negligence, attempts to kill, assaults to kill, suicides, and accidental deaths are excluded. The Program classifies justifiable homicides separately and limits the definition to: (1) the killing of a felon by a law enforcement officer in the line of duty; or (2) the killing of a felon, during the commission of a felony, by a private citizen. b.) Manslaughter by negligence: the killing of another person through gross negligence. Deaths of persons due to their own negligence, accidental deaths not resulting from gross negligence, and traffic fatalities are not included in the category Manslaughter by Negligence.

Forcible rape

The carnal knowledge of a female forcibly and against her will. Rapes by force and attempts or assaults to rape, regardless of the age of the victim, are included. Statutory offenses (no force used—victim under age of consent) are excluded.

Robbery

The taking or attempting to take anything of value from the care, custody, or control of a person or persons by force or threat of force or violence and/or by putting the victim in fear.

Aggravated assault

An unlawful attack by one person upon another for the purpose of inflicting severe or aggravated bodily injury. This type of assault usually is accompanied by the use of a weapon or by means likely to produce death or great bodily harm. Simple assaults are excluded.

Burglary (breaking or entering)

The unlawful entry of a structure to commit a felony or a theft. Attempted forcible entry is included.

Larceny-theft (except motor vehicle theft)

The unlawful taking, carrying, leading, or riding away of property from the possession or constructive possession of another. Examples are thefts of bicycles, motor vehicle parts and accessories, shoplifting, pocket-picking, or the stealing of any property or article that is not taken by force and violence or by fraud. Attempted larcenies are included. Embezzlement, confidence games, forgery, check fraud, etc. are excluded.

Motor vehicle theft

The theft or attempted theft of a motor vehicle. A motor vehicle is self-propelled and runs on land surface and not on rails. **Motorboats, construction equipment, airplanes, and farming equipment are specifically excluded from this category.**

Arson

Any willful or malicious burning or attempt to burn, with or without intent to defraud, a dwelling house, public building, motor vehicle or aircraft, personal property of another, etc.

Table 9.17 List of Part II Offenses of the UCR

Part II offenses of the UCR

The Part II offenses, for which only arrest data are collected[, include]

Other assaults (simple)
Assaults and attempted assaults which are not of an aggravated nature and do not result in serious injury to the victim. Stalking, intimidation, coercion, and hazing are included.

Forgery and counterfeiting
The altering, copying, or imitating of something, without authority or right, with the intent to deceive or defraud by passing the copy or thing altered or imitated as that which is original or genuine; or the selling, buying, or possession of an altered, copied, or imitated thing with the intent to deceive or defraud. Attempts are included.

Fraud
The intentional perversion of the truth for the purpose of inducing another person or other entity in reliance upon it to part with something of value or to surrender a legal right. Fraudulent conversion and obtaining of money or property by false pretenses. Confidence games and bad checks, except forgeries and counterfeiting, are included.

Embezzlement
The unlawful misappropriation or misapplication by an offender to his/her own use or purpose of money, property, or some other thing of value entrusted to his/her care, custody, or control.

Stolen property: buying, receiving, possessing
Buying, receiving, possessing, selling, concealing, or transporting any property with the knowledge that it has been unlawfully taken, as by burglary, embezzlement, fraud, larceny, robbery, etc. Attempts are included.

Vandalism
To willfully or maliciously destroy, injure, disfigure, or deface any public or private property, real or personal, without the consent of the owner or person having custody or control by cutting, tearing, breaking, marking, painting, drawing, covering with filth, or any other such means as may be specified by local law. Attempts are included.

Weapons: carrying, possessing, etc.
The violation of laws or ordinances prohibiting the manufacture, sale, purchase, transportation, possession, concealment, or use of firearms, cutting instruments, explosives, incendiary devices, or other deadly weapons. Attempts are included.

Prostitution and commercialized vice
The unlawful promotion of or participation in sexual activities for profit, including attempts. To solicit customers or transport persons for prostitution purposes; to own, manage, or operate a dwelling or other establishment for the purpose of providing a place where prostitution is performed; or to otherwise assist or promote prostitution.

Sex offenses (except forcible rape, prostitution, and commercialized vice)
Offenses against chastity, common decency, morals, and the like. Incest, indecent exposure, and statutory rape are included. Attempts are included.

Drug abuse violations
The violation of laws prohibiting the production, distribution, and/or use of certain controlled substances. The unlawful cultivation, manufacture, distribution, sale, purchase, use, possession, transportation, or importation of any controlled drug or narcotic substance.

Table 9.17 List of Part II Offenses of the UCR (continued)

Part II offenses of the UCR

Drug abuse violations

Arrests for violations of state and local laws, specifically those relating to the unlawful possession, sale, use, growing, manufacturing, and making of narcotic drugs. The following drug categories are specified: opium or cocaine and their derivatives (morphine, heroin, codeine); marijuana; synthetic narcotics; manufactured narcotics that can cause true addiction (Demerol, methadone); and dangerous non-narcotic drugs (barbiturates, Benzedrine).

Gambling

To unlawfully bet or wager money or something else of value; assist, promote, or operate a game of chance for money or some other stake; possess or transmit wagering information; manufacture, sell, purchase, possess, or transport gambling equipment, devices, or goods; or tamper with the outcome of a sporting event or contest to gain a gambling advantage.

Offenses against the family and children

Unlawful nonviolent acts by a family member (or legal guardian) that threaten the physical, mental, or economic well-being or morals of another family member and that are not classifiable as other offenses, such as Assault or Sex Offenses. Attempts are included.

Driving under the influence

Driving or operating a motor vehicle or common carrier while mentally or physically impaired as the result of consuming an alcoholic beverage or using a drug or narcotic.

Liquor laws

The violation of state or local laws or ordinances prohibiting the manufacture, sale, purchase, transportation, possession, or use of alcoholic beverages, not including driving under the influence and drunkenness. Federal violations are excluded.

Drunkenness

To drink alcoholic beverages to the extent that one's mental faculties and physical coordination are substantially impaired. Driving under the influence is excluded.

Disorderly conduct

Any behavior that tends to disturb the public peace or decorum, scandalize the community, or shock the public sense of morality.

Vagrancy

The violation of a court order, regulation, ordinance, or law requiring the withdrawal of persons from the streets or other specified areas; prohibiting persons from remaining in an area or place in an idle or aimless manner; or prohibiting persons from going from place to place without visible means of support.

All other offenses

All violations of state or local laws not specifically identified as Part I or Part II offenses, except traffic violations.

Suspicion

Arrested for no specific offense and released without formal charges being placed.

Curfew and loitering laws (persons under age 18)

Violations by juveniles of local curfew or loitering ordinances.

Runaways (persons under age 18)

Limited to juveniles taken into protective custody under the provisions of local statutes.

codes, geographic division, and population group; on the age, race, and sex of victims and offenders; and on the victim/offender relationship, weapon use, and circumstance of the crime. Within the SHR, homicide is defined as murder and non-negligent manslaughter, which is the willful killing of one human being by another. The categories exclude deaths by negligence, suicide, and accident; justifiable homicides; and attempts to murder. Justifiable homicides are analyzed separately within the SHR.

The strength of the SHR is that it is an incident-based system. Therefore, it is possible to compare the relationship between victim and actor and to compare type of weapon used by relationship status. The most significant weakness of the SHR is the growing number of unsolved homicides, resulting in no offender information.

National Incident-Based Reporting System (NIBRS)

In 1982 the FBI and the Bureau of Justice Statistics (BJS) began a detailed review and revision of the UCR to meet the needs of the twenty-first century. The redesign resulted in the NIBRS, which collects data on each reported crime incident by capturing 56 data elements via six types of data groupings: administration, offense, victim, property, offender, and arrestee. Over the years, new data elements have been added. In 1990, bias-motivated offenses were added; gang activity was added in 1997 and law enforcement officers killed and assaulted in 2003. NIBRS data come from local, state, and federal law enforcement authorities to the FBI on each criminal incident involving 46 specific offenses, including the eight part I crimes. Arrest information on the 46 offenses plus 11 lesser offenses is also provided in NIBRS.

The main advantage of the NIBRS is that it reports on each crime incident rather than reporting the total number of certain crimes for each specific law enforcement agency. The importance of shifting from aggregate numbers to reporting individual incidents is that a greater level of information is gained about the individual incident, the victim, the offender, and the offenses within each incident. Another advantage in the NIBRS over the UCR summary reporting system involves the hierarchy rule that governs multiple-offense reporting (see preceding section on the UCR). This rule is not used in the NIBRS. If more than one crime was committed by the same person or group of persons and the time and space intervals were insignificant, *all* of the crimes are reported as offenses within the same incident. An additional advantage of the NIBRS system over the UCR is the addition of the category of "crimes against society" to the previous two: "crimes against persons" and "crimes against property." Table 9.18 lists the types of crimes reported to NIBRS: group A offenses, group B offenses, and those for which only arrest data are reported, in addition to those collected in part I (Table 9.19).

Table 9.18 List of Group A Offenses of the NIBRS

Group A offenses of the NIBRS
1. Arson
2. Assault offenses—aggravated assault, simple assault, intimidation
3. Bribery
4. Burglary/breaking and entering
5. Counterfeiting/forgery
6. Destruction/damage/vandalism of property
7. Drug/narcotic offenses—drug/narcotic violations, drug equipment violations
8. Embezzlement
9. Extortion/blackmail
10. Fraud offenses—false pretenses/swindle/confidence game, credit card/automatic teller machine fraud, impersonation, welfare fraud, wire fraud
11. Gambling offenses—betting/wagering, operating/promoting/assisting gambling, gambling equipment violations, sports tampering
12. Homicide offenses—murder and non-negligent manslaughter, negligent manslaughter, justifiable homicide
13. Kidnapping/abduction
14. Larceny/theft offenses—pocket-picking, purse-snatching, shoplifting, theft from building, theft from coin-operated machine or device, theft from motor vehicle, theft of motor vehicle parts or accessories, all other larceny
15. Motor vehicle theft
16. Pornography/obscene material
17. Prostitution offenses—prostitution, assisting or promoting prostitution
18. Robbery
19. Sex offenses, forcible—forcible rape, forcible sodomy, sexual assault with an object, forcible fondling
20. Sex offenses, nonforcible—incest, statutory rape
21. Stolen property offenses (receiving, etc.)
22. Weapon law violations

Advantages and Limitations of Using ME/C Data and the DC

ME/C Data

ME/C offices contain a wealth of homicide data and present the best depository of information, secondary only to the transcripts of a court hearing. The main advantages include

Table 9.19 List of Group B Offenses of the NIBRS

Group B offenses of the NIBRS
1. Bad checks
2. Curfew/loitering/vagrancy violations
3. Disorderly conduct
4. Driving under the influence
5. Drunkenness
6. Family offenses, nonviolent
7. Liquor law violations
8. Peeping Tom
9. Runaway
10. Trespass of real property
11. All other offenses

1. a timely and complete list of homicide victims within a specific geographical area;
2. information on the basic epidemiological characteristics of the victim, the relationship between the victim and actors, the actions that led to the homicide, and a summary of the events surrounding the homicide on each case;
3. anatomical and photographic evidence on the types of injuries, the specific site, and the organs affected; and
4. the results from the subdivisions of the crime laboratory such as toxicology, ballistics, DNA, trace, and fingerprints.

ME/C offices amass this wealth of information because they are fully aware that the evidence and information collected will be used during the criminal trial.

The advantage of timely or current listing should not be overlooked. Deaths from possible drug OD may take months to certify as an accidental drug OD. However, deaths by homicide are typically certified within 24 hours, thereby providing an almost real-time picture of homicide in a particular region.

One of the few limitations of using ME/C data is the large amount of time required to ascertain the data. Many ME/C offices still use paper copies; they lack relational computer systems and each division has its own method of identifying the same case. In these cases, the individual files will have to be hand-searched and data abstracted to a data collection form and then entered into an analysis program.

Death Certificate Data

The DC is one of the most frequently used documents in mortality research. Advantages include (1) all deaths require a DC, (2) the causes of death are classified by ICD-10 codes, and (3) deaths are compiled by age, sex, race, state, and region. The limitations of using the DC in cases of homicide are that it does not contain the following data: (1) specific type of firearm used and number and caliber of bullets fired, (2) distance between the actor and victim, and (3) relationship between the actor and victim.

10 Stages of Decomposition Methods of Determining Identity, Cause of Death, and Undetermined Manner of Death

Introduction

All ME/C offices have two main functions: to ascertain a positive identification of the deceased and to determine the cause and manner of death. The level of decomposition of the body dictates the method used to confirm the identity of the individual. The simplest method used to identify the dead positively is also the most ancient: visual recognition by family and close friends. The other methods include fingerprints, dental comparisons, and DNA matching. Fingerprints are only effective if the dead individual's fingerprints are stored in a national database. Dental impressions require a short list of possible matches with which to compare the teeth. The newest and possibly the most definitive method, DNA, requires a sample of the victim's DNA for comparison. Each method of identification has strengths as well as limitations.

The second role of the ME/C is to determine the cause and manner of death by the forensic autopsy. However, even the best equipped office may fail in one or both of these functions. In a number of deaths, the end result of the completed forensic investigation fails to determine the positive identity of the body, and no cause or manner of death can be assigned.

This chapter will trace the stages of decomposition and the methods used for establishing a positive identification, starting with the most basic, visual identification and ending with the most sophisticated method of facial reconstruction. The process, advantages, and limitations of each method will be discussed. The chapter will describe cases where a positive identification cannot be made and scenarios where the cause of death is established but the manner of death remains undetermined. It will also discuss the circumstances in which the cause and the manner of death cannot be established, resulting in both being listed as undetermined and the impact of these types of cases on the forensic epidemiological analysis.

The Determination of Identity

The role of the ME/C office is to make a positive identification of the decedent. This is done for several reasons:

1. to establish the fact of death in a specific individual for official, statistical, and legal purposes;
2. to record the identity for administrative and ceremonial reasons;
3. to allow the discharge of legal claims and obligations, such as property, estates, and debts;
4. to allow claims for life insurance, survivor's pensions, and other financial matters;
5. to allow the initiation of a legal investigation and inquiry into criminal or suspicious deaths; and
6. to provide the surviving relatives with definitive proof of the death of their loved one to offer closure.

All of these actions can only take place after positive identification of the decedent is established.

Numerous methods can be used to establish the positive identification of an individual, ranging from simple visual identification to highly sophisticated techniques. The nonmedical methods include simple visual identification, clothing recognition, and document matching. Standard methods include the use of fingerprints, x-ray comparison (dental and other sites), surgical prostheses, medical implants, and evidence of disease conditions. The highly technical methods rely on DNA comparison, photo-overlaying, and physical reconstruction. The method employed is dictated by the circumstances of the death and the condition of the body.

Early Stages of Decomposition

A short time after death, the body begins to break down, or decompose. The early stages of death include livor mortis, rigor mortis, and algor mortis (a drop in the core body temperature). Livor mortis is the pooling of blood and begins to occur 30 minutes after death. Rigor mortis is a stiffening of the muscles due to their loss of ATP and begins about 2 hours after death; however, it starts to disappear 36 hours after death. After death, the body core temperature drops from its normal level of 98.6°F at a rate of 1.5°F per hour for the first 12 hours and 1°F for the next 12–18 hours until the body is close to the surrounding ambient air temperature. During the early stages of death, methods of identification include visual identification, clothing and personal effects, and fingerprints.

Visual Identification

The most often used method of determining the identity of an individual is through visual identification or visual comparison because it is simple and highly reliable in the majority of circumstances. In any death investigation, the first role of the death investigator is to ascertain the positive identification of the victim. The primary source of visual identification is the next of kin at the residence or scene. In cases where the body was transferred to the morgue prior to positive field identification, the next of kin can make this identification by viewing the body via a closed-circuit monitor or, on occasion, in person. If the decedent has no immediate family or no family at all, then positive identification must rely on close friends and/or neighbors.

Another form of visual identification is by visual comparison. In this method the face of the deceased is compare to the image on a driver's license or other official photo-identity card. These cards also provide other information such as an address, height, weight, hair color, and eye color of the individual. This method can only be used if the body, mainly the face region, is not distorted by decomposition, trauma, fire, or a chemical agent.

A tattoo is a form of body art in which ink is injected into the dermal layer of skin. Tattoos can be very simple—such as initials, a few words, or a phrase—or a full-body, multicolored, elaborate image. Because of their possible uniqueness, tattoos can be used to make a positive identification even in cases where the body is in advanced stages of decomposition. Because most tattoos are located on areas of the back, chest, and arms, they are less affected by the decomposition process. In these cases, the top loose epidermal layers are removed, revealing the unaffected skin and tattoo below. The process of using tattoos for identification of a disfigured body involves comparing the tattoo on the body to photographs of a possible match. To allow comparison and establish identity, these photographs should be sharp and recent, and they should clearly show the tattoo.

Clothing and Personal Effects

For deaths where positive visual identification by facial features is impossible, the clothing discovered on the body might be used to make a positive identification. These circumstances include cases such as suicide by a shotgun wound to the head, someone hit by a train, fire victims, or individuals exposed to chemical agents. During the autopsy, the clothing is described in great detail and in terms of type, color, manufacturer, collar size, trouser length, shoes, belt, and the nature of the fabric. Laundry marks and tailors' labels can also establish identity. The next of kin are asked to describe the types of clothing they last saw the missing person wearing. The next step is to compare the features to see if there is a match. However if the clothing on the body lacks uniqueness, other methods must be used to make the identification.

Personal effects found on the body can also aid in identification. All pockets are searched for any identifying papers. Wallets or purses are inspected for personal effects such as driver's license, social security card, photographs, or credit cards. Other effects include rings, watches, and necklaces, which can be examined for engravings that family members might identify as worn by a specific individual. Those in the military service wear personal identification systems around their neck in the form of "dog tags." These are a very effective means of identification, especially in cases where the solider was killed by a high-yield explosive or stripped of all uniform markings.

Although use of the visual comparison method provides a highly effective means of identification, it also has several limitations. First, it requires relatives or close friends to help make the identification. Second, the victim's clothing or tattoos must be unique enough to make a positive identification. Finally, in instances when there is advanced decomposition, mutilation, or thermal or chemical damage, facial recognition is impossible. Under these circumstances, more elaborate methods of identification such as fingerprints, internal features (dental, surgical/medical implants, and x-ray comparisons), DNA, and facial reconstruction must be used.

Fingerprints

The use of fingerprints as a means of identification can be traced to ancient times dating back to 1000–200 BC, when they were used on clay tablets for business transactions in Babylon. In 1823, a Czechoslovakian by the name of Jan Purkinje described the nine fingerprint patterns for the first time. The first use of fingerprint identification was conducted in 1870. The first use of criminal fingerprint identification was made by Argentinean police in 1892 when they were used to identify a woman who murdered her two sons. She then cut her own throat in an attempt to blame another. Her bloody prints on a doorpost proved her identity as the murderer. That same year the first book of its kind, *Fingerprints*, established the fingerprinting classification system. This book noted that fingerprints did not change over an individual's lifetime and that no two fingerprints were exactly the same.

In 1902, the first criminal identification using a fingerprint without a known suspect occurred when a print removed from a homicide scene was compared against fingerprints on file and matched to a suspect's fingerprints. In 1905, the U.S. Army started fingerprinting its troops; the U.S. Navy followed suit 2 years later and the U.S. Marines the following year. In 1924, the FBI established its Identification Division. Initially, fingerprints were collected and placed on cardboard cards; searches were conducted manually. In early 1999, the Automated Fingerprint Identification System (AFIS) technology was created, computerizing fingerprints and thus allowing for a rapid search through millions of records. For a more detailed history of fingerprints, see *The Encyclopedia of Forensic Science*.

Aside from matching fingerprints discovered at a crime scene to those on record, they can be used to help in the identification of unknown dead bodies. This method can be used if the body is discovered nude, without any identifiable clothing or tattoos, or in moderate stages of decomposition. In these cases, a latent fingerprint examiner from the crime laboratory will print the unknown individual. The conditions of the fingers can vary from fresh, stages of decomposition, mummified, or macerated (water soaked).

The technique of fingerprinting of the recently dead is similar to that used on the living. The basic equipment used to collect fingerprints consists of an inking plate, cardholder, printing ink (heavy black paste), and a roller. The ink is spread in a thin, even coat over the tip of the fingers and then each finger impression is transferred or "rolled" onto the card. In some locations, palm impressions are taken.

In advanced stages of decomposition, conditions such as putrefaction (rot), mummification, or maceration (submersion in water) are typically encountered. In situations where the body was in water and the fingers are wrinkled, this condition can be corrected by injecting tissue builder underneath the skin or by immersing the fingers by applying alcohol, benzene, or acetone to them and thus allowing them to be fingerprinted. If the hands are in early stages of decomposition, the skin can be removed and placed over the gloved hands of the examiner in order to print the hands. If the fingers are desiccated (dried out or mummified), they are removed and placed in a solution to rehydrate them.

Fingerprinting is a highly effective means of identification; however, there are two major limitations. First, the fingerprints of the unidentified individual must be on file with a law enforcement, government, or military agency. Second, fingerprint identification is of limited use if the body has sustained significant thermal injuries (burns).

Moderate Stages of Decomposition

A short time after death, two processes begin to occur within the body: autolysis and putrefaction. Autolysis is the breakdown of cells and internal organs by the actions of enzymes; putrefaction is a breakdown due to the action of bacteria and fermentation. About 24–36 hours after death, the body begins to take on a greenish discoloration; marbling due to hemolysis of blood within the vessels also begins. The body shows signs of bloating, swelling of the abdomen, and bulging eyes and tongue about 60–72 hours after death. As the body decomposes, the external features of the face and body are distorted; this makes a positive identification based on visual clues more difficult. In these cases, the method of identification turns to examination of the body for surgical prostheses, medical implants, and evidence of specific disease conditions.

Internal Identification

Methods of positive identification are not limited to the external features of the face or fingers; they can include internal identification methods through the examination of the body for surgical prostheses, medical implants, and evidence of specific disease conditions. These can offer clues to the identification of the individual.

Medical/Surgical Implants and Procedures

One form of internal identification is through the use of medical implants such as pacemakers, breast implants, or surgical pins discovered during the internal examination of the body. All medical implants are etched with a serial number. Once the implant has been located and removed, the manufacturer can be contacted to determine the name of the individual into whom it was implanted, the date of implant, and other medical information regarding that individual. These implants survive most mechanisms of death due to their position in the body and their material—typically, high-grade stainless steel. In addition, surgical procedures such as bypass surgery, stomach stapling, and removal of the appendix can also be matched to medical records and be used as a form of individual identification.

Disease Conditions

The internal examination of the organs can reveal medical conditions such as gallstones, silicosis, asbestosis, and congenital anomalies that would have been diagnosed during life. These conditions can be identified even among early decomposed bodies or victims of fire. This information can be used to compare with data contained in medical records.

Advanced Stages of Decomposition

The rate at which the body decomposes is affected by the air temperature, layers of clothing, types of wounds, and the location of the body. During the advanced stages of decomposition, the external features of the body are completely disfigured and at times unrecognizable. In these cases, positive identification requires the use of x-ray comparison.

X-ray Comparison

There are two basic types of x-ray comparison: skeletal structural and dental. Both methods rely on comparing similarities between the premortem and postmortem x-rays. During the forensic autopsy, whole-body x-rays are taken looking for features such as broken bones, fractures, or abnormal bone structures. A short list of possible matches is typically generated by the police from missing person reports. For each possible match, hospital records and x-rays are compared to postmortem x-rays. If the autopsy x-ray shows unique features, such as a compound fracture of the left femur, then the hospital records are reviewed to see if that individual was ever treated for a broken leg; if he or she was, the two x-rays are compared. Other features that allow comparison of x-rays taken before and after death include old fractures and congenital abnormalities of the bone structure such as sclerosis.

Dental Comparison

The second and more frequently used method of x-ray identification is that of dental comparison. The dentition is forensically significant in the identification process primarily because the teeth and jaws can resist even the most severe environmental conditions such as fire and trauma. The durability of the teeth is primarily due to the enamel (the outermost covering of the teeth) and the cementum (the outer covering of the roots of teeth). In addition, dental fillings and bridges also survive intact.

The skills of a forensic odontologist—forensic dentist—are called upon to determine the identity of individuals burned beyond visual recognition, in advanced stages of decomposition, skeletonized, or discovered in mass graves. For a more detailed history of forensic odontology, see *The Encyclopedia of Forensic Science*.

A forensic odontologist is a traditionally trained dentist with extensive knowledge of oral anatomy and experience within the forensic medicine field. The role of the forensic odontologist ranges from identification of human remains to assessment of bite marks and patterned skin injuries to the collection of DNA evidence from around the bite mark.

The main method of identification used by forensic odontology is pattern recognition and comparison, focusing the examination on the characteristics of the teeth, dental restoration, and anatomical variations. The teeth are described in terms of surface configuration, size, shape, wear patterns, missing teeth, extra teeth, and decay. Adults typically have 32 teeth, each with five surfaces; thus 160 possible configurations are provided. Dental prosthetic tooth replacements (dentures, bridges, partials) can also aid in identification and may potentially yield information such as geography of origin, approximate dating of construction, and even linkage to a particular dentist or dental laboratory.

The forensic odontology community has developed terminology and classification for body identification following a forensic odontology identification investigation (Table 10.1). The procedure of comparison involves the odontologist obtaining x-rays of the unknown individual and being provided with x-rays and charts of possible matches. He or she will then compare the two sets of x-rays and determine the degree of similarities between the antemortem dental records and postmortem x-rays. Based on this detailed examination, a level of identification will be assigned to the comparison (shown in Table 10.1). Therefore, the role of the forensic odontologist is to provide an expert opinion regarding the likelihood of a match between premortem and postmortem x-rays.

This method of identification has one major weakness. In the United States, there are many more dental records on file than fingerprint records and these records, unlike fingerprints, are not stored in a large, central, easily searchable database. Each dentist keeps his or her own x-rays and many have different methods of storing information. The ME/C office must provide the odontologist with a short list of possible matches. In addition, each possible match requires fairly current premortem dental x-rays to compare with the postmortem x-rays. Because of lack of insurance, fear, or the failure of dentists to maintain complete records, an individual's antemortem records may not be available. If a backpacker comes across a skull with a lower jaw containing a few teeth, there is nothing an odontologist can do until a list of possible matches is generated from the police or forensic investigation.

Table 10.1 Classification for Body Identification

Level of identification	Definition
Positive identification	The antemortem and postmortem data match in sufficient detail to establish that they are from the same individual. In addition, there are no irreconcilable discrepancies.
Possible identification	The antemortem and postmortem data have consistent features, but, due to the quality of the postmortem remains or the antemortem evidence, it is not possible to establish dental identification positively.
Insufficient evidence	The available information is insufficient to form the basis for a conclusion.
Exclusion	The antemortem and postmortem data are clearly inconsistent. However, it should be understood that identification by exclusion is a valid technique in certain circumstances.

Extreme Stages of Decomposition

If the body is exposed in the environment for a significant amount of time, the remains will be reduced to a collection of bones. In these circumstances, the ME/C office relies on the anthropologist or the science of superimposition and facial reconstruction to assist in determination of the victim's identity.

Skeletal Identification

In cases where the body has decomposed to bones, the skills of an anthropologist are required. The role of the anthropologist is to answer seven key questions:

1. Are these bones?
2. Are the bones human bones?
3. What is the sex?
4. What is the stature?
5. What is the race?
6. What is the age?
7. How long has the victim been dead?

Many objects can resemble bones, including stones, plastic, and even wood. When bones are delivered to the ME/C office, the forensic pathologist will conduct an examination to determine whether they are animal or human. During the year, hunters, hikers, and birdwatchers flood the ME/C office with what they are convinced are human bones. The vast majority turns out to be the bones of domestic or wild animals; however, from time to time human remains are located. One possible source of human bones is discarded bones from dental or medical schools.

Occasionally, human skeletal remains are discovered that require a full forensic investigation. After the scene is photographed, the next step is to recover all the bones from the surrounding environment. At the morgue, the anthropologist reassembles the collected bones into their normal anatomical positions and determines the victim's sex, race, age, and stature by examining and measuring them. If the skull has been located, the sex and, to a lesser degree, race can be determined. The sex can be confidently determined if the pelvis bone is recovered. If the femur bone (the long bone of the leg) has been discovered, an approximate height of the individual can be calculated. If the teeth are present, a dental odontologist can aid in the determination of the identity of the body. Once some basic characteristics have been determined, missing person reports will be reviewed to see whether any match the developed profile. Only after the identity has been positively made can a police investigation begin.

Superimposition Facial Reconstruction

Under extreme circumstances, when all the traditional methods of identification of the dead fall short, methods such as superimposition and facial reconstruction must be employed. In cases where only a complete skull and lower jaw are recovered, the process of photo superimposition can be used to determine identity. This method requires a large, fairly recent photograph of the face of a missing person from the front or slightly turned to the side with the teeth visible. The photograph is then adjusted to the correct scale and superimposed over the image of the skull. The matching is based on anatomical and dental features.

The method of facial reconstruction is also used on recovered skulls. Facial reconstruction is the process of using modeling clay, plastic eyes, and artistic and special anatomical knowledge to create a three-dimensional face to allow visual recognition by family or friends. The method employs applying modeling clay to the skull using information within a large database to estimate the correct tissue thickness. The end result is a three-dimensional bust complete with skin tone, eyes, eyebrows, lips, ears, hair, and scars. Once the reconstruction is complete, the created bust is shown on news broadcasts, in newspapers, and on flyers posted in surrounding areas.

Special Cases of Decomposition

In some cases, the body is dismembered due to an airplane crash, explosion, terrorist attack, or other natural or man-made disaster, thus preventing use of the identification methods listed previously. In these cases, the science of DNA comparison can be used to identify the remains.

DNA

Although based in science, the previously described methods of identification have some level of subjectivity. The discovery and development of DNA (deoxyribonucleic acid) profiling has revolutionized the method of identification. DNA analysis was thrust to the forefront due to its ability to link an individual to a crime scene, exonerate the innocent, or exclude suspects in criminal cases. However, DNA also has a role in identification.

In brief, within each human cell are chromosomes that contain the DNA. DNA can be recovered from blood, semen, skin cells, tissue, organs, muscle, brain cells, bone, teeth, hair, saliva, mucus, perspiration, fingernails, urine, and feces; it is the foundational building block for an individual's entire genetic makeup. It is composed of two strands of sugar and phosphate molecules that form a double helix bound together by links formed by adenine and thymine, and cytosine and guanine.

DNA has advantages over other methods of identification in that it is a highly stable compound; thus, it can be recovered from badly decomposed bodies, charred bodies, and even thousand-year-old mummies. Only a small amount is required for analyses and comparisons. The most powerful advantage is the uniqueness of one's DNA profile.

In the case of an unknown body, a small sample of blood is collected and, through a process of gel electrophoresis, a DNA profile is created for the unknown individual. This profile can be compared to the millions of profiles in CODIS (combined DNA index system). CODIS is an electronic database containing DNA profiles from federal, state, and local crime labs across the United States operated by the FBI.

A DNA identification methods system relies on matching the sample DNA profile with the profiles within the database; the probability of a match depends on the likelihood of being in the searched databases. Using the CODIS system has the major limitation that the database only contains DNA profiles of individuals convicted of sex offenses, rape, murder, child abuse, and other violent crimes; in many states, it also includes other felonies. Therefore, this system would only be helpful if the unknown victim has a criminal record.

DNA was instrumental in the identification of the remains of victims from the mostly unrecognizable masses of tissue after the terrorist attack of 9/11. Family members of possible victims supplied samples of DNA to be used to match with the remains recovered from the scene. DNA identification has also been used to determine the identity of the remains of soldiers recovered from Korea and Vietnam.

Cause of Death Known but Manner Undetermined

In many deaths examined by the ME/C office, the cause of death is easily and accurately established. In cases such as a single gunshot wound to the right temple, decapitation by a train, or the ingestion of 50 valium pills, the mechanism and the immediate cause of death are clear. However, determining the manner of death is, in some cases, almost impossible to establish. Table 10.2 shows the mechanism of death (cause of death) and the total number of such deaths when the manner was determined and when the manner was not ascertained. The table illustrates that the cause of death is associated with the ability to assign a manner to the death. Only a small percentage of deaths resulting from a fall or involving a firearm had the manner listed as undetermined. In these types of deaths, the intent is clear to the forensic pathologist. However, the intent (suicide or accident) among deaths resulting

Table 10.2 Number of Deaths Classified as Undetermined by Mechanism

Mechanism	Total number with known manner	Total number (%) with unknown manner
Drowning	4,006	242 (5.7%)
Falls	20,357	69 (0.34%)
Fire/flames	3,506	120 (3.3%)
Firearms	30,473	221 (0.7%)
Poisoning	29,451	3,240 (9.9%)
Suffocation	13,781	139 (0.9%)

from drowning or poisoning is less clear, resulting in a greater number of DCs with the manner checked as undetermined.

A death listing the manner as undetermined occurs in the following situations: (1) equal evidence has been discovered to support two different manners of death (e.g., accident vs. suicide); (2) there is insufficient physical evidence to support a death from natural, accidental, suicidal, or homicidal causes; or (3) remains are insufficient to conduct a thorough investigation to determine the manner. The first type is the most frequently encountered case.

Several examples will highlight this type of case. A 2-month-old infant was discovered in the morning hours unresponsive in the parents' bed. The forensic examination of the infant revealed no trauma, no congenital malformations, and no past medical conditions, and the police cleared the parents of any foul play. The cause of death by definition was listed as SIDS (see Chapter 6 for a detailed description of SIDS). The possible mechanism for the death included smothering caused by one of the adults in the bed placing an arm over the nose and month of the infant or positional asphyxia caused by the placement of an arm or leg over the chest of the infant, thus preventing breathing; in both of these, the manner would be accidental. The death could have been caused by the yet unidentified etiology collectively called SIDS, where the manner is classified as natural. However, no pathological or anatomical evidence supported either of the proposed mechanisms. In this case, the DC would be completed as immediate cause of death as SIDS and the manner as undetermined.

A badly decomposed body was discovered in an abandoned house during demolition. Examination of the body revealed an entrance wound in the chest region and an x-ray showed a bullet inside the body. No weapon was located near the body, but the condition of the structure made the search difficult. All possible methods of identification were employed, but no matches resulted. The cause of death was GSW to the chest but the manner was listed as undetermined. The fatal wound could have been inflicted during an act of suicide; it could be a homicide or even an accidental shooting. As for the firearm, it might still be in the rubble of the house or most likely taken by kids playing in the house. Without knowing the identity of the victim, no police investigation could proceed.

Cause of Death Undetermined and Manner Undetermined

In a small number of cases, the results of the death scene investigation and forensic examination of the body fail to ascertain the cause of death and the manner in which it occurred. These cases typically occur under three circumstances: (1) advanced decomposition, (2) skeletonized remains, or (3) bone fragments. Examples of these three cases are discussed next.

Remains in an advanced state of decomposition were discovered in an abandoned barn. The victim was dressed in a blue shirt and blue jeans but no identification was recovered on or near the body. X-rays found no bullets or other metal objects. Examination of the skin showed evidence of insect and small animal activity, making it impossible to conclude definitely that there was no evidence of puncture wounds or bullet holes in the skin. All the internal organs had decomposed to the point of being unidentifiable. Examinations by a forensic odontologist and an anthropologist concluded that the victim was a white male at an estimated age between 60 and 70. A search by police of the surrounding area and missing person reports failed to locate a match for this individual. Due to a lack of internal organs or body fluids to examine, the forensic pathologist could not provide a cause of death or the manner in which the man had died.

During the construction of a new house, workers unearthed what appeared to be bones. Investigators arrived from the ME/C office and began to clear away the soil, revealing a nearly complete skeleton. The surrounding soil was carefully sifted for rings, necklaces, fragments of clothing, bullets, and bullet casings; however, no clothing or jewelry was recovered. An anthropologist was called in to assemble and examine the bones for signs of trauma such as knife marks, bullet damage, or broken bones. In a struggle, a knife can be thrust deeply enough to leave cut marks on the bone. Examination of the bones can also show evidence of teeth marks made by small rodents after death. Location of these types of marks would indicate that the body was not buried after death but was exposed. The lack of these teeth marks would indicate that the body was buried shortly after death.

Although the anthropologist can provide the age, sex, and a rough estimate of the time of death, he or she cannot determine the victim's identity. A forensic odontologist can also provide a general state of health based on the condition of the teeth. The lack of physical evidence may indicate that the body was dead before being buried at this location. In this case, the most likely explanation is that the death was a homicide; however, with no internal organs to examine, body fluids, or a forensically provable mechanism of death, the cause of death and manner of death must both be listed as undetermined.

During the first few days of spring, hikers, birdwatchers, and naturalists come across bones that they believe are human. These bones are brought to ME/C offices and examined by forensic pathologists; 95% of the bones are from a deer, chicken, or some other small animal. A key factor in differentiating human from animal bones is the shape and size of the bones. Occasionally, the bones discovered in the woods are human; the bones typically are the large bones of the leg (femur, tibia), the pelvic bone, some vertebrae, ribs, mandible, or the skull. A few bone fragments do not allow for a complete forensic examination and the death must be classified as immediate cause of death undetermined and manner undetermined.

In the three examples listed earlier, the remains stay behind in the possession of the ME/C office forever. Without a means of positively identifying them, there is no one to release them to and, more importantly, the decedent may have been the victim of murder.

Forensic Epidemiological Investigation of Undetermined Deaths

A forensic epidemiologist must understand the reasons why the cause and/or manner of death is sometimes listed as undetermined, as well as the overall impact of this classification on the estimation of the other manner of death. These deaths can be grouped with those with an equivalent manner of death, those without a manner, and those without a cause or manner of death. In the equivalent category are those for which the forensic evidence can support two different manners of death. These are not cases where half the evidence points in one direction and the other in another. The forensic epidemiologist can review the available evidence and assign a probable manner of death. This is not an official designation but one used for research purposes. This type of recoding is most useful in an area where there is a high percentage of cases signed out as "undetermined."

An ME/C office may be overly cautious with the manner of suicide because of the stigma attached to the act and therefore may issue a substantial number of DCs with the cause of death as GSW to the head, suicide, with a manner undetermined. Another ME/C office may conduct a thorough SIDS investigation but feel that, because it did not discover the mechanism of the death, the DC for the death should indicate the mechanism as undetermined. This issue of determining a manner also arises in cases of Russian roulette (see Chapter 11). The same case of Russian roulette shown to three different forensic pathologists could result in three different conclusions as to the manner of death: suicide, accident, and undetermined.

The nonstandardization and autonomy of a forensic pathologist in determining the cause and manner of death can have the following epidemiological effects. Location-to-location (region-to-region or state-to-state) comparisons become very difficult with regard to certain types of deaths. The definition and data on homicides are fairly uniform across the United States and allow for a reliable comparison between the states and within the state. However, comparing the number of deaths from certain types of suicide or deaths from SIDS may not be possible. The heavy use of the manner "undetermined" has the effect of underestimating deaths from other manners.

For example, an ME/C office reported an average of 45 suicides, 35 homicides, and 57 undetermined deaths with the cause listed as GSW to the chest. The 57 cases require closer examination. Were some of these deaths actually suicides but equivocal circumstances made the determination difficult or was pressure placed on the ME/C to call them undetermined? Were they in reality homicides that lacked the hard forensic evidence to support that conclusion at this time? Resolving these 57 cases is important from a forensic epidemiological point of view because this region has either a significant suicide-by-firearm epidemic or a high homicide-by-firearm rate.

The research conducted by forensic epidemiologists can provide guidelines to assist medical examiners and coroners in resolving some of these equivocal deaths. They can collect large amounts of data on thousands of deaths by Russian roulette and create profiles of the victims, the features of the gunshot wounds, the toxicological levels, and the social and behavioral characteristics of the victims to assist in differentiating this type of self-inflicted death from others. This will result in a more accurate determination of the manner of death.

Special Types of Investigations

Introduction

The ME/C office encounters a wide range of death scenes. A number of special types of cases warrant some special attention; these include a homicide that is followed by a suicide and playing "Russian roulette." In a majority of investigations, a complete forensic autopsy is conducted; however, this physical examination may not be sufficient to determine the manner of death. In these types of cases, a psychological autopsy can be conducted to assist in the determination of the manner of death in ambiguous cases.

Homicide–Suicide

Death investigators routinely investigate deaths by suicide and homicide. However, in a small number of cases, the suicide is directly linked to the homicide. This dyadic death is also referred to as a murder–suicide, which is defined as the unlawful killing of one or more people quickly followed by the offender taking his or her own life, usually within 24 hours. This dyadic death commonly occurs between intimate partners. In most cases, the man (husband or boyfriend) will kill the woman (wife or girlfriend) and then turn the gun on himself. The scene typically occurs in the bedroom and the female homicide victim is typically discovered lying on the bed with a gunshot wound to the head or chest. The man will usually be found lying in close proximity, often right next to the female, with a fatal gunshot wound to the head. The role of the forensic death investigation is to determine the sequence of the shooting. This is important not only from the forensic and police investigation perspective, but also for insurance and inheritance purposes. It is important to determine whether both victims committed suicide (e.g., in a suicide pact) or whether a homicide–suicide incident occurred.

The forensic examination will primarily focus on the ballistics data: the entrance wound, the angle of the shot, blood splatter patterns, and the results of the gunshot residue (GSR) analysis. In the case of a double suicide, one would expect to find both entrance wounds to be contact or near-contact type wounds. The path of the bullets can be downward, upward, or linear.

Blood splatter patterns may offer a clue to the order of the suicides. Assuming both individuals were standing in close proximity to each other, when the first victim committed suicide, the blood splatter would be deposited on the second victim. The splatter blood would, due to gravity, flow in a downward direction, producing a tear-drop pattern on victim 2. In addition, if victim 2 was close to a wall, a pattern of the body's outline would appear. When victim 2 shoots himself or herself, the deposited splatter on victim 1 would be more circular and downhill, depending on the position of the body. Both victims' hands would be positive for GSR. A slightly higher concentration would be found on victim 2 if the same firearm was used.

In the case of a homicide–suicide, one would expect to find the entrance wound for the homicide most likely to be a contact or near-contact type wound and the path of the bullet to be downward, reflecting that the shooter was standing in front or to the side of a sitting victim. The blood splatter from victim 1 may deposit on the hands of the shooter and be tested by DNA analysis. The splatter blood from victim 2 during the suicide would deposit on victim 1 because the two are typically in close proximity to one another. Only the shooter's hands would be positive for GSR.

A major limitation for forensic epidemiologists that wish to study the phenomenon of homicide–suicide is that, at the state and national levels, the deaths are treated as two individual cases: one as a homicide and one as a suicide, with no mechanism of linking the two events. Part 30d of the DC for the homicide victim will read, "shot by husband" while the suicide victim's will read, "self-inflected GSW head." The only method to study these types of deaths is to go directly to the issuing ME/C office and begin by locating all the homicides, search the database for a suicide that occurred that same day or the following day, and finally read the death investigation report and police reports. Matching can also be done by the victim's last name, by addresses, or by location.

Russian Roulette—Death by Suicide or by Accident?

Another special type of death investigated by the ME/C office involves a death by a firearm that occurred while engaged in playing Russian roulette—a potentially lethal game of chance. "Russian" refers to the supposed country of origin and "roulette" to the element of risk taking and the spinning of the revolver's cylinder being analogous to that of a spinning roulette wheel.

Typically, the game is played by taking a revolver, placing a single round into one of the six chambers (resulting in a 1/6, or approximately 17%, chance of the revolver discharging the live round), spinning the cylinder, placing the end of the muzzle against the temple, and then pulling the trigger. If the weapon fails to discharge, it is passed to the next player. Between each player, the cylinder can be spun again or not, and the trigger can be pulled again. Variations on the game include fewer chambers (typically five) in a firearm or increasing the number of rounds in the cylinder—both of which increase the risk of death. The motivation for playing the game varies from displays of bravery, showing off to friends, or heightening the act of committing suicide. Russian roulette was made famous with the 1978 release of the movie *The Deer Hunter*, which featured three soldiers captured during the Vietnam War and forced to play Russian roulette as their captors gambled on the results.

The key question facing the forensic community after locating a victim with a self-inflicted gunshot wound to the head resulting from engaging in Russian roulette is whether to rule the manner of death as a suicide or as an accident. Although there are no clear-cut rules for the forensic pathologist in the determination of the manner, some guidelines have emerged. If the victim was alone while playing the game, most ME/C offices would rule that death a suicide. If the individual was playing the game with others and alcohol or drugs were involved, the office would rule the death an accident. The justification for this decision is based on the thinking that the individual was not trying to kill himself, but rather showing off to friends using judgment impaired due to the effect of alcohol.

Forensic epidemiologists studying death by Russian roulette should first inquire as to the guidelines used by that ME/C office regarding policy on how to determine the manner of death in these types of cases.

Psychological Autopsy

Introduction

Not all forensic investigations end after the forensic autopsy, which is essentially a physical examination of the deceased's internal organs. Further information can be obtained by performing a psychological autopsy, which is designed to determine the mental status of the deceased prior to death.

Definition

The psychological autopsy is defined as investigating a person's death by reconstructing what the person thought, felt, and did preceding death. This involves interviewing those close to the deceased and gathering information contained in written documents.

Brief History of Psychological Autopsies

The first psychological autopsy studies were carried out in the early 1940s by Gregory Zilboorg's investigation of 93 consecutive suicides by police officers in New York City between 1934 and 1940. In 1958, the chief medical examiner of the Los Angeles Coroner's Office asked a team of professionals from the Los Angeles Suicide Prevention Center to help in his investigations of equivocal cases where the cause of death and, in most cases, the manner of death were not immediately clear. The psychiatrist Edwin Shneidman coined the phrase "psychological autopsy" to describe the procedure he and his team of researchers developed during these investigations. The method involved talking in a tactful and systematic manner to key persons—a spouse, lover, parent, grown child, friend, colleague, physician, supervisor, or co-worker—who knew the deceased. This practice of investigating unclear deaths in Los Angeles continued for almost 30 years and allowed for a more accurate classification of equivocal deaths as well as contributed to experts' understanding of suicide.

In the 1970s and 1980s, researchers began using the psychological autopsy method to investigate risk factors for suicide. Psychological autopsies have confirmed that the vast majority of suicide victims could be diagnosed as having had a mental disorder—usually depression, manic depression, or alcohol or drug problems. Other studies have focused upon the availability of firearms in the homes of suicides, traumatic events in persons' lives, and other psychological and social factors.

The Use of Psychological Autopsy

Currently, psychological autopsies have two major uses: research investigation and clinical and legal use. Research investigations generally involve comparing the deaths of individuals that died from suicide with those of another group—for example, accident victims—in order to see what factors are important in discriminating between suicides and other deaths. The clinical and legal uses of psychological autopsies involve the investigation of a single death in order to clarify why or how a person died. These often involve descriptive interpretations of the death and may include information to help family and friends better understand why a tragic death occurred. Suggestions of means of preventing suicides, such as improving hospital treatment or preventing suicides in jails, can also be made.

A psychological autopsy is appropriate for a number of reasons, but the most common is typically to assist in determining the manner of the death. Estimates suggest that in up to 20% of cases presented to a medical examiner or coroner, the precise mode of death is unclear. A psychological autopsy can help address this ambiguity and establish whether death was a result of natural causes, suicide, accident, or murder.

Conducting a Psychological Autopsy

Within the context of a forensic investigation, a psychological autopsy is employed as a data collection tool; the most common source is interview data obtained from the family and friends of the deceased. Obtaining the medical history of the deceased is also a central component of the psychological autopsy. Interviewing the doctor of the deceased and/or examining medical records is therefore another important data collection source. The nature of the information collected would usually include the following:

- biographical information (age, marital status, occupation);
- personal information (relationships, lifestyle, alcohol/drug use, sources of stress); and
- secondary information (family history, police records, diaries).

It is important to note that, as with most data collection protocols conducted within a psychological framework, different methodological approaches exist. The goal was best described by Berman and Litman in 1993 as "postdictive analysis yielding an opinion giving a logical understanding of the relationship between the deceased and the events and behaviors that preceded the death."

Bioterrorism: Real-Time Surveillance

Introduction

In today's political climate, the threat from a biological terrorist attack is real. The methods behind these types of attacks are not always designed to kill thousands, but rather to paralyze the masses from engaging in their normal activities. Terrorist organizations can be located outside or within U.S. borders and can exist as well-organized and well-funded organizations to small groups of loosely affiliated individuals. Their motivation can be driven be radical religious dogma, antigovernment ideology, or protesting against a number of policies or laws the group feels are unjustified or unconstitutional. One method of bioterrorism is to introduce a biological agent into the air, ground, water, or food supply.

This chapter will define terrorism, provide a few examples of biological agents of terrorism, and discuss the role the ME/C office plays in investigating a possible terrorism event. In addition, the functions of the forensic epidemiologist in providing real-time surveillance of deaths investigated by the ME/C office will also be examined.

Definition

U.S. federal statute defines terrorism as "violent acts or acts dangerous to human life that appear to be intended (1) to intimidate or coerce a civilian population; (2) to influence the policy of a government by intimidation or coercion; or (3) to affect the conduct of a government by assassination or kidnapping." Terrorism is an act or acts of violence on a civilian population who are innocent or uninvolved in order to achieve political, religious, or ideological objectives. The means used can be high explosives, toxic chemicals, or biological agents including microbiological agents.

Brief History of Bioterrorism

In the not so distant past the use of bioterrorism was limited primarily because of lack of a means of manufacturing a sufficient amount of the toxic substance and limitations in the methods of delivery. Today, due to the instability of certain countries willing to produce and provide biological agents to terrorist groups and the increasing ease of introducing these agents into the general population, the risk of a biological attack has increased. Terrorism agents can be divided into two general types.

Biological Terrorism Agents

These agents are microbiological organisms or toxic substances that can be derived from members of the plant or animal kingdom and are capable of causing severe illness leading to death. The CDC has divided biological agents into three categories:

- high priority: anthrax, smallpox, plague, tularemia, botulism, and viral hemorrhagic fever;
- second priority: Q fever, brucellosis, *Burkholderia, mallei (glanders)*, alpha virus, ricin, toxic C1, *Clostridium perfringens, Salmonella, Shigella dysenteriae, Escherichia coli,* and Vibrio cholerae; and
- low priority: hantavirus, multidrug-resistant Mycoberterium tuberculosis, Nipah virus, and yellow fever virus.

Chemical Terrorism Agents

Such agents are toxic chemical substances capable of causing incapacity, severe illness, or death. The CDC has developed three categories of threat:

- category A: agents that are easily disseminated, are transmitted from person to person, result in a high mortality rate, are designed to cause social disruption, and require special public health preparedness;
- category B: agents that are moderately easy to disseminate, result in low mortality rates, and require specific enhancements of diagnostics; and
- category C: agents that include emerging pathogens that could be engineered for mass dissemination in the future.

A few examples of biological agents of terrorism are described next.

Anthrax is a disease of animals caused by a Gram-negative organism, *Bacillus anthracis*. This agent has a high potential for being a biological agent because (1) it is relativity easy to manufacture, (2) it is extremely difficult to eradicate from the environment in its spore form, (3) it has a high virulence factor, and (4) it is normally a ubiquitous disease, therefore initially obscuring the terrorist attack. Infection from anthrax can occur by contact, ingestion, or inhalation. Direct contact with anthrax results in a cutaneous disease characterized by pustules, ulcerates, eschars, fever, and malaise. This form of contact is rarely fatal. The ingestion of contaminated food causes hemorrhage of the intestines, enlarged lymph nodes, and high mortality. Respiratory exposure to anthrax has symptoms very similar to those of a common cold, so diagnosis is very difficult. Death from this type of exposure is rapid. Delivery can also be made by an aerosol delivery system.

Smallpox is caused by the variola virus and was eradicated from the planet in 1977. Vaccination for the virus ended in 1972. The virus only exists in two laboratories: one in the United States and one in Russia. However, there is a growing concern that terrorist states may have the virus. The risk from smallpox is that the world population has limited or no immunity against the virus. The risks from this virus are that (1) it is highly contagious with a rapid dissemination (spread) from person to person, (2) nearly 100% of those infected will become ill and 30% will die, (3) treatment options are limited, and (4) it is easily transported in a viral form or in an infected individual preclinically or presymptomatically. The spread of the virus is from inhalation of the infected particles during person-to person contact.

The most famous *plague* was the Black Death during the fourteenth and fifteenth centuries, which was responsible for killing 20–30 million people in Europe. The plague was caused by a Gram-negative bacterium, *Yersinia pestis*. The plague is a naturally occurring infection spread between rats by fleas; the spread to humans was due to their close proximity to rats. Symptoms of bubonic plague, septicemia, and pneumonia are mainly associated with the infection. Warning signs of a bioterrorism attack by the plague include occurrence of plague infection (1) in a community without prior episodes, (2) among individuals without proper risk factors, (3) in an area without associated rodent deaths. Methods of dissemination would most likely be by an aerosol agent.

Botulism is caused by the Gram-positive organism *Clostridium botulinum*. The disease is caused by the secretion of exotoxins from the organism. The toxins from this bacterium have been developed by the United States, Iraq, Iran, North Korea, Syria, and the former USSR as a bioweapon. The toxins are easy to manufacture and transport, and they have a high level of potency. They work by blocking the acetylcholine release at the neuromuscular junction, resulting in profound muscle weakness. Terrorist groups can contaminate food supplies and the outbreak is difficult to diagnosis.

For a more in-depth examination of the forensic aspects of biological terrorism, refer to *Forensic Aspects of Chemical and Biological Terrorism* by C. H. Wecht (see Bibliography).

The Role of the Forensic Community

The ME/C office plays a vital role in the war on terrorism. Medical examiners and coroners have the legal authority to investigate deaths that appear suspicious or criminal in nature. These deaths include people that die shortly after entering the county, deaths associated with an explosion, and people that died after exposure to microbiological agents. The role of the forensic autopsy in the investigation of a possible act of terrorism goes beyond determining the cause and manner of death to the collection of critical evidence of chemicals, micro-organisms, or pieces of explosive devices from the victim and death scene. Staff of the ME/C office see fatalities among individuals that might not be seen or examined by a physician or in an emergency room. Autopsies are critical for the surveillance of fatalities, especially those caused by infectious diseases, because they can provide an organ-specific diagnosis and determine the route of exposure.

The ME/C office plays a major role in providing information to determine whether an event was or was not an act of terrorism. For example, consider TWA flight 800, which exploded in 1996 above Long Island, New York, killing all 220 people on board. Many early reports pointed to a terrorist bomb. The forensic investigation resulted in recovery of all 220 victims and examination of the bodies and clothing. The injury patterns were compared to seat assignments and a detailed examination was made of foreign objects removed from the victims. The results of the forensic examination concluded that no explosive device was used and the injury patterns were not consistent with a bomb explosion. The final conclusion was that the cause of the airplane crash was an accidental explosion of an empty middle fuel tank rather than a terrorist attack.

The ME/C office also has a role in investigating bioterrorism in terms of providing real-time surveillance. This role falls to the forensic epidemiologist and surveillance generally consists of collecting, analyzing, and disseminating data. First, the types of deaths common in that particular area are determined; next, the baseline number of deaths is calculated and then an unusual spike in unusual deaths is noted.

The forensic epidemiologist examines and codes every death that is processed through the ME/C office and therefore becomes extremely familiar with the characteristics and distribution of these deaths. An ME/C office operating in an area with a high percentage of farms may see more deaths associated with livestock-to-human transfer than an ME/C office servicing a large city. Publishing annual reports is one of the duties of a forensic epidemiologist; these reports detail the number of deaths by cause and manner of death; using the data from 5 or more years, they can establish the baseline for every specific type and manner of death.

A baseline is the average number of deaths one would expect over a given time period. For example, based on 5 years of forensic data, one would expect, on average, five individuals to die from gastrointestinal hemorrhage each year. The main strength of the forensic epidemiologist lies in his or her ability to examine and code the specific death information on the date or date after the death occurred. This provides real-time surveillance of a region. The forensic epidemiologist can easily identify clusters of similar deaths in one area, similar symptoms among initially unrelated individual deaths, spikes in deaths typically occurring with low frequency, or deaths exceeding baseline.

For example, if, over a 2-week period, a large number of individuals from the same apartment complex presented to the ME/C and all were diagnosed with a severe respiratory infection, this would warrant further investigation. This type of outbreak would be missed if the individuals went to different hospitals or relied on over-the-counter medications for treatment. For example, suppose that a number of individuals from different parts of an area died from an intestinal virus. Further investigation would link the initially unrelated deaths to the restaurant at which all the victims ate at the same time, and the cause would be listed as food contamination. The investigator now has to determine whether this was due to poor food handling or terrorism. The surveillance also includes monitoring for unusual or atypical increases in certain types of diseases. The sudden increase of deaths that typically have a low baseline, the appearance of deaths not commonly seen, and the appearance of illness out of season should all be investigated further.

Structure of a Forensic Paper 12

Introduction

In the ME/C office, the role of transforming an idea to a completed manuscript falls to the forensic epidemiologist. The ideas can be generated from the forensic pathologist, medical examiner or coroner, or an individual from within any of the divisions of the crime laboratory. Forensic epidemiologists have the formal training to go from a concept or theory to a well designed manuscript. Training includes creating abstract forms, collecting data, entering the information into statistical programs, conducting the correct analyses, and preparing the various components of a manuscript. In addition, they understand the mechanism involved in submitting a paper and the review process.

This chapter will describe the typical structure of a manuscript, the six main components, the role of each section, how it should be prepared, writing style, and some common errors to be avoided. It will also provide an overview of the manuscript review process. In addition, the three most common types of papers produced within the forensic community will be described.

Structure of a Manuscript

The standard manuscript has six main parts: abstract, introduction, methods, results, conclusions, and references.

Abstract

The first section encountered in almost all manuscripts is the abstract, which may be the most important part of any paper. It is important because this may be the only part individuals will read and make a determination as to whether to read the entire paper. Conferences print only the abstracts of accepted papers, and search engines such as PubMed also provide only the abstract of the paper.

The purpose of an abstract is to provide a concise overview of the entire paper in a single paragraph, typically using between 250 and 500 words. The opening sentences should provide some limited, basic background information about the topic. The next sentence should state the problem or issues to be addressed by the paper. Next, the purpose of the study, the hypotheses to be examined, or the data to be described should be stated. The following sentences should provide information relating to the methodology—the study population, the years covered, the number of sites, and the study design. The results are presented next with only the most significant findings reported. The final sentence should state the significance of the study.

The goal of the abstract is to provide the reader with an understanding of the rationale behind the study, general approach to the problem, the results, and the importance of the findings. When any manuscript is prepared, the last section to be written is the abstract, which must stand alone and cannot refer to any other part of the paper.

Introduction

The introduction section of a manuscript is designed to provide the reader with background information, some theoretical context, the results of previous studies, the rationale behind the current study, and, finally, the goal of this study.

This section begins by providing a brief overview of the field or main topic covered by the article and includes the current methods used in that particular field. Background information should be presented only as needed in order to support the paper's position. The reader does not need to read everything the author knows about the subject. For example, "The traditional method of obtaining a depth of an impression in snow is by casting with gypsum."

The next section highlights the weaknesses of the current method or specific problems encountered when this method is applied to certain subpopulations. For example, casting with the traditional method of gypsum has the risk of destroying detailed identification characteristics due to its weight. Summaries of past studies that have addressed this same issue are presented next, and the results and weaknesses of these studies are noted. For example, "Prior studies using a lighter gypsum base still resulted in destroyed impressions and failed to work in colder temperatures."

The last section of the introduction is to provide the reader with the goal of the study. For example, "The goal of this study was to examine whether a three-dimensional surface scanning method is a practical and viable alternative for the documentation of impressions in snow at a crime scene."

One important factor to consider when writing this section is the audience. Consider the education, training, and occupations of the individuals most likely to read the article. If the audience mainly consists of individuals in the medical community, information regarding basic anatomical and medical information can be limited. The introduction should provide enough background information for the reader to understand the object of the study.

The main purpose of the introduction is to describe the importance (significance) and worthiness of the study, provide a rationale behind the design, state a specific hypothesis to be tested, and briefly describe the experimental design used to accomplish the stated objectives.

The style of the introduction typically uses past tense, except when referring to established facts. The length of the introduction is dictated by the journal guidelines, but the target length should be between two and three pages.

Materials and Methods

The materials and methods section contains the materials used during the study and the methodology employed to conduct the study. This section typically begins with the study type, location, and study period. The two basic study designs used in forensic epidemiological research—retrospective and prospective—are described in Chapter 1. The location can be one site or multiple sites depending on the design. If multiple sites are used, the study period for each site must be listed. The study period is the start and end date of the study. For example, "This is a retrospective study, conducted at the medical examiner's office in Pittsburgh, Pennsylvania, from January 1, 1990 to December 31, 1999."

The subjects selected for this study are defined next in terms of how they were selected from the general population and what the inclusion and exclusion criteria were. The case definition should be very clear and well defined. After the cases are defined, the methods that will be used to identify these cases are detailed. If certain types of cases are excluded from the study, the exclusion criteria must be described—for example:

> In this study we are defining suicide as a death that occurred as a result of intentional and self-inflicted injuries. Deaths listed as suicide by police officers will be excluded from this study. Cases will be located by a computer search of death certificates that list the manner of death as suicide.

If the study design consists of multiple sites, one of the most important factors is consistency of definition across all sites. If the rates of suicide by Russian roulette across several states are being compared using death certificate data, each issuing ME/C office should be contacted and the manner of death checked in such cases. In some jurisdictions, Russian roulette is coded as an accident; others code it as a suicide.

The documents that will be reviewed are listed next, including an exact list and their description. The individuals conducting the review and methods used to collect the data will be detailed—for example:

> For each suicide case, the forensic epidemiologist and forensic pathologist will review the following documents: death investigation report, police reports, medical and psychological records, autopsy and toxicological reports, and the DC. The data will be collected using an abstract form or the data will be entered directly into a laptop computer with an electronic data form.

The types of data and the methods used to code from the documents are listed—for example: age, sex, race, marital status, time and date of suicide, mechanism of suicide, suicide note, toxicology analysis, and type of autopsy preformed. The categories of race include white, black, Asian, Hispanic, Native American, and "other," which includes mixed race. Marital status is categorized as single, married, divorced, widowed, or unknown. Common-law marriages are not categorized as married but as single. The methods of suicide are classified into firearm, stabbing/incised wounds, hanging, smothering, carbon monoxide, smoke inhalation, drug OD, BFT from jumping from a height, drowning, suicide by train or motor vehicle, and electrocution. Suicide notes will be listed as present or absent. All legal and illegal compounds present will be listed by name and concentration. The examination will be defined as a complete autopsy or an external-only examination.

The last section describes the type of database the statistics will be entered into and the software used to conduct the analysis of the data. The specific statistical testing should be described—for example, "Statistical analysis of the Excel® database was performed using the SPSS Base 10.0 applications software (SPSS Inc., Chicago, IL)."

The majority of forensically based studies can involve using deceased subjects, body fluids, tissues, cells from humans, and forensic epidemiological data collected during the death investigation. Although the majority of forensic epidemiological studies involve data collected on deaths, forensic studies can also involve data about the living, such as rape analysis, breathalyzer results, fingerprints, bite mark analysis, forgeries, and trace evidence.

All studies involving live humans must first undergo a review by an institutional review board (IRB). The role of the IRB is to make certain that the study adheres to the standards of medical principles and to protect the subjects from unjustifiable risks. A statement declaring that the study underwent an IRB review before beginning must be contained within this section of the paper. If animals are involved, these studies also require an IRB review. Fluids such as blood or urine collected from the living during the course of routine medical evaluation may be used to conduct secondary research; however, the patient must be informed and consent to the research.

Studies involving deceased individuals typically are not covered under the jurisdiction of most IRBs. Some universities still require that the IRB receive a copy of the research methodology for its records. Fluids, tissue, and DNA recovered during the autopsy are routinely used in forensic medical research and papers.

The methods section contains the step-by-step process used to analyze the data. If the data were epidemiological—such as age, race, sex, and cause and manner of death, for example—how these data were grouped or classified would be described. Age could be grouped in the following age groups: 0–10, 11–20, 21–30, etc. If instrumentation was used, the type of system, the model number, how the sample was prepared for analysis, and the method used to interpret the results would appear in this section. For example, if analysis involved gas chromatography in combination with mass spectrometry, the methods section should include the following: the model number for the gas chromatography and mass spectrometry instruments, size and type of the column, the temperatures used, the carrier gas, the selected ion monitors, method used to determine peak standard, and the limits of detection. The methods section should provide a detailed protocol with sufficient information for others to reproduce the study.

The goal of this section is to document all specialized materials and procedures used in conducting this study. Note that this section should not contain any results or an interpretation of the results.

Results

After the study has been completed, the results section allows for presentation of the study results, which typically begins with basic epidemiological data, such as the total number of cases identified during the study period followed by a breakdown by age, sex, and race—for example, "During the 10-year study period, 1,447 deaths were identified as suicide. An examination of the 1,447 cases revealed that 1,164 were male and 283 female; 1,304 were white, 131 were black, and 12 were other."

These results can be displayed as figures or tables. Several variables can be displayed in one table, such as age versus sex and/or race. The data collected on each variable must be presented. The results must be described in a short paragraph detailing the breakdown within each category. A figure or table often accompanies this description. The text should point the reader to observation of what is most relevant in the figures or tables. The text should complement any table/figure and not repeat the same information. Each figure and/or table should be labeled in a manner in which it can stand alone and be understood.

The results section must not present interpretation of the data or discuss the relevance of the results. In addition, the same data should not be presented more than once within the results section. Raw data should not be presented within the paper. The past tense should be used when presenting data.

The goal of the results section is to provide the outcome values, or measurement of the study. The interpretation of the results will be used to support the conclusions.

Conclusion

In the discussion section, the results of the study are put into context of other studies or national data. This section can highlight consistency between the results of the current study and similar previous reports or national data. It can emphasize the results of other studies similar in methodology to the current study but with significantly different results. For example, many studies have reported that the predominant method of suicide by females is drug overdose, but the results of your study show firearms as the leading method of suicide among females. The goal of the discussion section is to interpret and explain the results obtained. Similarities between your results and published reports should also be described—for example, "Our results corresponded with previous reports that have shown single marital status was an increased risk factor for suicide."

For each variable, compare results to those cited within the medical literature and report similar findings, as well as differences. Then discuss the possible reasons to explain why this study reported something contrary to the literature. One of the important items of this section is to state the significance of the study's findings. Stress statements like "this is the first study to show…" or "this is the first time the link between…." The last paragraph typically presents a summary of the study findings and often offers recommendations for future studies.

The goal of this section is to provide an interpretation of your results and support for the conclusions. To interpret data if results differ from expectations, explain why and suggest future directions.

References

The methods of citing the source material vary from journal to journal. Authors must consult the journal guidelines for the specific citing style. All material within the article must be cited in the reference section. Information obtained from other journals, books, the Internet, and personal communication must be referenced.

Types of Manuscripts

One of the main goals of research is to share one's results with others in the scientific community and the general population. This is done through the publication of the results of the study. This allows others within the field to build on the work, to avoid the mistakes experienced by others, and to add to the knowledge base of that field. There are four basic types of manuscripts submitted for publication within the forensic science community: research articles, case presentations, review articles, and letters to the editor.

Research Articles

The key to a well designed and original research paper is to ask a specific question in science and test possible hypotheses in order to provide a possible answer. ME/C offices are ideal for this type of research, mainly because they contain a large amount of unique data in one central location. They are perfect for retrospective as well as prospective study designs. A research article consists of the following sections: abstract, introduction, methods/materials, results, conclusions, and references.

Case Presentations (Case Reports)

During the normal operation of most ME/C offices, aside from typical death cases, a small number of cases are either so unique or so rarely encountered that they are worthy of publication within a forensic medical journal. The forensic epidemiologist who normally reviews all deaths processed by the ME/C office can identify such cases. This case is first presented to the forensic staff of the ME/C office to determine whether it is indeed unique and atypical and warrants publication.

The purpose of a case report is to provide detailed information about a case that others within the forensic community may never encounter and to provide forensic investigative tools or protocols on how to investigate such cases if similar types of cases are encountered in the future.

The case presentation report can take two forms: a case report or a series case report. Case reports present the details of one death (e.g., a suicide by chainsaw). A case report is usually a brief, detailed description of the case. It is a stylized version of the death investigation report. The discussions section should provide aid to the forensic community in how to handle these types of cases if members of the community encounter them during their operations. In a series case report, a small number of similar cases are collected and presented together (e.g., deaths by ingesting antifreeze).

The format of a case presentation differs from that of a formal research article and varies depending on journal guidelines. Possible formats include: (1) abstract followed by a case report, a discussion section, and then references; (2) abstract followed by an introduction, a case report, the results of the autopsy, toxicological and microscopic examination results, a discussion section, and references; (3) introduction, multiple case reports, discussions, conclusion, and references; or (4) introduction, case history, autopsy findings, toxicological analysis, discussions, conclusion, and references.

Review Articles

Forensic researchers, forensic investigators, and forensic pathologists do not have the time to collect, read, and stay current on a specific topic of forensic medicine, so they rely on review articles. A review article is a full-length paper that can review the current state of the art of a procedure or methods within forensic science or provide a review on the published literature in a particular subject.

A state-of-the art review involves the author collecting all the major and relevant articles that focus on one specific topic to be reviewed. This review paper is designed to describe the current methods used to collect or analyze a specific type of evidence and then to summarize the varying methods. For example, a review paper on the methods of obtaining fingerprints would first provide the basic principles of fingerprinting, the varying methods of obtaining fingerprints, the advantages and disadvantages of each method, and possible implications for the future of the science.

In a review article of the published literature, the author first collects all relevant articles that address that topic and then provides a detailed summary of each article. In this type of review, the following data for each study are presented: the number of subjects, the study period, the location, the definition used to identify subjects, and the main findings of each study. An example is a review article on SIDS deaths. In this article, papers that address SIDS deaths would be described in terms of the total number of infant studies; the distribution by age, sex, and race; the length and significant findings of the study; and any weaknesses noted by the paper or by the author conducting the review.

The format of a review article includes the abstract, introduction, biological background, models, discussions, conclusion, and references.

Letters to the Editor

Letters to the editor offer a method for readers to respond to an article that was published within that journal. The letter starts by first referencing the article to which the letter is responding and then offering a brief summary or overview of that paper. Then the responding writer can present problems in the methodology, statistics, or issues that were not addressed in the published article. Often, the letter writer proposes alternative methods to conduct future studies. The name, title, and affiliation of the responding author are listed, followed by references. Most journals limit letters to the editor to a few hundred words and they are not subjected to a peer review.

Peer Review

The completed manuscript is then submitted to a forensic journal for publication consideration. The first key to getting published is to locate a journal that is most appropriate to the subject matter of the paper. Some journals are looking for highly technical articles; others are interested in pure research and others are more cutting edge. Examining the mission statement of the journal will give an indication of its focus. As described in Chapter 3, a number of journals operate within the field of forensics.

Once the most appropriate journal has been selected, the manuscript must be formatted for that specific journal. The author guidelines provide the formatting protocol. An increasing number of journals have an electronic submission format, which means that the document is submitted online. The submitted manuscripts are first reviewed by the editor of the journal to determine whether the article is within the scope of the publication, is formatted correctly, and up to the standards of the journal to warrant a peer review.

A peer-review process is an evaluation of a submitted manuscript. It is a process of subjecting an author's scholarly work, research, methodology used, and data analysis to the scrutiny of others who are experts within that field. Successful peer review therefore requires a community of experts in a given field who are qualified and able to perform an impartial review. Depending on the journal, the manuscript will be sent to three or four reviewers.

This process encourages authors to submit work that meets the accepted high standards of their discipline and to prevent the dissemination of unwarranted claims, unacceptable interpretations, or personal views. Publications that have not undergone peer review are likely to be regarded with suspicion by scholars and professionals in many fields.

A common rationale for peer review is that it is rare for an individual author or research team to spot every mistake or flaw in a complicated piece of work. Authors may be too close to their work to be able to step back and objectively review the work. With its special expertise or experience, the review team may spot areas that require corrections or expansion. For a publication in a scholarly journal, it is also normally a requirement that the subject be both novel and substantial. Therefore, showing work to others increases the probability that weaknesses will be identified and, with advice and encouragement, fixed.

Typically, to help foster unvarnished criticism, reviewers are anonymous and independent. In addition, because reviewers are normally selected from experts in the fields discussed in the article, the process of peer review is considered critical to establishing a reliable body of research and knowledge. Scholars reading the published articles can only be experts in a limited area; they rely, to some degree, on the peer-review process to support reliable and credible research that they can build upon for subsequent or related research. As a result, significant scandal ensues when an author is found to have falsified the research included in an article because many other scholars, as well as the field of study itself, may have relied upon the original research.

The Peer Review Process

To review the article, the journal's editor will select three or four reviewers from a large database of experts in areas that closely match the topic of the manuscript. These reviewers will be sent a copy of the manuscript, normally by e-mail or through a Web-based manuscript processing system. The names and the affiliations of the submitting authors are removed from the manuscript.

These reviewers are given 6–8 weeks to review the article. Then they are required to complete and return an evaluation report of the work to the editor. This evaluation report includes a general impression of the work, the strengths and weaknesses, and major problem areas within the study, such as small sample size, methodology problems, and analysis errors. Additionally, the role of the reviewers is to suggest ways to improve the study. These suggestions can be very detailed.

Aside from the written comments, most journals have a check box system requiring the reviewer to categorize the work from "ready for publication" to "rejection." Table 12.1 shows the options that reviewers have in grading the article.

The comments and ranking by the reviewers are all sent to the journal editor. The editor, who is usually familiar with the field of the manuscript (although typically not in as much depth as the reviewers, who are specialists), then evaluates the reviewers' comments. The editor may provide his or her own opinion of the manuscript with regard to the scope of the journal before passing a decision back to the submitting author, alone or with the comments of the reviewers. Although the editor relies heavily on the expert

Table 12.1 Ranking of a Manuscript by Peer Reviews

check one	Reviewer recommendation
—	Unconditionally accept the manuscript or proposal
—	Accept with minor changes
—	Reject, encourage revision, and invite resubmission
—	Reject

reviewers, he or she makes the final decision whether to publish the article. The role of the reviewers is advisory, and the editor is typically under no formal obligation to accept their opinions. In situations where the reviewers disagree substantially about the quality of a work, there are a number of strategies for reaching a decision. When an editor receives very positive and very negative reviews for the same manuscript, he or she can solicit one or more additional reviews or make the final decision as to whether to publish the work.

The author is then notified by e-mail or a letter as to the decision of the editor. The possible outcomes include acceptance without any revision, acceptance with minor revision, rejection but encouragement to rewrite and resubmit, or rejection. Acceptance without any revision indicates that the manuscript was up to the standards of the journal and contains no theoretical, methodological, grammar, or spelling errors that required correcting. Acceptance with minor revision is an indication that the editor and reviewers believe that the manuscript has merit, but they require some small changes in the way the data were presented or require more background information or rewording of certain sections. If the author submitting the manuscript follows the review suggestions, the article will be published. A rejection but encouragement to rewrite and resubmit is an indication that the reviewers liked the concept or idea within the paper, but that it lacked the proper structure, the sample size may have been too small, or the proper level of analysis was lacking. In other words, the submitter is on the right track but needs to do more. Finally, rejection indicates that the quality of the research is below the standards of that journal.

Reviewers are usually not paid and reviewing takes time away from the reviewer's main activities, such as his or her own research. The main reason that individuals choose to become reviewers is that they are authors—or at least readers—who know that the publication system requires that experts donate their time. Reviewers also have the opportunity to act as "gatekeepers" to prevent work that does not meet the standards of the field from being published, which is a position of some responsibility. Editors are at a special advantage in recruiting a scholar when he or she has overseen the publication of his or her work or if the scholar hopes to submit manuscripts to that editor's publication in the future.

Another difficulty that peer-review organizers face is that, with respect to some manuscripts or proposals, few scholars may truly qualify as experts. Such is the case of subspecialties such as forensic nursing, forensic entomology, or forensic botany.

The process of peer review does not end after publication within the journal. The process continues in the form of peer-review journal clubs' reviews. Here, groups of colleagues review literature and discuss the value and implications that it presents. Journal clubs will often send letters to the editor of a journal or correspond with the editor via an online journal club. In this way, all "peers" may offer reviews and critiques of published literature.

The Forensic Epidemiologist Consultant and Expert Witness

Introduction

Today's criminal justice cases are ever increasing in complexity, and daily advances in the science of forensics and the technology used in its analysis have also become extremely complicated. The major function of the forensic epidemiologist is to advise individuals, attorneys, and juries of the meaning, significance, and limitations of the forensic evidence in cases involving a death or other types of criminal cases. The role of the forensic epidemiologist as either a consultant or as an expert witness functions as a bridge between the scientific community and the legal community.

This chapter will define the role of a forensic epidemiologist functioning as a consultant or an expert witness, the federal rules of evidence, and the experiences faced by an expert witness during a trial.

Forensic Epidemiological Consultant

Private forensic epidemiologists are frequently hired by individuals, companies, and attorneys. The next of kin of the decedent or other family members are concerned because they have questions regarding the death of a loved one. They may not understand the reasons why the death was ruled as it was, information within the autopsy report, or whether the level of investigation was carried out correctly. The consultant begins the investigation by obtaining and reviewing all documents relating to the case; this may include medical records, death investigation reports, the autopsy report, and police reports. The role of the consultant is to assess whether the proper procedures were followed, the methods of testing the evidence were appropriate, and the conclusions reached by the testing laboratories were correct.

In addition, the consultant notes the weaknesses of the investigation. For example, if the death was due to a firearm, were the hands of the victim tested for gunshot residue (GSR)? If the last will and testament was in question, was an examination of the brain conducted? If a suicide note was located at the death scene, was the writing style compared to that of the deceased? In most cases, the concern revolves around the family not understanding what constitutes a proper death investigation and wanting to know that all possible explanations for the death were in fact explored. In many cases, the family refuses to accept the manner of death listed on the death certificate (usually death by suicide) and wants the forensic epidemiological consultant to review the case and provide a second opinion to that provided by the ME/C office. The major role of a forensic epidemiological consultant is to evaluate the scientific and forensic investigation and analysis of the evidence and provide a written report indicating the conclusions of that review. Furthermore, he or she will provide guidance if further investigation is warranted and, if so, advise the direction in which it should proceed.

Companies typically employ forensic epidemiological consultants to perform evaluations of their product in order to counter claims by outside organizations or assess the risk to their product under certain conditions. Many manufacturers and companies have to defend themselves against claims made by outside organizations. These claims are often based on nonscientific data analysis, small sample size, or, in most cases, simply anecdotal information; nevertheless, they do require a response from the company. The consultants are provided with complete access to the company's research and data.

Consider the following example. Company X has produced a new type of extension cord. The media have linked a number of fatal house fires to the extension cord. The consultant would start by obtaining all the information about all fires within a large geographic area where the new extension cord had been distributed. The following reports would be obtained: fire marshal's investigation reports containing the determination as to the cause of the fire, the death investigation reports, autopsy reports, and toxicology reports. The objective of the consultant would be to determine what percentage of the fires were directly attributed to the new cord and, in cases where the cord was identified as contributing to the fire, whether it was used properly or whether it overloaded the line. In addition, the consultant would obtain data regarding the national average of fires started by extension cords and compare them to other fire-related data for sources such as space heaters, TVs, toasters, and other electrical devices to place the risk of the extension cord in perspective with other household items.

Companies also hire forensic epidemiological consultants to perform evaluations of the potential risk to their product under specific conditions—for example, whether the introduction of a few strands of hair from an individual with a blood-borne disease poses any risk to the end product. When the consultant is hired by a company, he or she performs a statistical and scientific analysis of the data and provides a report that is unbiased and scientifically accurate.

Attorneys most frequently utilize the skills of a forensic epidemiological consultant. Primarily due to the increased complexity of current cases and the increased utilization of forensic science evidence in the courtroom, lawyers are increasingly seeking out and utilizing consultants to assist them in understanding and evaluating evidence, as well as to offer advice on ways to proceed. Lawyers are using these consultants to:

1. understand highly complicated, highly technical, complex scientific processes and procedures to analyze forensic data and the meanings and significance of the results;
2. assist them in pretrial evaluation of the strengths and weaknesses of the forensic evidence in a case; and
3. act as nontestifying consultants.

The goal of consultants is to help explain the meaning of detailed forensic analysis and the significance of these results, as well as to provide background to the death scene protocol and procedures. Their function is to review and evaluate medical records, autopsy reports, police reports, technical data, and the level of investigation and testing conducted on the evidence in order to provide a written report indicating the strengths and weaknesses of the cases, as well as technical advice on how to proceed with the case. Forensic epidemiological consultants do not testify in court.

Forensic Epidemiologist as Expert Witness

In contrast to a consultant, an expert witness is hired to testify in a court of law and to express his or her opinion regarding a particular aspect of a case. An expert witness is an individual who, through training, experience, or education, has special and precise knowledge in a specific field. With the advances in forensic science and the increased use of such technology, the justice system is relying on this field in the courtroom much more than ever before. In addition, with the popularity of television shows such as *CSI*, *Forensic Files*, and *Crossing Jordan*, reruns of the classic *Quincy* series, and the public airing of high-profile cases such as the O. J. Simpson trial, prosecutors, defense attorneys, and even jurors expect the presentation of forensic evidence during the trial. These experts are often sought out by members of the legal community because they are needed to assist during the pretrial evaluation of the evidence and to testify in a court of law.

There are two basic types of expert witness: the professional expert witness and the individual sought out by lawyers to testify in a case because of his or her special knowledge. The latter type typically comes from the world of academia or industry and has little experience in or understanding of the legal arena into which he or she is about to be drawn. Individuals in the traditional sciences of biology, engineering, chemistry, microbiology, epidemiology, and medicine normally have little or no experience with or exposure to the legal system. To them, the process of testifying can be alien or an experience filled with feelings of excitement, intimidation, or anger. This is especially true for those coming from the "ivory towers" of academia and, to a lesser degree, for those coming from industry. Although a forensic epidemiologist transitioning from the role of consultant to that of expert witness will possess a deeper understanding of the legal system, he or she is still entering a world much different from that of science.

One must ask, "Why is there such a great disconnect between the worlds of science and medicine and that of the legal community"? In general, this is because the two disciplines serve different purposes and share no common ground. Several reasons account for this great disconnect, including education, objectives, and terminology.

First, the educational backgrounds of the two disciplines differ. Lawyers are taught about laws, case law, procedures, and the mechanics of a trial. During their 3 years of formal education, they are not exposed to topics such as the scientific method, statistical evaluation, or hypotheses testing. In addition, they are not instructed on how fields of science can assist in their cases. Conversely, individuals emerging from engineering or medical schools, PhD programs in forensics or epidemiology, or other fields within public health have no exposure to the legal system. In turn, in their training programs, forensic epidemiologists and physicians have no familiarity on how to prepare and present an opinion in court, the mechanism of testifying, or the techniques used by the opposition during the trial.

Second is the concept of objective. The law is concerned with ordering human conduct in accordance with certain standards, values, and societal goals. Science, on the other hand, is designed to describe and explain occurrences and data in neutral, objective terms. The goal of the scientist is to try to ask specific questions and discover the truth or facts with regard to a particular question. Lawyers are trying to win a case by presenting the jury only information favorable to their case; they have no interest in presenting all sides of an issue or alternate explanations. There is a purposeful difference between science and medicine and the law. The goal of science and medicine is to follow objective methodology to find the cause or multiple causes of a condition, while the purpose of the legal system is to settle disputes.

Third is the terminology. Those in the scientific community use words and phrases like "relative risk," "bias," and "statistically significant"; the law dictionary contains terms such as "admissibility," "beyond a shadow of doubt," and "reasonable doubt." In addition, the word "significant" has a different meaning in the legal context compared to its meaning within the scientific community. The scientist or physician and the attorney speak two different languages. The term "causation" illustrates this point the best. The law assumes that the expert can quantify his or her opinion in such terms as "reasonable medical certainty" or "reasonable probability." This is driven by the fact that causation in the legal world is testimony that is sufficient to support a verdict in favor of the plaintiff even though it may not meet the scientific level of causation.

The Court Experience

The experience faced by the academician, scientist, or industrial expert during a trial is totally foreign in terms of procedural and intellectual milieu. We next describe the typical experiences an expert witness may face in a court of law.

The first novel experience comes in the form of the cross-examination. The purpose of a cross-examination of the expert witness is twofold. The first is to elicit as many facts from the expert as possible that are favorable to his or her client's theory. Within the academic and scientific setting, it is the accepted practice to present all aspects of a theory. By contrast, in a cross-examination, the expert witness is only allowed to provide opinions regarding limited aspects of a particular issue. The sequence of questioning, the phrasing, and the limits placed on the answers are in contrast to the open-ended format that usually prevails during scientific conferences and symposia. The use of a "yes–no" response does not afford the expert an opportunity to discuss all possible explanations.

Second, the examiner tries to destroy the expert's credibility by bringing out any facts that would tend to lessen the weight of the expert's opinion. This is accomplished by attempting to show that the witness is overcompensated, is biased in favor his or her client's cause, is not really knowledgeable in the field, or holds a different view from that of other experts generally recognized as authorities within the same field. This attempt to destroy creditability is totally foreign to a witness coming from the academic and scientific universe. Within the academic world, credibility is determined by educational degrees, number of publications, and faculty appointments. These are rarely questioned. In contrast, when a forensic epidemiologist takes the witness stand, every grade (back to high school) and published paper (especially with conflicting views) may be called into question. In a court of law, every opinion may be subjected to a blistering dissection on cross-examination.

Third, the examiner attempts to cast doubt on the expert's theories while trying to have the expert admit that an alternative explanation can be possible. This is done by intensity, rapidity, and sometimes adversarial questioning during the cross-examination. Academic and scientific debates are designed to determine facts and separate out fiction or mere assumptions in order to support a hypothesis. In contrast, in the courtroom, opposing counsel attempts to have the expert admit the possibility that a particular event could have occurred in a different manner or that the conclusions expressed by the witness could have an alternative explanation. The end result is to cast doubt on the truthfulness and credibility of that particular witness. This goal is diametrically opposed to the training of epidemiologists and basic science theory.

Currently, the teaching of future epidemiologists in graduate programs remains focused on basic course work that will lend itself to conducting and designing future research studies. The majority of these studies are geared to implementation in the university academic setting. The results of these studies are then presented in relatively nonadversarial settings such as conferences and peer-reviewed publications. Consequently, although recent graduates emerge with knowledge of the fundamentals of epidemiology, such an educational background does not adequately prepare the graduate for the legal arena.

The Federal Rules of Evidence

A forensic epidemiologist hired as an expert witness is expected to testify in a court of law and express his or her opinions regarding a particular aspect of a case. The forensic epidemiologist who plans to function as an expert witness must understand two key concepts: (1) the Federal Rules of Evidence, and (2) admissibility of expert evidence and testimony. The Federal Rules of Evidence codifying the requirements and limitations of an expert witness within Rules 701–706 are described in detail in Table 13.1. Rule 702 specifically addresses the definition of an expert.

The Admissibility of Expert Evidence and Testimony

Outside the courtroom, attorneys can choose forensic epidemiological consultants based solely on their experience, education, and references. However, in a courtroom, the admission of an individual to present expert testimony as an expert witness is at the discretion of the presiding judge. Prior to the trial, a *Daubert hearing or motion is held*. The primary purpose of this hearing is to exclude the testimony of those who are not truly expert witnesses. The reasons to disallow the testimony of so-called expert witnesses include their lack of the specific expertise required to testify at that level of expertise or use of questionable methods to obtain information that is unacceptable within the field of science.

This hearing is conducted before the judge, who becomes the "gatekeeper" of scientific evidence. The expert must prove to the judge that (1) he

Table 13.1 The Federal Rules of Evidence

Rule	Features
Rule 701 Opinion testimony by lay witnesses	If the witness is not testifying as an expert, the witness' testimony in the form of opinions or inferences is limited to those opinions or inferences which are (a) rationally based on the perception of the witness; (b) helpful to a clear understanding of the witness' testimony or the determination of a fact in issue; (c) not based on scientific, technical, or other specialized knowledge within the scope of Rule 702
Rule 702 Testimony by experts	If scientific, technical, or other specialized knowledge will assist the trier of fact to understand the evidence or to determine a fact in issue… A witness qualified as an expert by knowledge, skill, experience, training, or education, may testify thereto in the form of an opinion or otherwise, if (1) the testimony is based upon sufficient facts or data, (2) the testimony is the product of reliable principles and methods, and (3) the witness has applied the principles and methods reliably to the facts of the case
Rule 703 Bases of opinion testimony by an experts	The facts or data in the particular case upon which an expert bases an opinion or inference may be those perceived by or made known to the expert at or before the hearing. If a type reasonably relied upon by experts in the particular field in forming opinions or inferences upon the subject, the facts or data need not be admissible in evidence in order for the opinion or inference to be admitted. Facts or data that are otherwise inadmissible shall not be disclosed to the jury by the proponent of the opinion or inference unless the court determines that their probative value in assisting the jury to evaluate the expert's opinion substantially outweighs their prejudicial effect
Rule 704 Opinion on ultimate issue	(a) Except as provided in subdivision (b), testimony in the form of an opinion or inference otherwise admissible is not objectionable because it embraces an ultimate issue to be decided by the trier of fact; (b) no expert witness testifying with respect to the mental state or condition of a defendant in a criminal case may state an opinion or inference as to whether the defendant did or did not have the mental state or condition constituting an element of the crime charged or of a defense thereto. Such ultimate issues are matters for the trier of fact alone
Rule 706 Court-appointed experts	(a) Appointment: The court may on its own motion or on the motion of any party enter an order to show cause why expert witnesses should not be appointed, and may request the parties to submit nominations. The court may appoint any expert witnesses agreed upon by the parties, and may appoint expert witnesses of its own selection. An expert witness shall not be appointed by the court unless the witness consents to act. A witness so appointed shall be informed of the witness' duties by the court in writing, a copy of which shall be filed with the clerk, or at a conference in which the parties shall have opportunity to participate. A witness so appointed shall advise the parties of the witness' findings, if any; the witness' deposition may be taken by any party; and the witness may be called to testify by the court or any party. The witness shall be subject to cross-examination by each party, including a party calling the witness

Table 13.1 The Federal Rules of Evidence (continued)

Rule	Features
	(b) Compensation: Expert witnesses so appointed are entitled to reasonable compensation in whatever sum the court may allow. The compensation thus fixed is payable from funds which may be provided by law in criminal cases and civil actions and proceedings involving just compensation under the fifth amendment. In other civil actions and proceedings the compensation shall be paid by the parties in such proportion and at such time as the court directs, and thereafter charged in like manner as other costs
	(c) Disclosure of appointment: In the exercise of its discretion, the court may authorize disclosure to the jury of the fact that the court appointed the expert witness
	(d) Parties' experts of own selection: Nothing in this rule limits the parties in calling expert witnesses of their own selection
Rule 705 Disclosure of facts or data underlying expert opinion	The expert may testify in terms of opinion or inference and give reasons therefore without first testifying to the underlying facts or data, unless the court requires otherwise. The expert may in any event be required to disclose the underlying facts or data on cross-examination

or she is appropriately qualified to provide expert testimony; (2) the opinion presented is valid, reasonable, and based on sound methodological foundations; and (3) his or her testimony fits the specific circumstances of the case. Therefore a forensic epidemiologist wishing to testify in court as an expert witness must first prove to the judge that he or she has the education, experience, and specific knowledge relevant to that case so as to be able to offer an expert opinion.

Becoming a Forensic Epidemiologist

Those thinking of hiring a forensic epidemiologist as a consultant or an expert witness must make a detailed examination of the individual's background and experience. Most forensic epidemiologists gain their forensic field experience by starting as death scene investigators, followed by assisting in the postmortem examination, learning the proper methods of identifying and collecting evidence, and then finally gaining an understanding of varying methods of analysis. Concurrently, they obtain an advanced degree in forensic epidemiology in order to perform a comprehensive and creditable review of the medical and scientific evidence.

This type of experience and education is difficult to obtain, and locations where such a background can be acquired are limited. Logically, it would be most beneficial for individuals interested in a career as a forensic consultant or expert to begin their careers as death scene investigators (e.g., deputy coroner) followed by formal education awarding a PhD in a forensic science and epidemiology program. Unfortunately, a number of forensic consultants obtain their PhD but lack any type of practical field training or experience. This places them at a disadvantage as consultants and expert witnesses.

Bibliography

Allegheny County Office of the Coroner. 2005. Statistical report.
Altamura, C., A. VanGastel, and R. Pioli. 1999. Seasonal and circadian rhythms in suicide in Cagliari, Italy. *Journal of Affective Disorders* 53:77–85.
American Academy of Pediatrics, Task Force on Infant Sleep Positioning and SIDS. 1992. *Pediatrics* 89:1120–1126.
_____. 1996. Positioning and sudden infant death syndrome (SIDS). *Pediatrics* 98:1216–1218.
_____. 2000. Changing concepts of sudden infant death syndrome: Implications for infant sleeping environment and sleep position. *Pediatrics* 105:650–656.
American Medical Association (AMA) Council on Ethical and Judicial Affairs. 1992. Confidentiality of HIV status on autopsy reports. Presented to the AMA House of Delegates, Chicago, IL.
Aufderheide, D. H. 2000. Conducting the psychological autopsy in correctional settings. *Journal of Correctional Health Care* 7:5–36.
Ayala, F. J. 1994. On the scientific method, its practice and pitfalls. *History and Philosophy of Life Sciences* 16:205–240.
Bailey, R. 2008. Carbon monoxide. Available at http://biology.about.com/library/blco.htm?p=1
Baker, F. M. 1990. Black youth suicide: Literature review with a focus on prevention. *Journal of the National Medical Association* 82:495–507.
Baker, S., and W. Spitz. 1970. An evaluation of the hazard created by natural death at the wheel. *New England Journal of Medicine* 283:405–417.
Barraclough, B. M., J. Bunch, and B. Nelson. 1974. A hundred cases of suicide; clinical aspects. *British Journal of Psychiatry* 125:355–373.
Beaumont, G. 1989. Suicide and antidepressant overdose in general practice. *British Journal of Psychiatry* 155 (suppl.6): 27–31.
Bennett, A. T., and K. A. Collins. 2001. Elderly suicide: A 10-year retrospective study. *American Journal of Forensic Medicine and Pathology* 22 (2): 169–172.
Benos, D. J. 2007. The ups and downs of peer review. *Advances in Physiology Education* 31:145–152.
Bergman, A. B., C. G. Ray, M. A. Pomeroy, P. W. Wahl, and J. B. Beckwith. 1972. Studies of sudden infant death syndrome in King County, Washington. *Pediatrics* 49:860–870.
Black, H. C. 1990. *Black's law dictionary,* 6th ed. St. Paul, MN: West Publishing Co.
Blair, P. S., P. J. Fleming, I. J. Smith, M. W. Platt, J. Young, P. Nadin, P. J. Berry, and J. Golding. 1999. Babies sleeping with parents: Case-control study of factors influencing the risk of the sudden infant death syndrome. *British Medical Journal* 319 (7223): 1457–1461.
Bootman, J. 2000. To err is human. *Archives of Internal Medicine* 160 (21): 3189–3192.

Buchholz, U., J. Mermin, and R. Rios. 2002. An outbreak of food-borne illness associated with methomyl-contaminated salt. *Journal of the American Medical Association* 288:604–610.

Buck, U., N. Albertini, S. Naether, and M. Thali. 2007. 3D documentation of footwear impressions and tire tracks in snow with high resolution optical surface scanning. *Forensic Science International* 172:157–164.

Buehler J. W., L. F. Smith, and E. M. Wallace. 1985. Unexplained deaths in a children's hospital: An epidemiological assessment. *New England Journal of Medicine* 313:211–216.

CDC medical examiner/coroner's map. Available at www.cdc/gov/mmwr/Preview/mmwrhtml/rr5308a1.htm

CDC SIDS data. Available at www.cdc/gov/SIDS/PDF/SUIDSIforms.pdf

Coping with peer rejection. 2003 16 October. Nature 425 (6959), 645. doi:10.1038/425645a

Criminal and epidemiological investigation handbook. FBI and Department of Justice.

Diekstra, R. F. W. 1993. The epidemiology of suicide and parasuicide. *Acta Psychiatrica Scandinavica* 371 (suppl): 9–20.

DiMaio, V. J. 2001. *Forensic pathology,* 2nd ed. Boca Raton, FL: CRC Press.

Drug Abuse Warning Network. August, 2002. Development of a new design. Available at www.samhsa.gov

Editorial. 2008. Working double-blind. *Nature* 451:605–606.

Elfawal, M. A. 1990. Cultural influence on the incidence and choice of method of suicide in Saudi Arabia. *American Journal of Forensic Medicine and Pathology* 20 (2): 163–168.

Facts: Vehicular homicide and the impaired driver. 2004. Available at http://www.nhtsa.dot.gov/people/outreash/safesobr/13qp/facts/facthom.html

FARS. 2008. *Analytic reference guide 1975–2007.* U.S. Department of Transportation, National Highway Traffic Safety Administration. DOT HS 810 937.

Fatality analysis reporting system. Available at http://www:nrd.nhtsa.dot.gov/departments/nrd-01/summaries/FARS_98.html

Fatality analysis reporting system. Available at http://www:iihs.org/research/fatality_facts_2006/fars.html

Felthous, A. R., and A. Hempel, A. 1995. Combine homicide–suicide: A review. *Journal of Forensic Science* 40 (5): 846–857.

Felthous, A. R., A. G. Hempel, A. Heredia, E. Freeman, K. Goodness, C. Holzer, T. J. Bennett, and W. E. Korndorffer. 2001. Combined homicide–suicide in Galveston County. *Journal of Forensic Science* 46 (3): 586–592.

Filiano J. J., and H. C. Kinney. 1994. A perspective on neuropathologic findings in victims of the sudden infant death syndrome: The triple-risk model. *Biology of the Neonate* 65:194–197.

Flick, L., D. K. White, C. Vemulapalli, B. B. Stulac, and J. S. Kemp. 2001. Sleep position and the use of soft bedding during bed sharing among African American infants at increased risk for sudden infant death syndrome. *Pediatrics* 138 (3): 338–343.

Ford, R. 1997. *The world's great handguns: From 1450 to the present day.* Edison, NJ: Chartwell Books, Inc.

Franks, A., J. J. Sacks, and J. D. Smith. 1987. A cluster of unexplained cardiac arrests in a surgical care unit. *Critical Care Medicine* 15:1075–1076.

Gallerani, M., F. M. Avato, and D. Dal Monte. 1996. The time for suicide. *Psychological Medicine* 26:867–870.
Gitanjali, B. 2001. Peer review—Process, perspectives and the path ahead. *Journal of Postgraduate Medicine* 47:210–214.
Goldman, M. B. 1994. Sudden infant death syndrome: back to sleep campaign. *Caring* 13 (Pt. 2): 52–55.
Goodman, R. A. 2003. Forensic epidemiology: Law at the intersections of public health and criminal investigation. *Journal of Law, Medication & Ethics* 31:684–700.
Griffith, E. E., and C. C. Bell. 1989. Recent trends in suicide and homicide among blacks. *Journal of the American Medical Association* 16:2265–2269.
Groenewold, M. Forensic epidemiology. 2007. *Kentucky Law Enforcement* Fall: 30–34.
Gunnell, D., and M. Nowers. 1997. Suicide by jumping. *Acta Psychiatrica Scandinavica* 96 (1): 1–6.
Hanzlick, R. 2007. *Death investigation: Systems and procedures.* Boca Raton: CRC Press.
Hanzlick, R., and R. G. Parrish. 1993. The failure of death certificates to record the performance of autopsies. *Journal of the American Medical Association* 269:27.
Hauck, F. R., S. M. Herman, M. Donovan, S. Iyasu, C. Merrick Moore, E. Donoghue, R. H. Kirschner, and M. Willinger. 2003. Sleep environment and the risk of sudden infant death syndrome in an urban population: The Chicago infant mortality study. *Pediatrics* 111 (5): 1207–1214.
Hauck, F. R., C. Merrick Moore, S. Herman, M. Donovan, M. Kalelkar, K. Kaufer Cristoffel, H. Hoffman, and D. Rowley. 2002. The contribution of prone sleeping position to the racial disparity in sudden infant death syndrome: The Chicago infant mortality study. *Pediatrics* 110 (4): 772–780.
Hayward, R., and T. Hofer. 2001. Estimating hospital deaths due to medical errors: Preventability is in the eye of the reviewer. *Journal of the American Medical Association* 286 (4): 415–420.
Healey, M., S. Shackford, and T. Osler. 2002. Complications in surgical patients. *Surgery* 137 (5): 611–618.
Ho, T. P., P. S. F. Yip, and C. W. F. Chiu. 1998. Suicide notes: What do they tell us? *Acta Psychiatrica Scandinavica* 98 (6): 467–473.
Homicide trends in the U.S.: Additional information about the data. 2008. U.S. Department of Justice, Office of Justice Program, Bureau of Justice Statistics. Available at http://www.ojp.usdoj.gov/bjs/homicide/addinfo.htm
Hoyert, D. L., E. Arias, and B. L. Smith. 2000. Deaths: Final data for 1999. *National Vital Statistics Reports* 49 (8): 1–114. Available at http://www.cdc.gov/nchs/data/nvsr/nvsr49
Hunt, L. W., M. D. Silverstein, and C. D. Reed. 1993. Accuracy of the death certificate in a population-based study of asthmatic patients. *Journal of the American Medical Association* 269:1947–1952.
Innes, B. 2005. *Body in question.* New York: Sterling Publishing Co.
Iserson, K. 1994. *Death to dust.* Tucson, AZ: Galen Press, Ltd.
Isometsa, E. T. 2000. Suicide. *Current Opinion in Psychiatry* 13 (2): 143–147.
Isometasa, E. T., M. Heikkinen, and M. Henriksson. 1997. Differences between urban and rural suicides. *Acta Psychiatrica Scandinavica*, 95 (4): 297–305.

Isometsa, E. T., M. E. Heikkinen, and M. J. Marttunen. 1995. The last appointment before suicide: Is suicide intent communicated? *American Journal of Psychiatry* 152 (6): 919–922.

Istre, G. R., T. L. Gustafson, and R. C. Baron. 1985. A mystery cluster of deaths and cardio pulmonary arrests in a pediatric intensive care unit. *New England Journal of Medicine* 313:205–211.

Measuring the quality of editorial peer review. *Journal of the American Medical Association* 287:2786–2790.

Kemp, J. S., B. Unger, D. Wilkins, R. Psara, T. Ledbetter, M. A. Graham, M. Case, and B. T. Thach. 2000. Unsafe sleep practices and an analysis of bed sharing among infants dying suddenly and unexpectedly: Results of a four-year, population-based, death-scene investigation study of sudden infant death syndrome and related deaths. *Pediatrics* 106:3–9.

Kevan, S. M. 1978. The seasonal behavior of Canadians. *Canadian Mental Health* 26:16.

———. 1980. Perspectives on season of suicide: A review. *Social Science & Medicine* 14:369–378.

Kircher, T., and R. E. Anderson. 1987. Cause of death: Proper completion of the death certificate. *Journal of the American Medical Association* 258:349–352.

Kircher, T., J. Nelson, and H. Burdo. 1985. The autopsy as a measure of accuracy of the death certificate. *New England Journal of Medicine* 313:1263–1269.

Klerman, G. L. 1984. Clinical epidemiology of suicide. *Journal of Clinical Psychiatry* 48 (suppl 2): 33–38.

Knight, B. 1996. *Forensic pathology*, 2nd ed. New York: Oxford University Press, Inc.

Koehler, S. A. 2005a. Using medical examiner/coroner-generated death certificates in research: Advantages and limitations. *Journal of Forensic Nursing* 1:133–135.

———. 2005b. The use of coroner's/medical examiner's data by forensic nurses. *Journal of Forensic Nursing* 1:37–38.

———. 2005c. Autopsy report. In *Medical-legal aspects of medical records*, ed. P. W. Iyer, B. Levin, and M. A. Shea. Tucson, AZ: Lawyers and Judges Publishing Co.

———. 2007. The role of suicide notes in death investigation. *Journal of Forensic Nursing* 3 (2): 87–88, 92.

———. 2008. SIDS deaths: The role of forensic nurses. *Journal of Forensic Nursing* 4 (3): 141–142.

Koehler, S. A., A. Shakir, S. Ladham, L. Rozin, and C. H. Wecht. 2004. Cardiac concussion: Definition, differential diagnosis, case presentation and legal ramification of a misdiagnosis. *American Journal of Forensic Medicine and Pathology* 25:205–208.

Koehler, S.A., H. B. Weiss, A. Shakir, S. Shaeffer, S. Ladham, L. Rozin, J. Dominick, and C. H. Wecht. 2006. Accurately assessing elderly fall deaths using hospital discharge and vital statistics data. *Journal of Forensic Medicine and Pathology* 27:30–35.

Kung, H. C., D. L. Hoyert, J. Q. Xu, and S. L. Murphy. 2008. Deaths: final data for 2005. National Vital Statistics Report, vol. 56, no. 10. Hyattsville MD: National Center for Health Statistics.

Lane, B. 2004. *The encyclopedia of forensic science*. London: Magpie Books.

Last, J. M. 1988. *A dictionary of epidemiology*, 2nd ed. New York: Oxford University Press.

Leenaars, A. A., E. J. Wilde, and S. Wenckstern. 2001. Suicide notes of adolescents: A life span comparison. *Canadian Journal of Behavioral Science* 33 (1): 47–57.

Leonard, B. E. 1986. Toxicity of antidepressants. *Lancet* ii:1105.
Lester, D. 1994. Estimates of prescription rates and the use of medicaments for suicide. *Pharmacology & Toxicology* 75:231–232.
Lester, D., and K. Abe. 1989. The effect of controls on sedatives and hypnotics on their use for suicide. *Clinical Toxicology* 27:299–303.
Loue, S. 1999. *Forensic epidemiology.* Carbondale: Southern Illinois University Press.
_____. 2002. *Case studies in forensic epidemiology.* New York: Kluwer Academic/Plenum Publishers.
Mainguy, G., M. R. Motamedi, and D. Mietchen. 2005. Peer review—The newcomers' perspective. *PLoS Biology* 3 (9): e326.
Marzuk, P. M., K. Tardiff, and C. S. Hirsch. 1993. Increase in suicide by asphyxiation in New York City after the publication of *Final Exit. New England Journal of Medicine* 329 (20): 1508–1510.
Matson, J. V., S. F. Daou, and J. G. Soper. 2004. *Effective expert witnessing,* 4th ed. Boca Raton, FL: CRC Press.
Maxfield, M. G., and E. Babbie. 2008. *Research methods for criminal justice and criminology.* Southbank, Victoria, Australia: Thomson Wadsworth.
McCook, A. 2006. Is peer review broken? *The Scientist* February 2006.
Meyer, C. 1999. *Expert witnessing: Explaining and understanding science.* Boca Raton, FL: CRC Press.
Minino, A. M., and B. L. Smith. 2000. Deaths: Final data for 2000. *National Vital Statistics Reports* 49 (12): 1–40. Available at http://www.cdc.gov/nchs/datawh
Mino, A., A. Bousquet, and B. Broers. 1999. Substance abuse and drug-related death, suicidal ideation, and suicide: A review. *Crisis* 20 (1): 28–35.
Montague, P. 2008. Medical mistakes: Health and beyond. Available online at http://www.chetday.com/medmistakes.html
Mortensen, P. B. 1999. Can suicide research lead to suicide prevention? *Acta Psychiatrica Scandinavica* 99 (6): 397–398.
Moscicki, E. K. 1989. Epidemiologic surveys as tools for studying suicidal behavior: A review. *Suicide & Life Threatening Behavior* 19 (1): 131–146.
_____. 1994. Gender differences in completed and attempted suicides. *Annals of Epidemiology* 4:152–158.
_____. 1995. Epidemiology of suicidal behavior. *Suicide & Life Threatening Behavior* 25 (1): 22–35.
_____. 1997. Identification of suicide risk factors using epidemiologicstudies. *Psychiatric Clinics of North America* 20 (3): 499–517.
Musshoff, F., K. Lackenmeier, D. W. Lachenmeier, H. Wollersen, and B. Madea. 2005. Dose–concentration relationships of methadone and EDDP in hair of patients on amethadone-maintenance program. *Forensic Science and Medical Pathology* 1 (2): 97–104.
Nakamura, S., M. Wind, and M. A. Danello. 1999. Review of hazards associated with children placed in adult beds. *Archives of Pediatric and Adolescent Medicine* 153:1019–1023.
National Institutes of Child Health and Human Development, National Institutes of Health. 2001. *From cells to selves, targeting sudden infant death syndrome (SIDS): A strategic plan.* Bethesda, MD.

National SIDS/Infant Death Resource Center. 2004. *What is SIDS?* Vienna, VA: U.S. Department of Health and Human Services, Health Resources and Services Administration.

———. 2004. *SIDS deaths by race and ethnicity 1995–2001.* Vienna, VA: U.S. Department of Health and Human Services, Health Resources and Services Administration.

Neeleman, J., V. Mak, and S. Wessely. 1997. Suicide by age, ethnic group, coroners' verdicts and country of birth. A three-year survey in inner London. *British Journal of Psychiatry* 171 (11): 463–467.

Neeleman, J., and S. Wessely. 1999. Ethnic minority suicide: A small area geographical study in south London. *Psychological Medicine* 29 (2): 429–436.

Nordenberg, T. September–October 2000. Make no mistake: Medical errors can be deadly serious. *FDA Consumer Magazine.* Available online at http://www.fda.gov/fdac/features/2000/500_err.html

O'Gorman, L. January 2008. The (frustrating) state of peer review. *IAPR Newsletter* 30 (1): 3–5.

Ohberg, A., A. Penttila, and J. Lonnqvist. 1997. Driver suicides. *British Journal of Psychiatry* 171 (11): 468–472.

Oliver, P. 2007. A psychological autopsy study of nondeliberate fatal opiate-related overdose. *Research Briefing* 24:20.

Omalu, B. I., K. M. Macurdy, S. A. Koehler, U. H. Agumadu, A. M. Shakir, L. Rozin, and C. H. Wecht. 2005. Forensic pathology and forensic epidemiology of suicides in Allegheny County, Pennsylvania: A 10-year retrospective review 1990–1999. *Forensic Science Medicine and Pathology* 1:125–137.

Panigraphy, A., J. Filiano, L. A. Sleeper, F. Mandell, M. Valdes-Dapena, H. F. Krous, L. A. Rava, E. Foley, W. Frost White, and H. C. Kinney. 2000. Decreased serotonergic receptor binding in rhombic lip-derived regions of the medulla oblongata in the sudden infant death syndrome. *Journal of Neuropathology and Experimental Neurology* 59 (5): 377–384.

Parikh, C. K. 1985. *Medicolegal postmortems in India.* Colaba, Bombay, India: Medical Publications.

Pear, R. T. December 20, 1999. Report details medical errors in V.A. Hospitals. The National Gulf War Resource Center, Inc. Available online at http://www.ngwrc.org/news/content/mondec201200021999.asp

Pestaner, J. P., and D. Schomburgh. 1997. Suicidal gunshot wounds of the head. *Lab Investigation* 76 (1): 6.

Peterson, B., and C. Petty. 1962. Sudden natural death among automobile drivers. *Journal of Forensic Science* 7:274–279.

Petit-Zeman, S. 2003. Trial by peers comes up short. *The Guardian,* Thursday January 16, 2003.

Pharmacology: Half-life of drugs. 2008. Available at www.nottingham.ac.uk/nursing/sonet/rlos/bioproc/halflife/index.html

Physicians' handbook on medical certification of death. 2003, April. Revision. Department of Health and Human Services. Center for Disease Control and Prevention. National Center for Health Statistics DHHS Publication No. (PHS) 2003-1108. Hyattsville, MD.

Postmortem procedures 1970. Chicago: American Hospital Association.

Ramsay, S. 1996. Suicides among elderly on the up in USA. *Lancet* 347 (8995): 182.

Bibliography

Rasinski, K., A. Kuby, S. Bzdusek, J. Silvestri, and D. Weese-Mayer. 2003. Effect of a sudden infant death syndrome risk reduction education program on risk factor compliance and information sources in primarily black urban communities. *Pediatrics* 111 (4): e347–e354.

Rennie, A. 2003. *Journal of the American Medical Association*—Fifth International Congress on Peer Review and Biomedical Publication: Call for Research 11: 1438.

Retterstol, N. 1992. Suicide in Nordic countries. *Psychopathology* 25:254–265.

Robbins, C. 1989. *Robbins pathologic basis of disease*, 4th ed. Philadelphia: W. B. Saunders Company.

Robins, E., G. E. Murphy, and R. H. Wilkinson. 1959. Some clinical considerations in the prevention of suicide based on a study of 134 successful suicides. *American Journal of Public Health* 49:888–898.

Rosewater, K. M., and B. H. Burr. 1998. Epidemiology, risk factors, intervention and prevention of adolescent suicide. *Current Opinion in Pediatrics* 10:338–343.

Sacks, J. J., J. L. Herdon, and S. H. Lieb. 1988. A cluster of unexplained deaths in a nursing home in Florida. *American Journal of Public Health* 78:806–808.

Sacks, J. J., D. F. Stroup, and M. W. Will. 1988. A nursing-associated epidemic of cardiac arrests in an intensive care unit. *Journal of the American Medical Association* 259:689–695.

Saferstein, R. 2007. *Criminalistics: An introduction to forensic science.* Upper Saddle River, NJ: Prentice Hall.

———. 2009. *Forensic science: From the crime scene to the crime lab.* Upper Saddle River, NJ: Pearson Prentice Hall.

Scheers, N. J., G. W. Rutherford, and J. S. Kemp. 2003. Where should infants sleep? A comparison of risk for suffocation of infants sleeping in cribs, adult beds, and other sleeping locations. *Pediatrics* 112 (4): 883–889.

Scott, C. L., E. Swartz, and K. Warburton. 2006. The psychological autopsy: Solving the mysteries of death. *Psychiatric Clinics of North America* 29:805–822.

Scragg, R. D., E. A. Mitchell, B. J. Taylor, et al. 1993. Bed sharing, smoking, and alcohol in the sudden infant death syndrome. *British Medical Journal* 307:1312–1318.

Sigurdson, E., D. Staley, and M. Matas. 1991. A five year review of youth suicide in Manitoba. *Canadian Journal of Psychiatry* 39:397–403.

Spicer, R. S., and T. R. Miller. 2000. Suicide acts in 8 states: Incidence and case fatality rates by demographics and method. *American Journal of Public Health* 90 (12): 1885–1891.

Spier, R. 2002. The history of the peer-review process. *Trends in Biotechnology* 20:357–358.

Spitz, W. U., and R. S. Fisher. 1980. *Medicolegal investigation of death*, 3rd ed. Springfield, IL: Charles C Thomas Publisher.

Stross, J. K., D. M. Shasby, and W. R. Harlan. 1976. An epidemic of mysterious cardiopulmonary arrest. *New England Journal of Medicine* 295:1107–1110.

Taylor, B. 1991. A review of epidemiologic studies of SIDS in Southern New Zealand. *Journal of Pediatric Child Health* 27:344–348.

Torok, T. J., R. V. Tauxem, and P. R. Wise. 1997. A large community outbreak of salmonellosis caused by intentional contamination of restaurant salad bars. *Journal of the American Medical Association* 278:389–395.

Tortora, G. J. 1983. *Principles of human anatomy*, 3rd ed. Cambridge: Harper & Row, Publishers.

Trapp, A. M. 2004. Vehicular homicide laws. Available at http://www.topgunlawyer.com/veh_homicide.htm

Unger, B., J. S. Kemp, D. Wilkins, R. Psara, T. Ledbetter, M. Graham, M. Case, and B. T. Thach. 2003. Racial disparity and modifiable risk factors among infants dying suddenly and unexpectedly. *Pediatrics* 11 (2): e127–e131. Available at http://pediatrics.aappublications.org/cgi/content/full/111/2/e127

U.S. Census Bureau [State and National Data (C2SS)]. Washington, D.C.: United States Department of Commerce; 2001. Updated September 11, 2001.

U.S. Consumer Product Safety Commission. Soft bedding may be hazardous to babies. *Consumer product safety alert, 1999* (publication number 5049). Retrieved from http://cpsc.gov/CPSCPUB/PUBS/5049.html on June 30, 2004.

———. Safe sleep campaign 2000. SIDS awareness survey. Retrieved from http//www.cpsc.gov/LIBRARY/SIDSsurvey.pdf on June 30, 2004.

———. Office of Information and Public Affairs. April 8, 1999. *Recommendations revised to prevent infant deaths from soft bedding.* Retrieved from http://www.cpsc.gov/CPSCPUB/PREREL/PRHTML99/99091.html

U.S. Drug Enforcement Administration. Available at http://www.usdoj.gov/dea/agency/mission.htm

U.S. Public Health Service. 1999. *The surgeon general's call to action to prevent suicide.* Washington, D.C.

Vermulapalli, C., K. Grady, and J. S. Kemp. 2004. Use of safe cribs and bedroom size among African American infants with a high rate of bed sharing. *Archives of Pediatric and Adolescent Medicine* 150:286–289.

Wecht, C. H. 2002. *Allegheny County Coroner's Office, statistical report for 2002.* Coroner's Office, 542 Fourth Avenue, Pittsburgh, PA, 15219.

———. 2004a. *Crime scene investigation: Crack the case with real-life experts.* Pleasantville, NY: Reader's Digest.

———. 2004b. *Forensic aspects of chemical and biological terrorism.* Tucson, AZ: Lawyers and Judges Publishing Company.

Wecht C. H., and S. A. Koehler. 2001. Bioterrorism—Investigation, medical, and societal considerations RE: anthrax and smallpox. In *Proceedings of Bioterrorism Symposium,* Duquesne University School of Law, Pittsburgh, Pennsylvania, November 14, 2001.

———. 2003. Case studies in forensic epidemiology. *Journal of Legal Medicine* 24:587–597.

———. 2005. Effective expert witnessing. *Journal of Legal Medicine* 26(4).

———. 2007a. History of the death investigation system. In *U.S. encyclopedia of forensic and legal medicine.* Oxford: Elsevier Ltd.

———. 2007b. Determination of fitness to drive. In *U.S. encyclopedia of forensic and legal medicine.* Oxford: Elsevier Ltd.

———. 2007c. Determination of fitness to drive: Driving offenses. In *U.S. encyclopedia of forensic and legal medicine.* Oxford: Elsevier Ltd.

———. 2005. Death in vehicular accidents. In *Forensic sciences,* ed. C. H. Wecht. New York: Matthew Bender Co.

Wedgwood, R. J. 1972. Review of USA experience. In *Sudden and unexpected death in infancy (cot deaths),* ed. F. E. Camps and R. G. Carpenter. Bristol, England: Wright.

Welch, S. S. 2001. A review of the literature on the epidemiology of parasuicide in the general population. *Psychiatric Services* 52 (3): 368–375.

Weller, A. C. 2001. *Editorial peer review: Its strengths and weaknesses.* Medford, NJ: American Society for Information Science and Technology, ISBN 1573871001
West, I., G. Nielsen, and A. Gilmore. 1968. Natural death at the wheel. *Journal of the American Medical Association* 205:266–272.
What's your real risk? June 1998. *American Demographics.* Available online at http://www.defendu.com/realrisk.htm
Wigfield, R., P. Fleming, P, Berry, P. Rudd, and J. Golding. 1992. Can the fall in Avon's sudden infant death rate be explained by changes in sleep position? *British Medical Journal* 304:282–283.
Willinger, M., H. Hoffman, K. T. Wu, J. R. Hou, R. C. Kessler, S. L. Ward, T. G. Keens, and M. J. Corwin. 1998. Factors associated with the transition to non-prone sleep positions of infants in the United States. The National Infant Sleep Position Study. *Journal of the American Medical Association* 280 (4): 329–335.
Willinger, M., J. J. Hoffman, and R. B. Hartford. 1994. Infant sleep position and risk for sudden infant death syndrome: Report of meeting held January 13 and 14, 1994, National Institutes of Health, Bethesda, MD. *Pediatrics* 93 (5): 814–819.
Willinger, M., L. S. James, and C. Catz. 1991. Defining the sudden infant death syndrome (SIDS): Deliberations of an expert panel convened by the National Institute of Child Health and Human Development. *Pediatric Pathology* 11:677–684.
Willinger, M., C. W. Ko, H. Hoffman, R. Kessler, and M. Corwin. 2000. Factors associated with caregivers' choice of infant sleep position, 1994–1998: The National Infant Sleep Position Study. *Journal of the American Medical Association* 283 (16): 2135–2142.
World Health Organization. 1996. Prevention of suicide: Guidelines for the formulation and implementation of national strategies. Geneva: World Health Organization.

Appendix A

Normal Weights of Internal Organs, Standard Deviations, and Ranges for Males

Organ Weight (grams) Standard Deviation Range	Age: 11–20	Age: 21–30	Age: 31–40	Age: 41–50	Age: 51–60
Brain	1315	1340	1337	1334	1309
	133.14	113	110	120	118
	870–1500	1040–1600	1080–1640	1030–1550	1000–1590
Right lung	445	579	609	621	607
	99	151	163	162	171
	195–530	210–580	210–835	260–755	230–760
Left lung	411	532	548	555	540
	104	146	156	160	183
	172–510	180–545	205–810	235–730	210–745
Heart	248	289	301	315	319
	62	55	58	68	81
	90–420	140–440	180–465	120–480	130–490
Right kidney	114	129	137	133	131
	24	22	32	30	32
	50–145	56–180	78–265	60–260	80–290
Left kidney	124	139	146	141	142
	25	23	31	35	30
	55–160	65–190	75–295	70–280	100–260
Liver	1420	1494	1545	1591	1486
	175	169	361	269	109
	909–1645	835–1816	903–1890	1120–2032	830–1588
Spleen	130	162	164	169	146
	30	43	63	70	28
	70–180	76–270	89–316	110–330	102–310
Pancreas	106	131	132	133	130
	14	33	19	22	10
	80–127	80–144	71–165	112–190	115–145

Note: Female organs weigh 10% less than male organs.

Index

A

Abdominal region, 41
Accidental death(s), 21, 105–164
  drowning, 159–164
    defined, 159
    forensic epidemiological
      investigation of, 161–164
      advantages and limitations of, 164
      basic data collected, 162
      fundamentals of, 160–161
      mechanism of, 161
      statistics, 160
  drug overdose, 105–122
    defined, 105
    drugs used, 107, 108
    forensic analysis of, 111–112
    forensic epidemiological
      investigation of, 112–122
      advantages and limitations of, 118–122
    forensic investigation of, 107–111
    fundamentals of, 106–107
    mechanism of, 109–111
    statistics, 106
  by falls, 138–146
    autopsy report, 144
    biological causes of, 141
    blood alcohol levels of victims, 143, 144
    chemical causes of, 141
    death report, 143
    environmental causes of, 141
    forensic epidemiological
      investigation of, 141–146
      advantages and limitations of, 145–146, 152
      basic data collected, 142
    location of, 144
    statistics, 142–143
  in fires, 146–152
    carbon monoxide poisoning in, 148
    defined, 146
    forensic epidemiological
      investigation of, 149–152
      basic data collected, 149
    fundamentals, 146–147
    mechanisms of, 148
    statistics, 146, 149, 150
  industrial (*See* Accidental death(s), occupational)
  by medical misadventure, 155–159
    forensic epidemiological
      investigation of, 158
      advantages and limitations of, 158
    time of error, 159
  motor vehicle, 122–137
    autopsies performed, 137
    blood alcohol levels of victims, 133
    causes of, 123
    factors for consideration, 130–133
    forensic epidemiological
      investigation of, 127–137
      advantages and limitations of, 137
    forensic investigation of, 125–127
      data for, 127
    front impact, 124
    fundamentals of, 123
    rear impact, 125
    rollover, 124–125
    seatbelt or helmet status of operators and passengers, 134
    side impact, 124
    statistics, 122
    types of, 123–125
  occupational, 152–155
    defined, 152
    forensic epidemiological
      investigation of, 153–155, 156
      advantages and limitations of, 154
      basic data collected, 155
    fundamentals of, 153
    mechanisms of death, 157
Alzheimer's disease, 7
American Academy of Forensic Sciences, 27

American Journal of Forensic Medicine and Pathology, 29
Arthritis, 7
Atomic absorption analysis kit, 42
Autopsy, 21, 22

B

Bioterrorism, 15, 241–246
   biological agents, 242, 243
   brief history, 242
   chemical agents, 242–243
   defined, 242
   role of forensic community in war on, 244–246
Blunt-force trauma, 41–42, 138, 212
Body
   examinations
      complete forensic, 43–49
         brain, 47–48
         CNS, 47–48
         gastrointestinal tract, 46–47
         heart, 43–44
         kidneys, 46
         liver, 45
         lungs, 44–45
         pancreas, 45–46
         Rokitansky technique, 43
         skeletal system, 48–49
         spinal cord, 48
         spleen, 46
         stomach contents, 46–47
         Virchow technique, 43–49
      external, 40–42
         abdominal region, 41
         genitalia, 41
         neck region, 41
         nose, 41
         pelvic region, 41
   identification, classification, 228
   preservation of, 40–41
   special processing, 42
Brain, 47–48
   fixing the, 48
Bruise, 41–42

C

Cancer, 7
   control, 7
   epidemiology, 7–8
   prevention, 7–8
Carbon monoxide, 148, 172–173
   effects of different concentrations of, 173
Cardiovascular disease, 7, 8
Central nervous system (CNS), 47–48
Chronic disease, 8
Clinical Forensic Medicine, 29
Clinical trial, 3
Clothing, 40
Complete forensic examinations
   body, 43–49
      brain, 47–48
      CNS, 47–48
      gastrointestinal tract, 46–47
      heart, 43–44
      kidneys, 46
      liver, 45
      lungs, 44–45
      pancreas, 45–46
      Rokitansky technique, 43
      skeletal system, 48–49
      spinal cord, 48
      spleen, 46
      stomach contents, 46–47
      Virchow technique, 43–49
Coroner(s)
   office, 31, 32
      death cases handled by, 35–39
   qualifications, 31

D

Data
   collection, 19–23
      for accidental deaths
         drowning, 162
         falls, 142
         fires, 149
         occupational, 155
         vehicular, 127
   death certificate, 89–90, 220
   death investigation, 19–20, 34
Data collection
   for homicides, 202
   for natural deaths, 83, 89–90
   for SIDS, 100
   for suicides, 176
DAWN. *See* Drug Abuse Warning Network (DAWN)
DEA. *See* Drug Enforcement Administration (DEA)

Index

Death(s)
  accidental, 21, 105–164 (*See also* Accidental death(s))
  cause known but manner undetermined, 231–233
  cause undermined and manner undetermined, 233–234
  homicidal, 21
  in hospital, 36–37
  investigated by coroner or medical examiner, 34–35
  manner of, 21
  natural, 21, 75–103 (*See also* Natural death(s))
  at nonresidence, 37–38
  reportable, 33–34
  at residence, 35–37
  suicidal, 21
  undetermined
    forensic epidemiological investigation of, 234–235
Death call, 32–35
Death certificate(s), 51–74
  advantages, 73
  completion, 52–53
  defined, 51
  disadvantages, 74
  fetal and stillborn, 53
  final pathological diagnosis *vs.*, 50
  functions, 51–52
  homicide, 220
  medicolegal, 64–71
  pathway of, 71–73
  standard, 53–64
  types of, 53
Death investigation data, 19–20, 34
Death investigation report, 35
Death review boards, 25–26
Decomposition
  early stages, 222–225
  extreme stages, 229–230
  moderate stages, 225–229
  special cases of, 230–231
Determination of identity, 222
Diabetes, 8
Drug Abuse Warning Network (DAWN), 23–24
Drug Enforcement Administration (DEA), 23, 24
Drug prevention programs, 18

E

Epidemiology
  aging, 7
  cancer, 7–8
  chronic disease, 8
  defined, 2
  environmental, 8
  factors considered, 2
  forensic, 11
  genetic, 10
  history, 1–2
  infectious disease, 8–9
  injury, 9–10
  physical activity, 10
  psychiatric, 10
  reproductive, 9
  scientific method in, 2
  studies
    experimental, 4
    limitation of, 6
    observational, 4
    prospective, 5
    purposes of, 3
    retrospective, 4–5
    strength of, 5–6
  types of, 7–11
External examination, 39–43
  body, 40–42
  purpose, 42–43
  types of, 42–43

F

FARS. *See* Fatality analysis reporting system (FARS)
Fatality analysis reporting system (FARS), 135–137
  partial list of variables, 136
  report, 135
Federal Rules of Evidence, 264, 265
Final autopsy report, 49
Final pathological diagnosis, 49–50
  death certificate *vs.*, 50
First-degree murder, 188
Food and Drug Administration, 27
Forensic epidemiological consultant, 259–261
Forensic epidemiologist(s)
  becoming a, 266–267
  conferences, 27

as consultant, 259–261
contacts with outside agencies, 23–26
court experience, 263–264
data collection, 19–23
   crime laboratory, 22–23
   death investigation, 19–20
   forensic medicine, 20–22
in drug prevention programs, 18
as expert witness, 18
   court experience, 263–263
   evidence presented, 264–266
   key concepts for, 264
in health department, 17
in medical examiner's or coroner's office, 16, 19–29
mentoring programs, 26–27
as private consultant, 18
in public and private organizations, 17–18
research and publications, 27–29
role in investigation of natural deaths, 83–90
teaching, 27
Forensic epidemiology, 11
bioterrorism and, 15
case studies, 276
defined, 15
development, 14–16
fundamentals, 11
internship and mentoring programs, 26
Forensic paper(s), 247–258
abstract, 247–248
case reports, 253–254
conclusion, 252
introduction, 248–249
material and methods, 249–251
peer review, 255–258
   process of, 256–258
   ranking of manuscript by, 257–258
references, 252
research articles, 253
results, 251–252
review articles, 254
structure of manuscript, 247–253
types of manuscripts, 253–255
Forensic pathology, 32
Forensic photographer, 40
Forensic science
brief history, 13–14
journals, 28
Forensic Science, Medicine, Medicine and Pathology, 29

Forensic Science International, 29
Funeral home, 39

G

Gastrointestinal tract, 46–47
Genetic epidemiology, 10
Genitalia, 41

H

Heart, 43–44
Homicide(s), 21, 187–220
activity prior to, 206
by day of week, 209
death certificate data, 220
defined, 187
excusable, 188
felonious, 188–189
forensic epidemiological investigation, 201–212
   advantages and limitations of using data from, 218–219
   basic data collected, 202
investigation, 189–192
justifiable, 188
mechanisms, 192, 193, 211
   by arson, 212
   by asphyxiation, 212
   by assault, 212
   by blunt force trauma, 212
   by drowning, 212
   by firearm, 212
   forensic analysis by, 193–201, 212
   by stabbing, 212
by month of occurrence, 208
race of actor compared to that of victim, 210
by sex and race, 189, 204
sex of actor compared to that of victim, 210
statistics, 189, 203, 204
by time of day, 209
types of, 188–189
Homicide-suicide deaths, 237–238

I

Infant death, 90–103. *See also* Sudden infant death syndrome (SIDS)

Index

Injury epidemiology, 9–10
International Association of Forensic Nursing, 27
Involuntary manslaughter, 189

J

Journal of Forensic and Legal Medicine, 29
Journal of Forensic Nursing, 29
Journal of Forensic Sciences, 29

K

Kidneys, 46

L

Law enforcement agencies, 24
Liver, 45
Lungs, 44–45

M

Medical examiner(s)
  office, 32
    death cases handled by, 35–39
    qualifications, 32
Morgue cases, 38–39
  steps to separate, 22

N

National Center for Injury Prevention and Control, 27
National Center for Statistics and Analysis (NCSA), 136
National Conference on Science and the Law, 27
National Highway Traffic Safety Administration (NHTSA), 136
National Incident-Based Reporting System (NIBRS), 217–218
  group A offenses, 218
  group B offenses, 219
National Medical Examiner Association (NMEA), 27
National Violence Data Reporting System, 212–218
  national databases, 212–218

Natural death(s), 21, 75–103
  Blood disease-related, 87
  cancer-related, 88
  cardiovascular related, 86
  data, 83
    death certificate, 89–90
    strength and weaknesses of, 89
  defined, 75
  demographic characteristics, 84
  endocrine system-related, 87
  forensic investigation, 78–79
    cardiovascular system, 80–81
    hepatobiliary system, 81
    nervous system, 82
    organ weights, 82
    respiratory system, 81
    role of epidemiologist in, 83–90
    stored tissue and microscopic slides, 82
  gastrointestinal system-related, 87
  hepatobiliary system-related, 87
  infant, 90–103 (*See also* Sudden infant death syndrome (SIDS))
  infection-related, 88
  investigated by ME/C office, 77–78
  nervous system-related, 87–88
  not reported to ME/C office, 76
  by organ systems, 85
  pancreatic system-related, 87
  psychiatrically-related, 88
  renal system-related, 87
  respiratory system-related, 86–87
  statistics, 75–76
  systematic-related, 87
  types of, 80–83
NCSA. *See* National Center for Statistics and Analysis (NCSA)
Neck region, 41
News agencies, 23
NHTSA. *See* National Highway Traffic Safety Administration (NHTSA)
NIBRS. *See* National Incident-Based Reporting System (NIBRS)
NMEA. *See* National Medical Examiner Association (NMEA)
Nose, 41

O

Office will issue, 38

P

Pancreas, 45–46
Peer-reviewed journals, 28–29
Pelvic region, 41
Photographing, 40
Psychiatric epidemiology, 10
Psychological autopsy, 239–241
   brief history, 240
   conducting, 241
   defined, 239–240
   use of, 240–241

R

Release to funeral home, 39
Reproductive epidemiology, 9
Risk factors, 2
Rokitansky technique, 43
Russian roulette—death by suicide or accident, 238–239

S

Second-degree murder, 188
SHR. *See* Supplementary Homicide Report (SHR)
SIDS. *See* Sudden infant death syndrome (SIDS)
Skeletal system, 48–49
Spinal cord, 48
   removal of
      anterior approach, 48
      posterior approach, 48
Spleen, 46
Stomach contents, 46–47
Stroke, 7
Sudden infant death syndrome (SIDS), 17, 90–103
   age sex and race statistics, 101
   back to sleep campaign and, 99
   bed sharing and, 98
   defined, 90–91
   ethnicity and socioeconomic factors associated with, 98–99
   factors for consideration
      birth, 93
      infant characteristics, 94
      postbirth environment, 93
      postbirth parental behaviors, 94
      prebirth, 93
   forensic epidemiological investigation, 95–103
      application of, 95–99
      basic data collected, 100
      significance of, 99
   forensic investigation
      complete examination of infant, 94
      death scene reports, 94
      methods of, 93–94
   foundations, 91–92
   natural or undetermined, 94–95
   sleep position and, 97
   soft bedding and, 97–98
   statistics, 91, 101, 102
   time, day of week, and month of discovery statistics, 102
Suicide(s), 18, 21, 165–186
   by asphyxiation, 171–172
   biomechanics of, 169
   by carbon monoxide, 172–173
   defined, 61
   demographic characteristics by, 177, 178
   by exsanguination, 174–175
   by firearm, 170
   forensic epidemiological investigation, 175–186
      advantages and limitations of, 184
      basic data collected, 176
      factors associated with, 183
   fundamentals of, 166–168
   investigation of, 168–169, 175–186
   living arrangements at time of, 179
   location of, 181
   mechanism of, 169–175, 179
      by age, 185
      asphyxiation, 171–172
      carbon monoxide, 172–173
      exsanguination, 174–175
      firearm, 170
      overdose, 173–174
      ratio of complete autopsy to external-only examination based on, 186
   statistics, 182
   train, 174

Index

vehicle, 174
by overdose, 173–174
review board, 25
statistics, 78, 165, 166
time of, 180
by train, 174
by vehicle, 174
Supplementary Homicide Report (SHR), 213, 217

T

Third-degree murder, 188

U

UCR. *See* Uniform Crime Report (UCR)
Uniform Crime Report (UCR), 212–213
part I offenses, 214
part II offenses, 215–216
weaknesses, 213
United States and Canadian Academy of Pathology, 27

V

Virchow technique, 43–49
Voluntary manslaughter, 188–189